hotels • restaurants • spas • golf resorts • villas

caribbeanchic

hotels • restaurants • spas • golf resorts • villas

caribbeanchic

text joe yogerst • kerry o'neill • richard nichols

·K·U·P·E·R·A·R·D·

publisher's acknowledgements

At last, the long overdue *Caribbean Chic*—the 11th book in the *Chic* series—is finally here. The *Chic* series started three years ago with *Mexico Chic*. Given the Caribbean's popularity as a fabulous chic destination, I am surprised it took this length of time for *Caribbean Chic* to be published. Maybe we thought the Caribbean was already well known. Maybe we had to wait to find the best writer. The author we found for this book, Joe Yogerst, is certainly worth the wait. He has been named Caribbean Travel Writer of the Year for 2006 by the Caribbean Travel Organization (CTO). I congratulate Joe on his award and thank him for agreeing to write this book.

As always, a book such as this makes demands on the wonderful *Chic* team and I would like to thank James McLeod and Isabelle DuPlessix for working tirelessly to put the chic into *Caribbean Chic*. Inevitably, the team at Editions Didier Millet has done its job superbly, including unsung heroes such as Sin Kam Cheong and Bobby Teh. I would also like to thank Sally Booth and her team at luxury tour operator Seasons in Style for the suggested itineraries (page 248) and sponsorship of the z-card map; Arsene Weishaupt of Air France who provided tickets; Neil Forrester of Antigua Hotels and Tourist Association and of course all of the properties that you see in *Caribbean Chic* for their support of this project.

The Caribbean is a dream destination and we hope this book will make you want to visit it. If you want more information, please visit our website, www.thechicseries.com.

Nigel Bolding
editor-in-chief

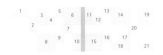

COVER CAPTIONS:

1: Garden bath at Goldeneye.
2: Francis Ford Coppola's Turtle Inn.
3: A seafront guestroom at Jake's.
4: Steel drums in Trinidad.
5: Concord Falls at Central Grenada.
6: Grottoes beneath the cottage-lined clifftop at The Caves.
7: Cropover Festival in Barbados.
8: Magnificent view from Shirely Heights at English Harbour.
9: Close-up of the Turk's head cactus.
10: Sunset at Necker Island, British Virgin Islands.
11: A mural depicting idyllic island life.
12: Sample gastro-chic at Maroma Resort and Spa.
13: Rafting on the Rio Grande river.
14: Aerial view of Tobago Cays.
15: Lifeguard on duty.
16: A beach hammock tempts.
17: Balloonfish with tube sponges.
18: Private plunge pool at Blue Waters.
19: Amanyara's open-concept design.
20: Impeccable service at Grace Bay Club, Turks and Caicos.
21: Relaxation at the waters' edge.

THIS PAGE: *Scuba divers circling corals.*
OPPOSITE: *Royal Plantation, Jamaica.*
PAGE 2: *Sailboats off Windward Islands.*
PAGE 8 AND 9: *Crystal-clear waters off Petit St. Vincent, St. Vincent and the Grenadines.*

executive editor
melisa teo

editors
wu xue yi • ibrahim tahir • lavinia ng

designer
chan hui yee

production manager
sin kam cheong

first published in 2007 by
bolding books
49 wodeland avenue,
guildford gu2 4jz, united kingdom
enquiries : nigel.bolding@theworldsbesthotels.com
website : www.theworldsbesthotels.com

©2007 bolding books
design and layout © editions didier millet pte ltd

first published in great britain 2007 by
kuperard
59 hutton grove, london n12 8ds
telephone : +44 (0) 20 8446 2440
facsimile : +44 (0) 20 8446 2441
enquiries : sales@kuperard.co.uk
website : www.kuperard.co.uk

Kuperard is an imprint of Bravo Ltd.

Printed in Singapore.

isbn-10: 185-7334-13-2
isbn-13: 978-185-7334-13-5

contents

10 **maps**of**the**caribbean · 12 **introduction**

jamaica 22
The Caves 38 · Goldeneye 40 · Jake's 42 · Jamaica Inn + Spa 44 · Rockhouse 46 ·
Round Hill Hotel + Villas 48 · Royal Plantation 50 · Strawberry Hill 52

dominicanrepublic 54
Casa Colonial Beach + Spa 66 · Sivory Punta Cana 68 · Victorian House 70

turks+caicosislands 72
Amanyara 82 · Grace Bay Club 84 · The Palms 86 · Parrot Cay 88 ·
Turks + Caicos Club 90 · The Somerset on Grace Bay 92

leewardislands 94
The Villa Book 108 · Blue Waters 110 · Carlisle Bay 114 · The Copper + Lumber Store Hotel 116 ·
Curtain Bluff 118 · The Inn at English Harbour 120 · Siboney Beach Club 122 · Biras Creek 124 ·
Necker Island 126 · Caneel Bay 128 · Gallows Point Resort 130

132 frenchantilles

Le Christopher 144 • François Plantation Hotel + Restaurant 146 •
Sibarth Villa Rentals + Real Estate 148 • Le Domaine de Lonvilliers 150 •
Marquis Hotel Resort + Spa 152 • La Samanna 154 • Le Cap Est Lagoon Resort + Spa 156

158 windwardislands

The Crane Resort + Residences 174 • mangobay 176 • Sandy Lane Hotel + Resort 178 • Treasure Beach 180 •
Fustic House 182 • Leamington Pavilion 184 • Port St. Charles 186 • Sandalo 188 •
Laluna 190 • True Blue Bay Resort + Villas 192 • Anse Chastanet Resort 194 • Ladera 196 •
Raffles Resort Canouan Island 198 • Tamarind Beach + Yacht Club 202 •
Mustique Villas 204 • The Palms Villa Resort 206

208 aruba+dutchantilles

Bucuti Beach 218 • Tierra del Sol Resort, Spa + Country Club 220

222 continentalcaribbean

Turtle Inn 236 • Hotel Básico 238 • Deseo [Hotel + Lounge] 242 • Maroma Resort + Spa 246

248 itineraries • 254 index • 255 picturecredits • 256 directory

thecaribbean

Gulf of Mexico

USA

Atlantic

THE BAHAMAS

TURKS + CAICOS

CUBA

MEXICO

Greater Antilles

JAMAICA

HAITI

DOMINICAN REPUBLIC

Hispaniola

BELIZE

Caribbean Sea

HONDURAS

NICARAGUA

Dut

ARUBA

COSTA RICA

PANAMA

COLOMBIA

O c e a n

Continental
Caribbean

Turks +
Caicos Islands

Leeward Islands

Jamaica

Dominican
Republic

French Antilles

Aruba + Dutch Antilles

Windward Islands

thecaribbeanbychapter

Leeward Islands

L e s s e r

BRITISH
VIRGIN
ISLANDS

PUERTO RICO

ANGUILLA
ST. MARTIN/ST. MAARTEN
ST. BARTHÉLEMY
BARBUDA

U.S.
VIRGIN
ISLANDS

ST. KITTS

ANTIGUA

A n t i l l e s

NEVIS

MONTSERRAT

GUADELOUPE

DOMINICA

MARTINIQUE

Windward Islands

ST. LUCIA

N

ntilles

ST. VINCENT +
THE GRENADINES

BARBADOS

ÇAO

BONAIRE

GRENADA

TOBAGO

Legend

○ Lake
● 2000 - 3000 m
● 1000 - 2000 m
● 500 - 1000 m
● 200 - 500 m

TRINIDAD

VENEZUELA

0 km   100   200   300   400 km

introduction

The Caribbean is an abode for thousands of islands and an inspiration for countless paradise island dreams. Its sparkling sapphire sea is a watery siren that lures with the promise of adventure. The Caribbean evokes images of coconut palms and white-sand strands, aquamarine bays and plenty of sunshine, set against the irresistible sound of calypso or reggae. It is a region that intrigues with its intoxicating blend of cultures, overwhelms with its boundless beauty, and infatuates.

The Caribbean mystique is not a recent phenomenon. For as long as people have been venturing to the Caribbean, they have been swept away by the experience. Of all the things that could have been on Christopher Columbus' mind on his fifth day in the New World, the thing he chose to describe in his captain's log was the underwater life: 'Here the fish are so dissimilar to ours that it is wonderful. Some are shaped like dories, of the finest hues in the world, blue, yellow, red, and every other colour, some variegated with a thousand different tints, so beautiful that no one on beholding them could fail to express the highest wonder and admiration.'

Samuel Taylor Coleridge, who spent six months sailing the Caribbean in the 1820s, waxed lyrical on the region's overt sensuality. After an amusingly raunchy account of how it is impossible for a woman not to sweat while dancing the night away in the Caribbean, the Englishman advised his readers not to drink too much in the hot tropical clime. 'Restrain yourself till twelve o'clock or so, and then eat some cold meat and absorb a pint of porter cup, which is perfectly innocuous to the system, and more restorative to the animal spirits than punch, wine or sangaree.'

Today, the Caribbean is still the epitome of sensual escape, guiltless bliss and tropical island chic. It is the paradise of choice for thousands who crave the sun on their backs, a cool breeze on the face, and a piña colada within easy reach. Perhaps the Spanish explorer, Ponce de León, was really onto something when he roamed the region in search of the mythical Fountain of Youth. He never realized that it was all around—the spirit of rebirth and renewal that overcomes everyone when they venture to the Caribbean.

THIS PAGE (FROM TOP): **The placid waters off St. Martin are especially alluring; Belize boasts an amazing marine biodiversity.**
OPPOSITE: **Islands in the Caribbean Sea.**

defining the caribbean

In geographical terms, the Caribbean is a basin of the Atlantic Ocean located between North and South America. It sprawls across 3 million sq km (1 million sq miles) of water. The basin is dotted with about 7,000 islands—not including the sandbars and rocky outcrops that only appear at low tide. Beneath the surface of the water, the Caribbean boasts about a tenth of the world's coral formations, including the planet's second longest barrier reef after the Great Barrier Reef in Australia.

Although the region encompasses islands that hug the coast of Mexico, Belize, Venezuela and other continental nations, the heart of the Caribbean is the Antilles islands, a meandering chain which stretches from Cuba to Trinidad. The larger islands in the west—Cuba, Hispaniola (Haiti and the Dominican Republic), Jamaica and Puerto Rico—are called the Greater Antilles. The smaller islands in the east are the Lesser Antilles, and these in turn are divided into the Leeward Islands in the north and the Windward Islands in the south.

Each island in the Caribbean is a world unto itself. Though similar to neighbouring islands in many ways, the experience on each island is distinct. This, in essence, is what keeps people coming back, year after year. If you tire of one island, there is always something intriguing—and thoroughly different—on another island, just over the horizon. There you could schmooze in Spanish rather than English or French; savour flying-fish sandwiches rather than conch fritters; or, that ultimate paradise delight, explore an empty beach or virgin reef.

cultural cornucopia

Five hundred years of cultural fusion have made the Caribbean what it is today—one of earth's most diverse regions. Over the course of its history, Africans, Amerindians, Europeans, and even pirates have given rise to the extraordinary blend that created many of the things we now take for granted in the Caribbean—culinary genius, artistic brilliance and infectious music.

The thing that most sets the Caribbean apart from other regions is its extraordinary rich culture. The islands are unique, right down to each islander. He or she may be Christian, Muslim, Hindu or Rastafarian; and may be descendents of African slaves, European indentured servants, Arab or Jewish traders, East Indian sugarcane workers, or South American cowboys. Jamaica's national motto—'Out of Many, One People'— actually applies to the entire Caribbean.

Out of this multitude have come many remarkable individuals who have shaped the history of the Caribbean. From Haitian independence leaders Toussaint L'Ouverture and Jean Dessalines to Jamaican nationalist Marcus Garvey, the region has had a long and colourful history of activism and political awakening. This streak has spilled over to the arts, producing Nobel laureates like Derek Walcott of St. Lucia, and musical icons like Bob Marley of Jamaica. The Caribbean spirit also found expression in the athletics arena, with a long list of champions that includes baseball legend Sammy Sosa, cricket star Sir Garfield Sobers, boxer Telefilio Stevenson, and sprinter Marion Jones.

the first islanders

Mankind first came to the Caribbean around 7,000 years ago, probably making their way from the South American mainland via Trinidad rather than southward from Florida. By the dawn of the European discovery of the West Indies, there were three major Amerindian groups—the Cibony in western Cuba; the Arawak (or Taino) in the Bahamas, Greater Antilles and Leeward Islands; and the Caribs (after whom the region was named) in the Windward Islands.

THIS PAGE (FROM TOP): Turtle Inn by acclaimed film director Francis Ford Coppola; Olympic champion Marion Jones in her element.

OPPOSITE (FROM TOP): The romantic Caribbean provides the perfect setting for honeymoon couples; Caribbean-style al fresco dining on the chic Necker Island, British Virgin Islands.

There is every reason to believe that the early islanders lived an idyllic existence. 'They are very gentle and do not know what evil is,' wrote Columbus on his first voyage. 'Nor do they kill others, nor steal; and they are without weapons.' Although wars did occur—the Caribs tried to expand their domain at the expense of the other two groups—life was much easier here than on the mainland. Between cassava cultivation in the rich volcanic soil and the endless supply of fish from the surrounding sea, islanders were never without food. There was thus plenty of time to develop various means to while away tropical days, including a handy little invention—the hammock.

paradise found

There are many stories about who might have been the first 'outsiders' to come into contact with the indigenous islanders. Some believe the ancient Egyptians made the trans-Atlantic voyage and imparted the knowledge of pyramid-building to the Maya. Others claim the ancient Greeks established a colony in the Caribbean, called Atlantis, that later sank beneath the sea—perhaps destroyed by a hurricane—in what is now the Bahamas. The Norsemen certainly reached North America, and it is not impossible that some adventurous Viking might have even ventured as far south as the Caribbean. However, the only concrete evidence of first contact is the arrival of Columbus' three-ship Spanish fleet in 1492.

The Spanish quickly put down roots in what was then known as the 'West Indies', establishing Santo Domingo on Hispaniola as a base to explore and eventually conquer the entire Caribbean. With the arrival of the Europeans, the population of Amerindian island inhabitants quickly dwindled, due to the lack of immunity to infectious European diseases, such as smallpox, and their cruel enslavement by the Spanish. As the Amerindian numbers plummeted, the Spanish filled the labour void by importing slaves from Africa. When King Ferdinand authorized the first shipment of slaves from Africa to the New World in 1510, he probably had no idea that he was about to alter the economics, culture and politics of the Caribbean for centuries to come.

THIS PAGE (FROM TOP): Peaceful island life is depicted in this mural on the façade of a home at Grand Case Bay, St. Martin; churchgoers in colourful hats attend mass at a cathedral in Basse Terre, Guadeloupe.

OPPOSITE (FROM TOP): Snoozing in a beach hammock is one of the privileges of being in the restful Caribbean; Christopher Columbus' Lighthouse in Santo Domingo in the Dominican Republic was built in 1992 to celebrate the 400-year anniversary of Columbus' landing.

sugar + molasses

The Europeans were the first to plant sugarcane in the Caribbean and it rapidly became the most important commercial crop in the region. Sugarcane was harvested and processed to produce sugar and molasses, which were shipped across the Atlantic to sweeten bland European foods. Sugar trade was extremely lucrative and formed a major component of the inter-connected Triangular Trade in the 18th century between the Caribbean (exporting sugar and rum), Europe (exporting manufactured goods) and West Africa (exporting slaves).

The import of thousands of African slaves to work on the sugarcane plantations, together with the installation of a wealthy European or Creole aristocracy, changed the entire social fabric of the Caribbean. Many of the things that we now consider intrinsically Caribbean—such as carnival, calypso and Creole cuisine—evolved from plantation society. Sugar also radically changed the landscape; the forest was replaced by green sugarcane fields.

Sugar production in the Caribbean peaked in the decades after World War II, but has been in steady decline over the last 40 years. However, the sugar production remains an important source of employment and revenue for many Caribbean islands. Barbados, Cuba, Guyana, Jamaica and Trinidad are the foremost sugar producers in the region. In Jamaica alone, more than 40,000 find work in sugarcane plantations and factories, and nearly a quarter million people derive at least some of their financial sustenance from the sugar economy. But declining prices worldwide could spell doom for the Caribbean sugar industry. In response, there have been initiatives on some islands to restructure the industry by shifting the focus to producing ethanol from sugarcane to be used as fuel.

rum: light, dark or flavoured

Molasses and sugarcane juice can be fermented and distilled into rum, which, in the absence of wine, became the drink of choice amongst the region's European habitués.

Although you can quaff rum straight from the still, the raw liquid is normally aged in an oak cask for at least a year. Like scotch and cognac, the best rums are aged for 20 or 30 years. Caramel is added to give rum its characteristic golden colour, although this can also be accomplished via long ageing. Several distinct varieties have evolved over the centuries. Light rum has almost no natural taste, very little colour and is thus perfect for cocktails—including legendary Caribbean drinks like daiquiri, mojito, cuba libre and piña colada. Dark rum is generally golden to light brown in colour, with a hint of molasses flavour. While found in cocktails, it is the rum most favoured for cooking. Flavoured rums have become all the rage in recent years, with coconut and various citrus concoctions among the most popular. Premium rums are the best. They are exquisite liquids that are carefully blended and aged to perfection.

Even though the large breweries now make a wide variety of rums, regional distinctions persist. English-speaking islands like Jamaica and Barbados are more renowned for darker rums. Spanish-speaking islands like Cuba and Puerto Rico tend to produce the best of the lighter lot. Rum from the French isles tends to retain more of its natural cane flavour. Bacardi, founded in Santiago de Cuba in 1862 and relocated to Puerto Rico after Castro came to power, is the largest rum producer in both the Caribbean and the world. In Jamaica, the king of the hill is Appleton, an upcountry distillery that makes what aficionados swear is the best rum in the West Indies—Estate 21. Malibu rum, bottled in Scotland and named after a place in California, is produced in Barbados and was the first to ignite the worldwide craze for flavoured rums.

pirates + plunder

One could make the argument that rum was responsible for the plague of pirates in the Caribbean, although European geopolitics also bears a fair share of the blame. Having been beaten to the punch in the exploitation of the New World by the Spanish and Portuguese, the French, Dutch and British authorized piracy as a means to harass, weaken and outright steal from their opponents. However, many of these maritime mercenaries had more interest in lining their own pockets. The British did not have more pirates than everyone else—they were just better at pillaging and plundering. It is no coincidence that most of the region's famous buccaneers—Henry Morgan, Edward 'Blackbeard' Teach, 'Calico' Jack Rackham—had Anglo-Saxon names.

Caribbean piracy started with Sir Francis Drake's marauding on Spanish treasure galleons in the 1560s. Port Royal in Jamaica, Tortola in the Virgin Islands, and Campeche on the Yucatán coast were amongst the most notorious pirate havens. In the 1720s, the European nations that had originally unleashed the pirates finally decided to stop the seafaring peril, effectively ending the age of piracy.

getting into the carnival groove

After the age of pirates, the Caribbean islands changed hands between various colonial powers. With the exception of Haiti, Cuba and the Dominican Republic, none of the islands gained full independence until after 1960. To this day, France, Britain, Holland and the United States continue to hold on to various insular dependencies. The Caribbean is the most highly colonized region in the world.

Many Caribbean cultural elements emerged during the drift towards independence. The most important of these is carnival. Carnival is a blend of the pre-Lent bacchanalian celebrations imported by the Europeans and the harvest festivals created for slaves. By the end of the 19th century, these celebrations had merged on islands such as Trinidad and Martinique. They became the forerunners of the exuberant carnivals we see today throughout the Caribbean.

THIS PAGE: Ageing in oak casks, the best rums are worth the wait.

OPPOSITE (CLOCKWISE FROM TOP): Sugarcane plantations have transformed the landscapes on many Caribbean islands; the sugar industry has had a huge impact on the daily lives of islanders; rum cocktails are best served chilled, and on a beach.

The climax of carnival is a series of parades during the week before Ash Wednesday. The participants, dressed in outrageous costumes, dance and sing their way through the streets. Musical competitions are another integral part of carnival. Last but not least, no carnival is complete without copious amounts of rum, beer and traditional island food. Although carnival takes place prior to Lent, there are actually very few religious overtones. In fact, there are devil costumes, satanic masks and antics that would make a saint blush. Long overshadowed by the Trinidad Carnival, some of the other islands have moved their carnivals to other times of the year. Antigua and Barbados are among the islands that have carnivals in August.

calypso + reggae

Carnival gave the world Caribbean music. A fusion of African rhythms and the musical traditions of the Spanish, French and British colonials who ruled Trinidad, calypso emerged around the turn of the 20th century. Although early calypso was largely based on vocals and bamboo instruments, the invention of the steel drum in the early 1940s—fashioned from 55-gallon oil drums—added another layer of richness to calypso. This boosted calypso's appeal, especially the songs of Harry Belafonte who, in the 1950s, became the Caribbean's first international music star.

A similar musical evolution took place in Jamaica, where Afro-Jamaican music produced ska, which would much later influence the development of reggae. The emergence of Bob Marley as a global superstar in the 1970s took the music of the Jamaican tenements to a worldwide audience and helped make reggae the prevailing soundtrack of the entire Caribbean.

The Spanish isles have been especially prolific, producing mambo (Cuba), salsa (Puerto Rico) and merengue (Dominican Republic) over the past hundred years. But it is reggae—and in particular the ethereal voice of Bob Marley—that has the power to summon an instant image of the Caribbean no matter where you are in the world. 'Sun is shining, the weather is sweet, yeah. Make you wanna move your dancing feet...'

THIS PAGE (FROM TOP): Steel drums, which originated from Trinidad, are played on many islands especially during carnival; the I-Threes, wearing traditional Rastafarian colours, was the reggae backing band for Bob Marley and the Wailers.

OPPOSITE: Outrageous costumes and infectious music are the hallmarks of carnival.

Carnival gave the world Caribbean music...

jamaica

> The Caves
> Rockhouse
> Round Hill Hotel + Villas

> Jamaica Inn + Spa
> Royal Plantation
> Goldeneye

Lucea • Montego Bay
• Green Island
Negril
Negril Point
Little Bay
Savanna la Mar
Black River
Treasure Beach
Port Kaiser
Great Pedro Cape
Carlisle Bay
Rocky Point
Portland Point

Falmouth
Duncans
• Wakefield
Montpelier
• Maroon Town
The Cockpit Country
• Catadupa
▲748
986 Denham
Maggotty
• Santa Cruz
725
• Alligator Pond

Rio Bueno
Runaway Bay
St. Ann's Bay
Ocho Rios
Claremont 797
Dry Harbour Mounts
Moneague
838

Chapelton
836
Bog Walk
Mandeville
May Pen
Old Harbour
• Salt River
160
Portland Cave

Oracabessa
Galina
Port Maria

Eden Gully

Spanish Town
Portmore
Port Royal
Harbour
Polink Point

> Strawberry Hill
Annotto Bay
Orange Bay
Buff Bay
Hope Bay
Boston Bay
Port Antonio
Blue Mountain Peak
Gordon Town 2076 ▲2256
The Blue Mountains
Rio Grande
Long Bay
Manchioneal
Hectors River
Holland Bay
Morant Point

Stony Hill
KINGSTON
Bull Bay
Yallahs
Seaforth
Bath
Bowden
Morant Bay

> Jake's

N

Caribbean Sea

0 km   15   30   45 km

from xaymaca to jamaica

Jamaica might be the only place on earth that has preserved, as a national landmark, the spot where a love song was penned—the wooden shack in Trench Town where Bob Marley wrote 'No Woman, No Cry' for future wife Rita Anderson. Jamaicans have always held music close to their hearts, and years of homegrown calypso, reggae and rap have painted the island as a magical place. Much of this is no more than melodic storytelling; the vivid imaginations of songwriters. But a good deal is based on fact. From postcard-perfect beaches with swaying coconut palms to cool-running waterfalls and swanky hideaway hotels, this is an island that oozes romance.

Many things associated with the Caribbean such as reggae, banana boats, barbecue jerk, Blue Mountain coffee and Red Stripe beer, were born on this island. Jamaica was the cradle of Caribbean cruise and the all-inclusive beach resort. In recent years, it has been at the cutting edge of yet another trend—hip boutique hotels that spoil guests with quiet luxury and impeccable service.

Largest of the former British West Indies, Jamaica stretches 240 km (150 miles) from east to west. The Arawak Amerindians called their homeland Xaymaca, 'land of wood and water', and to a large extent the island remains this way. From jungle-shrouded peaks that are amongst the highest in the Caribbean, rivers and waterfalls plunge. In the rugged highlands, there are villages where time seems to have stopped. Vast stretches of the interior, like the Black River Morass and the impenetrable Cockpit Country, remain largely uninhabited—a stark contrast to the Jamaican coast, with its chic beach retreats and edgy urban jungles. There is something for almost everyone in this Caribbean island paradise.

where caribbean tourism began

When American steamship captain Lorenzo Dow Baker was returning from South America in the 1870s, he put into Jamaica for provisions. On the spur of the moment, he filled the empty space in the hold with bananas. They sold like hotcakes back in

PAGE 22: Cool and soothing Y.S. Falls, located in the foothills of St. Elizabeth Parish.

THIS PAGE: Jamaican icon Bob Marley took reggae to a worldwide audience.

OPPOSITE: Lifeguard on duty at one of Jamaica's strands.

Boston, and Baker sank his life savings into the fruit business. Within a decade, he had 80 banana boats plying back and forth to Jamaica and was wealthy beyond his wildest dreams.

Baker could have drifted into his twilight years on his banana bonanza, but he realized he could make even more money by sending something back to Jamaica in the empty banana boats. It seemed crazy at the time, but it turned out to be a stroke of genius; he filled the boats with American tourists. The Caribbean cruise was born.

Half a century later, the all-inclusive resort was also conceived in Jamaica. This time the pioneer was Canadian 'biscuit king' Garfield Weston, who built a retirement home at Frenchman's Cove near Port Antonio. Much like Baker, he just could not leave things alone. Rather than bask in tropical bliss, Weston decided to transform his estate into an upscale seaside retreat for his wealthy friends and anyone else who could spare the money. For a set daily price, guests could grab as much champagne and caviar as they could slide down their gullets, then step into a horse-drawn carriage to be brought back to their private villas. Jamaican jack-of-all-trades Butch Stewart picked up where Weston left off, evolving the all-inclusive concept into the rowdy Sandals resorts that have revolutionized tourism in the region.

writers' abode

For nearly a century, Jamaica's north shore was the epicentre of tropical chic, a place where bored socialites, celebrities and creative types came to escape the winter blues. The coast was especially attractive to writers seeking a tranquil place to write. It was also an out-of-the-way haven for lifestyles not quite acceptable back home. It is believed that English writer Rudyard Kipling penned *Ode to a*

Firefly while lounging on the patio of the old Titchfield Hotel in Port Antonio. Robin Moore, the American writer, was said to have written much of his book, *The French Connection*, while reclined beneath a mango tree at Blue Hole, which is also located at Port Antonio.

Ian Fleming first came to Jamaica during World War II while on assignment for the British military intelligence and was so taken by its natural beauty that he returned immediately after the war. He built a house near Oracabessa and dubbed it Goldeneye, the place where he would parlay his inside knowledge of espionage and fascination with military gadgets into 13 James Bond novels. Three of these novels—

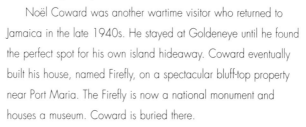

Live And Let Die, *Doctor No* and *The Man With The Golden Gun*—were partially set in Jamaica.

Noël Coward was another wartime visitor who returned to Jamaica in the late 1940s. He stayed at Goldeneye until he found the perfect spot for his own island hideaway. Coward eventually built his house, named Firefly, on a spectacular bluff-top property near Port Maria. The Firefly is now a national monument and houses a museum. Coward is buried there.

Truman Capote, the American writer and bon vivant, was a frequent visitor to the Jamaican vacation home of actress Audrey Hepburn, allegedly because he had a crush on another expat—Australian actor Errol Flynn. The always-adventurous Flynn spent much of the 1950s in Jamaica, living on a three-mast schooner anchored off Port Antonio. He also had a sprawling coconut plantation and cattle ranch near Boston Bay. Flynn whiled away his days in paradise honing the fine art of the beach party and taking rum-splashed raft trips down the Rio Grande. In one of these notorious escapades, Capote fell overboard and nearly drowned. Nowadays Jamaica provides inspiration for singers and songwriters such as Jimmy Buffett, Gwen Stefani and Joe Cocker.

THIS PAGE (CLOCKWISE FROM TOP):
Monkey Island near Port Antonio was once the domain of Princess Nina Aga Khan; statue of Nöel Coward at Firefly, near Port Maria; Sean Connery and Ursula Andress in a scene from Dr. No, filmed at Bond Beach.
OPPOSITE: Bamboo rafting on the Rio Grande river.

reggae + dreadlocks

Jamaica is best known for its homegrown music. A creative explosion started in the early 1960s, and the music has never ceased. It started with ska, a buoyant blend of traditional island styles like mento and calypso with snazzy jazz, rock and R&B riffs imported from the United States. Ska's highly danceable rhythm and upbeat lyrics matched the optimistic mood of the time—the years when Jamaica was earning its independence from Britain.

By the middle of the 1960s, ska had evolved into a slower and more sober style called rocksteady which had more soulful vocals and lyrics that reflected the growing discontent of Jamaica's underclass. By the late 1960s, rocksteady had spun into reggae with a slow hypnotic beat and an even harder lyrical edge. It was the music that would soon become the backdrop for the cry for self-determination, adopted by oppressed peoples everywhere. Heavily influenced by Rastafarian traditions, such as dreadlocks and ganja smoking, reggae became the living, breathing symbol of Jamaica around the globe. From Peter Tosh and Third World to Yellow Man and Burning Spear, reggae has produced many international stars; none so formidable as Bob Marley who rose from poverty to cultural phenomenon in just 30 years.

Robert Nesta Marley came into this world in 1945. He was born in a modest clapboard house in a hamlet called Nine Mile in the mountains above Ocho Rios. The property is still owned by his family, but in a spiritual sense it belongs to the entire nation. It is the spot where the nation's most renowned citizen was born, raised, and ultimately buried. The mausoleum stands poised on the flanks of Mt. Zion, right behind the house. While Marley wrote and recorded most of his songs while living in Kingston, Nine Mile is the place of his childhood, where he felt the bitterness of poverty and oppression. This experience burns through so many of his lyrics. Two decades after his death from cancer in 1981, Marley's music continues to flourish and remains influential. His image—ebullient dreadlocks, boyish grin and defiant eyes—has become a symbol of Jamaica and the Caribbean.

THIS PAGE (FROM TOP): Reggae singer Jimmy Cliff shot to fame as an actor before hitting it big in the music business; ganja smoking, part of the Rastafarian tradition.

OPPOSITE (FROM TOP): Diving with barracudas off the north shore; exploring the coast on horseback near Montego Bay.

north shore chic: montego bay

The antics of Errol Flynn and the musings of so many writers sparked overseas interest in Jamaica's north shore, helping to transform a coast that had traditionally relied on the banana trade and sugarcane plantations into a holiday playground. Three distinct resort areas have emerged—Montego Bay, Ocho Rios and Port Antonio.

Montego Bay has evolved into Jamaica's outdoor recreation mecca, a place where you could quite conceivably saddle up for a game of polo, scuba through a school of barracuda, raft down the Martha Brea River and sail between Jamaica and Cuba within a single day. But 'Mo Bay' is best known for golf. Links like Tryall, Three Palms and White Witch, are all ranked amongst the top hundred in the world. While all of these courses have lush tropical scenery and breathtaking landscapes, they are by no means just good-looking; many of the holes are difficult and unpredictable. They present a challenge to even the most seasoned putter. Among the many prestigious tournaments

that have taken place in Montego Bay are the Johnnie Walker World Championship and the Alfred Dunhill Cup.

The bay area's biggest annual party is the Reggae Sumfest, a weeklong celebration of modern Jamaican music that unfolds in venues all over Montego. Among the highlights of the seven days are a massive street jam and a rowdy beach party. Top artists from around the world are also drawn to the July event.

ocho rios + port antonio

About an hour's drive to the east (along the new north coast highway), Ocho Rios is the island's major cruise port, a friendly seaside town with good shopping and great entertainment. Island Village along the waterfront unfolds as a jumble of craft stores and fashion boutiques, rowdy restaurants and music bars, as well as a chilly Devon House shop that scoops up the island's best ice cream.

'Ochie' is also home to Reggae Xplosion, a fascinating interactive museum that explores Jamaica's musical heritage through hundreds of videos, photos, sound clips and even dance lessons. The Jamaican National Gallery also maintains a small art museum near the cruise terminal, with revolving exhibits of the nation's indigenous painting and sculpture. On the outskirts of Ocho Rios are three of the island's most renowned natural attractions—Fern Gully, Dunn's River Falls and James Bond Beach (where Ursula Andress famously emerged from the surf in *Dr. No*).

Port Antonio is still dominated by British colonial architecture and the colourful Musgrave Market, as well as the legendary Rooftop Club where many movie stars have danced the tropical night away. Navy Island—Errol Flynn's old stomping ground—lies on the outer edge of a natural harbour that embraces a brand new mega-yacht marina with the finest facilities in the northern Caribbean. 'Porty' is also a focal point for sports fishing, including the annual Blue Marlin Tournament in September.

From Frenchman's Cove, with its rocky headlands, to the black sands of Orange Bay, the gorgeous beaches of surrounding Portland Parish are rarely crowded. Bear in mind that when locals mention 'jerk' they are not talking about some obnoxious fool but the finger-licking-good barbecue (pork, chicken or fish) sold at roadside stalls around Boston Bay to the east of town. In fact, jerk was invented by runaway Maroon slaves in the heavily wooded hinterlands right behind Port Antonio. Jerk is prepared by cooking meat marinated with tangy herbs and spices over a pimento-wood fire.

THIS PAGE: *Navy Island and the Titchfield Peninsula form the two sides of Port Antonio.*

OPPOSITE (FROM TOP): *Waterfalls and streams tumble through the Enchanted Garden in the hills above Ocho Rios; jerk pork roasting on a traditional pimento-wood grill at Boston Bay.*

It would be difficult, anywhere on the planet, to find better conditions for cultivating coffee...

the blue mountains: coffee + callaloo soup

The numerous rivers that pour into the sea near Port Antonio have their origins in the Blue Mountains, one of the most spectacular chains in the Caribbean. The range derives its name from the bluish light that colours its crags in the early mornings and late afternoons. The highest peak is the 2,250-m (7,400-ft) Blue Mountain Peak. Many of the highest peaks are within the confines of the Blue and John Crow Mountains National Park. Created in the early 1990s, the park is the island's most important nature reserve, protecting endangered species like the blue mahoe (Jamaica's national tree), the flamboyant doctor bird, an indigenous rodent called the Jamaican coney, and the Jamaican swallowtail butterfly which is the largest in the western hemisphere.

In addition to nature, the Blue Mountains are also celebrated for its coffee. It would be difficult, anywhere on the planet, to find better conditions for cultivating coffee—rich, acidic soil and a wet highland climate that doubles the growing season. The longer the berry stays on the tree, the bigger and harder the bean and the more concentrated the sugar content. This is what makes Blue Mountain coffee so good. While the bulk of the beans are slated for export, some of the smaller operations sell beans directly from the roaster. One of these operations is the Alex Twyman Estate where the aroma of the world's most expensive coffee wafts through the open windows of Victorian-era plantation houses. A cup of local java is the perfect complement to the fine food you will also find in the Blue Mountains at places like the Gap Café and Strawberry Hill. Gourmands should be on the lookout for traditional Jamaican dishes such as saltfish and ackee, callaloo soup or mackerel rundown.

kingston: where the music never stops

Jamaica's sprawling, seething, spirited capital city is the place that gave birth to reggae and rocksteady, dance hall and dub (the precursor to modern rap). Kingston is the musical melting pot that produced Bob Marley, Peter Tosh and so many other euphonious legends. Modern music would not be the same if this city had never existed.

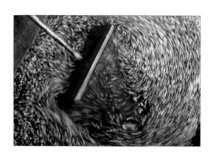

THIS PAGE (FROM TOP): Coffee beans about to be roasted on an estate in the Blue Mountains; entrance to the Bob Marley Museum in Kingston.

OPPOSITE: Much of the terrain of the Blue Mountains is within the boundaries of national parks and nature reserves.

The city's top attraction is the Bob Marley Museum at 56 Hope Road. The museum is located in a colonial house where Marley and his considerable entourage lived during most of the 1970s. Unlike Nine Mile with its spiritual overtones, Hope Road is much more down to earth. The museum is more of a tribute to a musical genius—and artistic eccentricity—than a shrine to a diffident prophet. Among the highlights are the kitchen where Marley cooked up his own Rastafarian Ital recipes, the pantry where he was nearly gunned down by political opponents (bullet holes still scar the plaster walls), the Tuff Gong recording studio where many of his later hits were cut, his glittering gold records and his favourite ganja pipe.

Another tribute to Bob Marley and the reggae movement is the Trench Town Cultural Yard. The Yard is the brainchild of former underworld 'don' Mikey Smith who came to realize that development rather than violence was the road to progress. The museum centres around the Trench Town 'yard'—a cluster of one-storey wooden tenement houses with a dirt courtyard where Marley spent his teenage years jamming with Vincent 'Tata' Ford, his first musical mentor. Tata's room, where he and Marley composed the legendary song, 'No Woman, No Cry', has been faithfully restored and has much of the original furniture as well as Marley's first guitar. Other homes around the yard have been converted into shops. There is now a Rastafarian restaurant and a craft shop filled with the work of Trench Town artists.

negril: hedonism + the black river morass

Nestled at the extreme western end of the island, Negril has gone from hippie haunt to hip hangout over the past three decades. Yet it has somehow managed to maintain its laidback manner. In so many ways, this serene beach resort is the epitome of 'no problem' Jamaican. From the cliff diving at Rick's to the nude volleyball games at Hedonism, you would not find another place in the Caribbean where you could let it all hang out to such an extreme. Just about anything goes at Negril. As one travel writer opines, '[Negril is] the vortex around which Jamaica's fun-in-the-sun vacation life whirls.'

Having developed into a holiday hotspot so late in the game, Negril was able to learn from the mistakes of others. There is, for example, a strict zoning ordinance that limits construction to nothing above the level of the highest palms. Instead of building up, Negril went sideways and now sprawls along 16 km (10 miles) of coast, all the way from Bloody Bay in the north to the lighthouse (built in the 1890s) at South Negril Point. The swankiest digs are along West End Road, where ultra-chic boutique hotels with infinity-edge pools and yoga pavilions perched on rugged limestone cliffs are located. With nothing but sapphire water between Seven Mile Beach and the Yucatán, the sunsets here are simply fabulous. The diving here is also stupendous. More than a thousand species of fish and coral inhabit Negril's offshore marine park.

Although life is largely focused on the shore, Negril is also a jumping off point for forays into the Jamaican interior to secluded spots like Y.S. Falls (Dunn's River without the crowds) and a vast tropical wetland called the Black River Morass. A southern cousin to the Florida Everglades, the Black River Morass is nourished by the island's longest navigable waterway, the slow-flowing Black River. The Morass boasts an incredible array of wildlife including osprey, egrets, barracuda, snook, snapper and tarpon that can weigh as much as 90 kg (200 lb). But the monarch of the morass is *Crocodylus acutus*—the rare and endangered American crocodile. A smaller, and reportedly much less aggressive, version of the man-eating crocs of Australia and Africa, these local crocodiles number around 300.

treasure beach: chic shacks + calabash

Separating the swamps from the open sea is a finger of sand called Treasure Beach, where 'old school' Jamaica is still alive and thriving. Chic little shacks, posh private villas and designer-savvy boutique hotels line the shore. Bare feet and bikinis are de rigueur in even the most expensive restaurants, a throwback to the Jamaica of 30 years ago; Negril before it became such a cause célèbre. Hang out at thatched-roof cafés and funky little bars near slivers of fine white sand where fishermen land their skiffs each morning. After a couple of days, you will definitely find yourself wishing that all of the Caribbean were still this way: simple, safe and completely unaffected by the machinations of the modern world.

Treasure Beach is also home to Jamaica's annual tribute to the written word—the Calabash Festival—a gathering of authors, poets and songwriters from all around the Caribbean. Spread across three days each spring, the festival unfolds in great billowy tents erected in goat pastures along the seafront, as thousands gather to hear readings, participate in literary workshops and hobnob with their favourite artists. Copious amounts of Red Stripe and jerk pork are also close at hand. It is a celebration of the many things that make Jamaica special.

THIS PAGE (CLOCKWISE FROM ABOVE):
Among the denizens of the Black River Morass is the rare American crocodile; fish for sale at Calabash Bay, near Treasure Beach; a casual beachside café along Treasure Beach.

OPPOSITE: Taking it easy, soaking up some sun—quintessential Jamaica at Negril.

Bare feet and bikinis are de rigueur...

The Caves

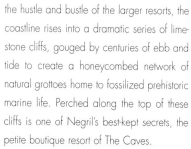

Negril, on the far western tip of Jamaica, is rich in natural beauty and best known for its 11-km (7-mile) stretch of pure, white sand. Southwest of the beach and removed from the hustle and bustle of the larger resorts, the coastline rises into a dramatic series of limestone cliffs, gouged by centuries of ebb and tide to create a honeycombed network of natural grottoes home to fossilized prehistoric marine life. Perched along the top of these cliffs is one of Negril's best-kept secrets, the petite boutique resort of The Caves.

Its lush, landscaped gardens hide many treasures, from cliffside sundecks and a salt-water pool to coral stairways leading down the cliff face to the water's edge, and a hot tub located in the cool interior of one of the grottoes. The resort's intimate size, ingenious architectural design and cleverly sequestered common spaces give guests the feeling that they always have the whole of paradise to themselves, regardless of the occupancy rate.

Accommodation at The Caves comprises 10 thatched-roofed cottages of wood and stone. With each set amid verdant tropical gardens by the edge of the sea, they offer breathtaking sea views and outdoor showers or baths which boast spectacular waterfront locations. As with the architecture and landscaping, the rooms were exquisitely decorated by the owners themselves—husband-and-wife team Bertram Saulter (the architect) and Greer-Ann (the interior designer)—with hand-carved furniture, batik fabrics and eclectic objets d'art. The beds are delicately draped with muslin mosquito nets for that romantic

...a honeycombed network of natural grottoes home to fossilized prehistoric marine life.

ambience, and a combination of high roofs, ceiling fans and constant sea breezes keeps the naturally ventilated rooms airy and cool. The food—an imaginative fusion of Jamaican and international cuisines—is another of The Caves' many attractions. Meals are served in an open-air gazebo and various locations around the property, most notably in one of its grottoes—candlelit and flower-strewn, with mysterious seawaters lapping the rocky edge mere metres from your table.

For those seeking physical and spiritual rejuvenation, The Caves has it all. Its Aveda Mini-Spa offers a wide array of facilities and services including a sauna, reinvigorating face and body treatments, massages and reflexology. Of course, there is the stirring Caribbean Sea itself. A magnificent tropical reef system stretches along the base of the cliffs, making it perfect for snorkelling, and a wide variety of water sports can be made available by arrangement. There's also the town of Negril, its beaches and nightlife, and while these are to be recommended, most guests will probably find that The Caves has everything—and quite possibly more—they need to make their holiday complete.

THIS PAGE (FROM TOP): The Caves offers new experiences that are hard to match elsewhere, from its organic interior design; and the fantastical wall murals; to candlelight dining in a grotto.

OPPOSITE: The resort's petit size doesn't keep it from pulling out all the stops. Making it one of the most original abodes in the region is the intriguing system of grottoes hidden beneath its cottage-lined clifftop.

FACTS		
ROOMS	10 suites	
FOOD	open-air gazebo: breakfast and lunch with intimate evening dining under the stars	
DRINK	open-air bar: premium brands (24-hour access, self-service after hours)	
FEATURES	spa • saltwater pool • cliffside jacuzzi • swimming in caves • kayaking • sea floats • snorkelling • bicycles • private dining in caves (by reservation) • wireless Internet (in lobby)	
NEARBY	Negril town	
CONTACT	PO Box 3113, Light House Road, Negril, Westmoreland, Jamaica • telephone: +1876.957 0270 • facsimile: +1876.957 4930 • email: thecaves@cwjamaica.com • website: www.islandoutpost.com	

PHOTOGRAPHS COURTESY OF ISLAND OUTPOST.

Goldeneye

THIS PAGE (FROM TOP): *Set on a sea-side bluff between a lagoon and the Caribbean Sea, Goldeneye is widely touted as one of the region's most alluring and romantic destinations; Ian Fleming's original house includes new luxuries today such as this garden bath.*

OPPOSITE: *The interior décor is a sensual blend of Oriental and European styles, with a slight touch of exotic Eastern mysticism worthy of a Bond novel and the hideaway's secluded tropical jungle oasis setting.*

In the last year of the Second World War, Ian Fleming found himself posted to Jamaica while serving with British Naval Intelligence. It wasn't long before he fell in love with the peaceful island paradise, its culture and its people, and the weary officer resolved to return one day to find the perfect hideaway where he would build a house for himself.

Returning after the war to scour the island for a suitable location, he eventually chose the idyllic waterfront site on which Goldeneye now stands. Fleming purchased the property in 1946 and, not long after his dream home was completed, went on to write 13 of his world-celebrated *James Bond* novels there, proclaiming that 007 himself would never have been born if not for the 'gorgeous vacuum' which Goldeneye provided.

And the place *is* gorgeous. Even on a beautiful tropical island renowned for some of the world's most picturesque landscapes, Goldeneye stands out as a very special place indeed. Located close to the sleepy banana port of Oracabessa, the famous property is a sprawling 7 hectares (18 acres) of lush gardens nestled into a seaside bluff which overlooks crystal clear waters—a lagoon on one side and the Caribbean on the other.

The namesake resort retains much of the original character and individuality that its creator intended and could, in fact, double as a setting for one of his books today. But

Goldeneye is anything but a museum piece. Although an exclusive address, the mood is relaxed and unstuffy; the interiors tastefully decorated in a clean, tropical style; and the clientele is as fashionable as any to be found in the Caribbean's most trendy and exclusive beach resorts.

In addition to Fleming's original three-bedroom house, there is a selection of villas each named after a character. Each room has been individually and exquisitely styled to blend well into its natural surroundings, also featuring outdoor showers and baths and, a high-tech media room to keep even the most ardent 007 fan happy (not least because the DVD library comes fully stocked with the super-spy's every film appearance).

For meals, guests can be served in the comfort of their villas and several garden and beach locations. The menu offers a note-worthy selection of Jamaican dishes and the service is efficient and pleasantly attentive without being intrusive.

For the adventurous and the water sport aficionado, the retreat offers a flood-lit tennis court and an extensive range of water sports which run the ground from kayaking and windsurfing to jet-skiing and snorkelling. For others, however, Goldeneye's attractions are perhaps the same as those that drew Fleming to it in the first place—the quiet tranquillity, exquisite shore and waters, and seclusion from the world beyond.

PHOTOGRAPHS COURTESY OF ISLAND OUTPOST.

FACTS		
	ROOMS	The exclusive Ian Fleming Villa and a selection of other villas ranging from one to six bedrooms
	FOOD	Jamaican
	FEATURES	flood-lit tennis court • beach • water sports • massage services • land and sea excursions
	NEARBY	airport at Boscobel (10 minutes by car) • Ocho Rios
	CONTACT	Oracabessa, St. Mary, Jamaica • telephone: +1876.975 3354 • facsimile: +1876.975 3620 • email: goldeneye@cwjamaica.com • website: www.islandoutpost.com

Jake's

THIS PAGE (FROM TOP): Jake's sports a quirky and eclectic style that gives it an intimate ambience of sensuality and romance; one of the boutique resort's three exuberantly coloured honeymoon cottages which overlook the Caribbean.

OPPOSITE (FROM LEFT): Each honeymoon cottage features a spacious patio on the upper deck complete with a daybed, lounge area and outdoor bath; in reflecting the idyllic lifestyle of the tiny fishing village where Jake's sits, many of the seafront guestrooms are designed with an extended deck over the water.

There's no escaping the fact—Jake's is a long way off the beaten track. It's a 2-hour drive from the nearest international airport and those making the trip for the first time will probably, at some point, find themselves wondering if they've made the right decision in selecting this—the most isolated of Island Outpost's collection of resorts—as their base.

In truth, Jake's secluded location on the unspoilt southern coast of Jamaica is just one of the many attractions that makes it one of the trendiest and most romantic 'chic shacks' on the planet, as the eclectic mix of rock stars, supermodels and billionaires who make the long trek to its doors goes to prove. Much of Jake's charm lies in its spot in the quaint, tiny fishing village of Treasure Beach, a part of the 'real' Jamaica that few visitors ever get to see, and an idyllic contrast to the mega-resorts that dominate the overdeveloped north coast.

What else makes Jake's so special? Some might say it's the colourful accommodation for which Jake's has earned the title as 'one of the Caribbean's funkiest resorts'. There are 23 one-of-a-kind seaside cottages nestled in the naturally landscaped gardens, each one thoughtfully appointed by theatre designer Sally Henzell in a groovy and eclectic mix of Jamaican, Mexican and, even Greek and Catalan elements. Sporting soothing rainbow hues, Moroccan-inspired roof decks and hand-crafted mosaics, some rooms feature private verandahs and others, wooden decks which are set right over the cerulean waters of the Caribbean. From the ocean- and garden-

view rooms to Calabash Bay—a six-bedroom luxury villa—each exudes, in its own way, an easy-going charm and personality.

Others might point to the quality of the food and drink. There are two restaurants to choose from. The first—Jake's—prides itself on its exquisite Jamaican delicacies with an international twist. Further along the beach is Jack Sprat, famous in the area for its oven-baked pizzas and locally caught seafood. If it's a refreshing rum punch you're after, there's

no better place in Jamaica to have one than at Dougie's Bar. The staff are fun, impeccably courteous and obliging. There's none of the formality associated with other exclusive world-class hotels, and it won't be long before you come to regard them as your friends.

Then there's the wide variety of amenities and activities, from snorkelling and deep-sea fishing to excursions to YS Falls, Appleton rum factory and Pelican Bar—dubbed 'the coolest bar in the Caribbean' by those in the know. For physical and spiritual well-being, Jake's offers a steam bath using fresh natural herbs and even massages by a Rastafarian healer. Or, simply soak up the rays on the private beach or cool off in the saltwater pool.

While all of these elements contribute to the near-legendary reputation that Jake's has earned for itself over the years, what makes the place really special is that rare, intangible quality of true class—an easy blend of urbane elegance and laid-back luxury that is hard to match. This is 'quirky chic' at its best.

FACTS		
	ROOMS	23 cottages
	FOOD	Jake's oceanfront restaurant: Jamaican cuisine with an international twist • Jack Sprat: pizza and seafood
	DRINK	Dougie's Bar
	FEATURES	beach • saltwater pool • land and sea excursions • spa and massage services • media room • boutique • cooking lessons
	NEARBY	Treasure Beach • YS Falls • Appleton rum factory • Pelican Bar
	CONTACT	Calabash Bay, Treasure Beach, St. Elizabeth, Jamaica • telephone: +1876.965 3000 • facsimile: +1876.965 0552 • email: jakes@cwjamaica.com • website: www.islandoutpost.com

PHOTOGRAPHS COURTESY OF ISLAND OUTPOST.

Jamaica Inn + Spa

Genteel, elegant and traditional, Jamaica Inn has enjoyed over 50 years at the top of the Caribbean hospitality league. Located in beautiful Ocho Rios on a private cove with an offshore reef not far from the town centre, this grand old classic overlooks the crystal-clear waters and champagne-coloured sands of one of Jamaica's premier private beaches.

The posh accommodations consist of 47 sumptuous suites (which include two recent additions, Cottages 3 and 4) as well as four separate, private cottages. Named by *Tatler* as 'Hotel Hotspot in the West Indies' (2005), this 'Caribbean Classic' is also adored by *Condé Nast Traveler* for bringing the best of Europe to the tropics. Impeccably furnished in charming colonial style with island-crafted mahogany, bamboo and Jamaican antiques, each expansive suite offers views of the sea

from its own terrace, which comes furnished with sofas, wing chairs and antique writing desks to serve as a living space.

For utmost exclusivity, the White Suite is perched on a private peninsula and offers its guests privileged views of the vast sea from anywhere within its airy rooms. Sir Winston Churchill, who once stayed here, declared the subtle light perfect for his watercolours.

Those seeking seclusion away from the Inn may choose to hole up in one of four tastefully appointed private cottages set on a bluff not far from the main hotel. Decorated in a unique tropical blend of Jamaican and Indonesian styles, each is an exquisite hide-away with a touch of old-fashioned idyll—there are no televisions, radios or clocks to upset the delicate atmosphere of tranquillity.

To ensure that gastronomic expectations are met with equal sensitivity and refinement, Jamaica Inn's award-winning chefs make a

THIS PAGE (CLOCKWISE FROM TOP LEFT):
The Dinner Terrace; uninterrupted horizon views from a superior suite balcony; a bedroom in Cottage 4, one of the two recently added suites.

OPPOSITE: Jamaica Inn's lush, sprawling grounds are graced by beautiful mature foliage and look out to the Caribbean Sea.

truly ambrosial affair out of every meal. The impressive cuisine's roots are firmly embedded in European styles, yet have absorbed many delicious Caribbean twists. Enjoy a gourmet breakfast at Shanty Town, where the sight of the shimmery, ever-changing sea surrounding the restaurant deck is reason enough to leave one's suite for an early morning start. Guests are also welcome to dine either in their own suite or in the comfort of their verandah.

As evening falls, the Dinner Terrace is beautifully illuminated by lamps, painting a soul-stirring view of the blue bay. Soak in the live entertainment (stars who include Nicole Henry have performed here) as you savour a six-course gourmet dinner beneath the stars. Fresh local seafood—lobsters in particular—plays a prominent role in proceedings, and menus vary by night. Enjoy sybaritic dining with Jamaica Inn's flawless service, which has been praised by industrial authorities such as *Travel + Leisure,* who ranked the Inn as Jamaica's number-one hotel (2006).

For guests with pampering in mind, visit KiYara Ocean Spa on Jamaica Inn's seaside cliffs, where native traditions are combined with ayurveda and exotic Fijian treatments. Spiritual wellness is sought through natural therapies from Apito Stone Energy Balancing (using volcanic river stones from the island) to multi-step body-mind experiences such as the Piña Colada Body Polish.

Those craving a little more exercise or adventure will take to the state-of-the-art pool and fitness facilities. Jamaica Inn also boasts on-property croquet, kayaking, sunfish sailing and snorkelling. Comfortably close by is the Caribbean's top equestrian centre, offering polo, dressage and show jumping lessons.

FACTS		
	ROOMS	47 suites • 4 cottages
	FOOD	Shanty Town: breakfast and lunch • Dinner Terrace: Jamaican cuisine
	DRINK	lounge • beach bar
	FEATURES	KiYara Ocean Spa • fitness room • pool • croquet • water sports • snorkelling
	BUSINESS	meeting room • audiovisual equipment
	NEARBY	windsurfing • sailing • diving • golf • tennis • polo • horse riding • Chukka Cove Farm • Blue Mountain bicycle tour • island eco-tours
	CONTACT	PO Box 1, Main Street, Ocho Rios, St. Ann, Jamaica • telephone: +1876.974 2514 • facsimile: +1876.974 2449 • email: reservations@jamaicainn.com • website: www.jamaicainn.com

PHOTOGRAPHS COURTESY OF JAMAICA INN + SPA.

Rockhouse

Perched on rugged cliffs over Negril Bay, Rockhouse is the sort of place that Robinson Crusoe might design if given the chance to create a 21st-century island escape. The laid-back ambience and 'no problem' attitude—together with sensational cuisine, comfy digs and killer sunsets—is just what the doctor ordered for wannabe castaways who find themselves 'washed up' on Jamaica's west coast. Just ask the Rolling Stones, who used to chill here back in the 1970s.

Owned and operated by a couple of affable Australians who fell in love with the Caribbean many moons ago, this small and trendy boutique hotel takes full advantage of its spectacular natural setting. Thatched-roof bungalows hug the clifftop, mere steps away from sundecks chiselled into the naked stone and ladders that lead down the drop of rocky palisades to half a dozen coves, where the swimming and snorkelling are marvellous.

Simply divine too are Rockhouse's new spa—think cliffside cabanas—and premium villas. Built on their own rocky promontories, the latter are individual thatched-roof cottages which boast wraparound terraces, gorgeous sunset vistas of Pristine Cove down below and private outdoor showers concealed by lush tropical vegetation. Featured among the timber furnishings are four-poster beds with delicate muslin netting and, this being music-crazed Jamaica, villas are outfitted with CD players.

THIS PAGE (FROM TOP): Carved into the edge of a cliff, the horizon pool offers a breathtaking vista; here, massages are delivered in open air by the sea; Rockhouse serves some of the best New Jamaican cuisine on the island and is even visited by guests from other hotels.

OPPOSITE: With island delights such as stairs cut into cliff rock leading straight into beautifully clear turquoise waters, it is easy to imagine Robinson Crusoe swimming here among fish.

Even those staying at other hotels make a point of coming to Rockhouse for dinner. The hotel's stylish restaurant and bar, set on a wooden verandah right above the water, serves Jamaican fusion fare that combines fresh local ingredients and European culinary flair. Seafood is the house specialty, although the jerk chicken is also a popular favourite.

The front desk can arrange all sorts of outdoor activities—from scuba diving trips, boat rental and parasailing to golf, tennis and horseback riding—as well as visits to Negril town or beach, and excursions into Negril's exotic hinterland, including safaris to find, photograph and, sometimes, even touch crocodiles in the Black River swamps.

Hewn into a cliff-top at the back of the property is an 18-m (60-ft) infinity pool that meets the horizon between sea and sky, flanked by sundecks with blue-cushioned loungers shaded by colourful umbrellas. The Red Stripe flows freely at the poolside bar, especially at sunset, when guests gather to toast the end of another day in paradise.

FACTS		
ROOMS	9 standard rooms • 5 studios • 13 villas • 7 premium villas • all rooms air-conditioned	
FOOD	Rockhouse Restaurant: New Jamaican cuisine	
DRINK	Rockhouse Bar • pool bar	
FEATURES	cliff-edge pool • Pristine Cove • snorkelling • kayaking • spa • yoga classes • lounge • boutique	
NEARBY	golf • tennis • water sports • night clubs • Seven Mile Beach • Black River Morass • Negril Royal Palm Reserve • YS Falls	
CONTACT	West End Road, Negril, Jamaica • telephone: +1876.957 4373 • facsimile: +1876.957 0557 • email: info@rockhousehotel.com • website: www.rockhousehotel.com	

PHOTOGRAPHS COURTESY OF ROCKHOUSE.

Round Hill Hotel + Villas

Launched in 1953 on the grounds of an old pineapple, spice and coconut plantation spread across a lush 45-hectare (110-acre) peninsula, Round Hill has long been one of the crown jewels of Jamaican tourism; a well-bred resort which successfully treads that fine line between laid-back and luxury.

Praised worldwide by travel writers and industrial authorities for its genteel, romantic ambience and seamless service, Round Hill features on *Condé Nast Traveler's* Gold List and *Travel + Leisure's* selection of the world's 500 greatest hotels and resorts. Celebrities too adore Round Hill for its quiet exclusivity, privacy and immaculate sense of discretion. The resort comprises a sumptuous seafront hotel—aptly named Pineapple House—and 27 private villas available for rent (either as

individual suites or complete cottages) when their owners are not in residence. Recently refurbished by Ralph Lauren, the Pineapple House guestrooms feature splashes of bright tropical colour against soothing white décor and linens. Bathrooms flaunt sleek chrome fittings and rain showers. Most of the villas boast private freshwater pools, and all are equipped with kitchens where housekeepers cook breakfast for guests each morning.

Master chef Trevor Duncan oversees a kitchen that creates a mouth-watering blend of international and Jamaican cuisine, with dishes like Shrimp Rundown, Medallions of Veal with Port and Almonds, and Pumpkin Risotto with Portobello Mushrooms. Guests can choose from several dining venues such as the elegant Georgian Room or the breezy seaside terrace overlooking the beach—or they can opt for personalized room service around their own private pool.

Set inside an elegant and meticulously restored 18th-century plantation house, the Spa at Round Hill offers sanctuary for both mind and body. Exotic massages, facials and wraps using natural tropical ingredients are rendered in cool indoor treatment rooms or an al fresco area overlooking the sapphire sea. On the other side of the bay, the new Thomas Woltz-inspired pool also integrates ancient stones (from the island's historic Golden Grove Sugar Works) into a stunning work of modern architecture and intelligent eco-friendly landscaping, the water cascading over the palm-lined outer lip into a wading pool beside the beach.

Scattered around the grounds are five tennis courts, including two equipped with night lighting. Round Hill's pro is happy to arrange a casual tournament. Guests can also arrange tee times at five Montego Bay golf courses including the famous Tryall links (host to PGA events like the Johnnie Walker World Championship) and the challenging new White Witch course near Rose Hall.

THIS PAGE: Sensitively designed to honour the ecological integrity of the surrounding natural land-scape, award-winning architect Thomas Woltz's centrepiece pool features two vanishing edges over the sea, water cascading into a spa pool below.

OPPOSITE (CLOCKWISE FROM TOP LEFT): Round Hill's charming façade reflects its air of easy grace; the plantation-style architecture offers plenty of spacious, breezy areas for guests' privacy; stunning panoramic views await in the hotel's oceanfront rooms.

FACTS

ROOMS	Pineapple House Hotel: 36 oceanfront rooms • 27 private villas: superior, deluxe or master suites
FOOD	seaside terrace: international and Jamaican cuisine
DRINK	Ralph Lauren cocktail bar • beach bar • pool bar
FEATURES	spa • fitness centre • tennis courts • pool • beach • water sports • boat charters • library • art gallery • beauty salon • kid's club
BUSINESS	business centre
NEARBY	golf • river rafting • Mayfield Falls & Mineral Springs • Doctor's Cave Beach
CONTACT	PO Box 64, Montego Bay, Jamaica • telephone: +1876.9567 0505 • facsimile: +1876.956 7505 • email: reservations@roundhilljamaica.com • website: www.roundhilljamaica.com

PHOTOGRAPHS COURTESY OF ROUND HILL HOTEL + VILLAS.

Royal Plantation

The Royal Plantation in Ocho Rios is a palm-lined paradise on the spectacular north coast of Jamaica. One of the Leading Small Hotels of the World, the exquisite tropical gardens and classic Colonial Caribbean style will captivate from the very first glance.

Voted 'Jamaica's Leading Resort' at the 2005 World Travel Awards, the baronial Royal Plantation radiates genuine Jamaican warmth, from the epicurean settings where unparalleled haute cuisine is served, to each of its 74 secluded oceanfront hideaways.

THIS PAGE (FROM LEFT): Built half a century ago in the soigné style of British colonial architecture, the Royal Plantation was recently refurbished and boasts today, modern luxuries found only in the world's most eminent hotels; each suite is elegantly furnished with lavish amenities and offers breathtaking ocean panoramas —this is a hotel which plays host to royalty and world leaders.

OPPOSITE: The freshwater pool of the exclusive three-bedroom Villa Plantana, situated on the Royal Plantation's east beach.

Beautifully designed with no detail in sumptuous comfort overlooked, the Royal Plantation's suites are sheer heaven. Floating linens skim mellifluous mahogany four-poster beds upon which down-filled duvets and a plethora of pillows repose. The only sounds that will reach your private balcony are the rustling of tropical leaves and the soothing lapping of the Caribbean. If such beauty inspires an interest in the arts, the hotel's new 'Artist In Residence' scheme introduces guests to the native heritage and culture through art lessons with renowned Jamaican painters.

This elegant first-class retreat gets everything just right, from the pomp and circumstance of English High Tea on the Terrace to the white-gloved discretion of a sublime seafood extravaganza at Le Papillon, the Royal Plantation's own Master Sommelier on hand to aid your fine wine selection. For a culinary treat appealing for its sights,

sounds and smells, opt for a tableside flambé on the terrace overlooking the breathtaking Caribbean Sea at dusk.

Royal Plantation bars too, are no mere events. Round off the day with a hand-rolled cigar in the warming glow of the Cognac Bar. If the night is yet young, let the champagne bubbles race straight to your head at C Bar, where sword-opened Veuve Clicquot and exclusive Iranian caviar reign supreme.

If physical and spiritual rebalancing are top of the agenda, then the stylish enclave of the Red Lane Spa is the place to be, hailed as one of only 48 Leading Spas of the World. With excellent complimentary water sports facilities, yoga classes, invitations to exclusive cocktail parties and Caribbean cookery demonstrations, the Royal Plantation will happily help you fill an empty hour. If you'd rather enjoy all of the above safe in the knowledge that you've an absolutely exclusive haven to retire to, then the 5-hectare (14-acre) Rio Chico Estate, complete with

waterfalls and flood-lit tennis courts, is the discerning choice. For a sensation tantamount to owning your own island—with personal chef, butler, beach and freshwater pool—

Villa Plantana is a microcosm of the Royal Plantation proper. Whichever your choice of a luxurious stay, you can expect nothing less than royal treatment.

PHOTOGRAPHS COURTESY OF ROYAL PLANTATION.

FACTS		
ROOMS	74 suites • Villa Plantana (private three-bedroom villa) • Villa Rio Chico (private estate)	
FOOD	Le Papillon: gourmet cuisine and white-glove service • The Royal Café: à la carte • Bayside Restaurant: à la carte classic and contemporary • Flambé on the Terrace	
DRINK	Appleton Lounge • C Bar: caviar and champagne • drawing room	
FEATURES	Red Lane Spa • fitness centre • freshwater pool • whirlpool • tennis courts • 2 beaches • Upton Golf & Country Club • water sports • scuba diving • snorkelling	
BUSINESS	Plantation Room • Wi-Fi access • conference facilities	
NEARBY	2 international airports (90 minutes by car) • Boscobel Aerodrome (15 minutes by car)	
CONTACT	Main Street, PO Box 2, Ocho Rios, Jamaica • telephone: +1876.974 5601 • facsimile: +1876.974 5912 • email: rpres@jm.royalplantation.com • website: www.royalplantation.com	

Strawberry Hill

Anyone who has ever been to Jamaica will know the natural beauty of its coastline for which the island is justly famous. But there's more to Jamaica than beaches. Towards the eastern end runs the majestic Blue Mountains range (home of the world-renowned coffee), rising dramatically out of the Caribbean Sea. Nestled amid its foothills at an altitude of just over 914 m (3,100 ft) is the exclusive mountaintop retreat of Strawberry Hill.

Sweeping across a breathtaking, lavishly landscaped estate of 20 hectares (50 acres), this is where the wealthy retreat to for divine repose and gilt-edged indulgences. Cradled by lush, mist-swathed rainforest surroundings and overlooking a spectacular cityscape at the foot of the mountains, Strawberry Hill has an almost ethereal air about it, seeming to hang in space midway between heaven and earth. Indeed, on arrival one could almost be forgiven for thinking you've entered a world created for gods—and here, naturally, your every wish is immediately granted by the attentive and quietly efficient staff.

The accommodations consist of deluxe rooms, studios and private villas distributed between 12 Georgian-style cottages, each individually styled by award-winning interior designer Tanya Mellich to create a nostalgic atmosphere of period romance and refined luxury. True to the style of the era, all rooms are furnished with dark mahogany four-poster

THIS PAGE (FROM TOP): Standing nobly on Jamaica's Blue Mountains range, veiled by a fine muslin of mist, Strawberry Hill has an almost celestial air about it; incorporated in the architecture and interior design are intricate hand-carved fretwork, spacious verandahs and rattan furniture; the décor reflects a nostalgic taste for 19th-century elegance.

OPPOSITE: Awaiting over the brink of the resort's negative-edge pool is a breathtaking vista of the island's capital, Kingston.

beds draped in delicate muslin-thin netting, hardwood floors, 19th-century furniture and elegant French doors which open out onto spacious private verandahs with hammocks. All rooms are tastefully adorned by hand-carved fretwork, each featuring a different aspect of Jamaican culture and life. A fully equipped kitchen completes each cottage and allows for a degree of self-sufficiency.

Tempting as it may be not to leave the comforts of the cottages, guests often find it hard to resist the delectable New Jamaican innovations of the resort's first-rate restaurant.

Difficult to ignore too is Strawberry Hill's intuitive philosophy of providing a balanced holiday lifestyle which embraces all facets of living. The resort's vast grounds are a tropical wonderland of winding pathways with over 350 species of recorded flora and fauna; and to help guests attain a blissful state of total relaxation and optimum self-awareness, they are actively encouraged to enhance their spiritual experiences through bird watching,

nature walks or a visit to a coffee estate to learn about its cultivation. For meditation and peaceful comtemplation, there is the resort's one-of-a-kind negative-edge pool, yoga deck and famous Aveda spa—the only full-service facility of its kind in the Caribbean.

As befits such a magnificent property, the panoramic views from the estate are simply spectacular. On one side the Blue Mountains rear up into the distant heavens; on the other side and far below lies the capital city of Kingston and, beyond it, the Caribbean Sea. Sunsets here have to be seen to be believed and, as dusk approaches, there is no finer way to enjoy the evening than by lounging on your own private verandah—rum punch in hand—savouring the magic of one of Jamaica's most privileged destinations.

FACTS		
	ROOMS	5 deluxe one-bedrooms • 5 deluxe studios • 3 deluxe villas
	FOOD	Strawberry Hill restaurant: New Jamaican cuisine
	DRINK	lounge bar
	FEATURES	full-service Aveda spa • yoga deck • freshwater negative-edge pool • plunge pool • gardens • library • boutique
	BUSINESS	conference facilities
	NEARBY	Irish Town • Blue Mountains • Kingston
	CONTACT	Newcastle Road, Irish Town, St. Andrew, Jamaica • telephone: +1876.944 8400 • facsimile: +1876.944 8408 • email: strawberry@cwjamaica.com • website: www.islandoutpost.com

PHOTOGRAPHS COURTESY OF ISLAND OUTPOST.

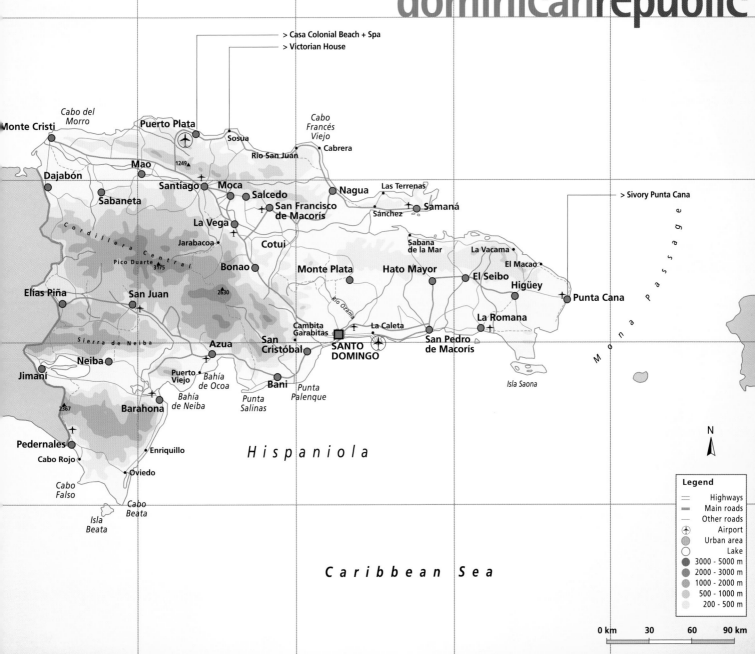

dominicanrepublic

Atlantic Ocean

> Casa Colonial Beach + Spa
> Victorian House

> Sivory Punta Cana

Cabo del Morro

Monte Cristi
Puerto Plata
Sosua
Cabo Francés Viejo
Cabrera
Rio San Juan
Dajabón
Mao
Santiago
Moca
Salcedo
Nagua
Las Terrenas
Sabaneta
San Francisco de Macorís
Sánchez
Samaná
1249▲
La Vega
Jarabacoa
Cotui
Sabana de la Mar
La Vacama
Pico Duarte 3175
Bonao
Monte Plata
Hato Mayor
El Macao
2630
El Seibo
Higüey
Elías Piña
San Juan
Río Ozama
Punta Cana
La Romana
Neiba
Cambita Garabitas
La Caleta
San Cristóbal
SANTO DOMINGO
San Pedro de Macorís
Jimaní
Azua
Bani
Isla Saona
Puerto Viejo
Bahía de Ocoa
Punta Palenque
2367
Barahona
Bahía de Neiba
Punta Salinas

Cordillera Central

Sierra de Neiba

Pedernales
Cabo Rojo
Enriquillo
Cabo Falso
Oviedo

Isla Beata
Cabo Beata

Hispaniola

Mona Passage

Caribbean Sea

N

Legend
Highways
Main roads
Other roads
Airport
Urban area
Lake
3000 - 5000 m
2000 - 3000 m
1000 - 2000 m
500 - 1000 m
200 - 500 m

0 km   30   60   90 km

a spanish heritage

The nation that gave the world baseball slugger Sammy Sosa and merengue, the Dominican Republic, or 'D.R.', defies description. One of the region's three Spanish-speaking nations, along with Cuba and Puerto Rico, the D.R. occupies the eastern half of Hispaniola island. French-speaking Haiti is located on the western half of the same island. The D.R. has a population of 9 million people spread across an area the size of the Netherlands. It has more dry land than all of the Leeward and Windward islands combined. The D.R. is graced with a mosaic of rainforest and arid desert-like regions, sugarcane plantations and cattle-grazing grasslands, golden beaches and unspoilt coral reefs, slumbering villages and a great simmering city called Santo Domingo.

Like much of the Caribbean, the island was 'discovered' by Columbus, who regarded it as the most beautiful place he had ever seen. Rather than speed past in pursuit of more discoveries, Columbus actually put down roots here. His brother Bartolomeo was the founder of Santo Domingo and Columbus' son Diego was one of the first governors of a colony that would serve as the base for the conquest of Mexico and Central America. Columbus' famous flagship, the *Santa Maria*, was probably wrecked along the coast of Hispaniola. Dominicans have long claimed that the Genovese explorer is buried within the imposing Faro a Colón (Columbus' Lighthouse) in the capital, although DNA tests of remains in the Cathedral of Seville in Spain seem to indicate that Columbus might actually be entombed there.

Centuries after Columbus, the D.R. has emerged as one of the great tourism success stories of the Caribbean. Almost overnight, the country has gone from holiday backwater to the front line of modern jet-set travel. Punta Cana in the east and the Costa Plata in the north are now amongst the swankiest beach resorts in the entire Caribbean. Despite the boom, the Dominican Republic is still large enough to have its quiet corners and secluded beaches.

PAGE 54: Children at the Pink House, an orphanage run by Catholic nuns in downtown Santo Domingo.

THIS PAGE (FROM TOP): Fuerte de San Felipe is Puerto Plata's last Spanish colonial relic; Christopher Columbus looks down on Parque Colón in the heart of old Santo Domingo.

OPPOSITE: Colourful cabanas line the shore at Isla Saona, a prime scuba and snorkelling spot, off the southeast coast.

games people play

Rather than knocking down wickets like kids elsewhere in the Caribbean, Dominican boys hone their skills at pitching, batting and fielding baseballs. To say that Dominicans are passionate about the sport is a gross understatement: these people eat, sleep and drink 'beisbol'. Contrary to popular opinion, baseball was not introduced by U.S. Marines who temporarily occupied Hispaniola after World War I, but rather by Cuban exiles who lived there in the 1870s. Dominican baseball was further bolstered by the presence of African American stars like Satchel Paige and Josh Gibson who played in the D.R. in the 1930s, before racial integration was introduced to U.S. baseball.

Since the 1950s, more than 200 players from the Dominican Republic have played in U.S. major leagues including pitchers Juan Marichal and Pedro Martinez, the three Alou brothers, Vladimir Guerrero, Albert Pujols and the incomparable Sammy Sosa—the only Latin player to hit more than 500 career home runs. One of the great joys of visiting the D.R. today is seeing many of the current Dominican stars play in the

ABOVE: Baseball players warm-up before a game at Quisqueya Stadium, Santo Domingo.

OPPOSITE: Porfirio Rubirosa in a car with Woolworth heiress Barbara Hutton, one of the many famous women with whom he shared a romance.

country's highly competitive winter league. Games at Liga Stadium in Santo Domingo and Tetelo Vargas Stadium in San Pedro de Macorís (Sosa's hometown) are more like carnivals than sporting events; a cacophony of drums, whistles, horns and ever-shouting vendors that often overwhelms the action on the diamond.

Another Dominican 'superstar' was Porfirio Rubirosa, who played the game of seduction like no one before or since. Born in the village of San Francisco de Macorís in 1909, he earned his stripes as a racecar driver, polo player and diplomat. But more than anything else he was known as an international Casanova. For nearly three decades, he was a staple of the tabloid press which called him the 'ultimate playboy' and the 'world's greatest lover'. Among Rubirosa's countless paramours were Woolworth heiress Barbara Hutton, controversial New York socialite Doris Duke, Hungarian actress Zsa Zsa Gabor and Hollywood starlet Kim Novak. Having lived such a fast life, it was perhaps inevitable that Rubirosa would die relatively young, slamming his Ferrari into a tree in Paris in 1965.

merengue + mofongo

Rubirosa's emergence on the international party scene coincided with the rise of another Dominican sensation—merengue. Both a music and dance form, people were grooving to merengue long before salsa became queen of the Latin beat. Although its precise origins are lost in history, merengue was no doubt influenced by Afro-Latin dances imported from Cuba and Puerto Rico in the early 19th century. Appalled by the sensual body movements and risqué lyrics, Dominican high society initially ignored merengue.

It was not until the 1930s that merengue gained wider acceptance, thanks in no small part to radio broadcasts and its prominent place in the political campaigns of Dominican dictator Rafael Trujillo. Several variants of merengue dancing have emerged since then, including the slightly formal salon (ballroom) form during which partners never separate, and the much more sensual club form with its freestyle dance moves (à la salsa). Many resort hotels organize Latin dance classes. You can go to merengue workshops and other events sponsored by Kalalú—the Afro Caribbean Cultural Research and Creative Action Lab—in the Zona Colonial in Santo Domingo. Merengue also takes the stage during the annual Dominican Republic Jazz Festival, which unfolds at various venues along the north shore in October.

Dominican cuisine is equally exotic, with dishes like mofongo, mondongo, sancocho. Like so much of the West Indies, the local cuisine is largely Creole—a mix of local ingredients, Afro-Caribbean seasoning and ancient Iberian cooking methods.

Mofongo is a delicious dish that combines mashed pork rinds and plantains (green bananas) in a deep-fried ball or patty that resembles green crab cake. Variations include mofongo camarones (with shrimp) and mofongo langosta (with lobster). Mondongo is basically stewed tripe made with peppers, onions, garlic, lemons and Tabasco sauce. Sancocho is a stew made with seven different types of meat. It is prepared during fiestas and special occasions. The nation's most beloved dessert is majarete, a type of custard made with fresh corn, coconut milk, vanilla and cinnamon.

THIS PAGE (CLOCKWISE FROM ABOVE):
Dancers doing the merengue, the Dominican national dance; mofongo, an island delicacy made from pork and bananas; traditional grinding bowls used to make mofongo.

OPPOSITE (FROM TOP): The majestic Alcázar de Colón was built in 1510 by Diego Columbus, son of Christopher Columbus; an outdoor café in the refurbished Zona Colonial.

santo domingo

It perhaps goes without saying that the finest Dominican cuisine is found in the capital, Santo Domingo, which in fact has the oldest Creole cooking tradition in the Caribbean. Founded in 1496 by Bartolomeo Colón, it was the first European settlement of any kind in the New World. Santo Domingo became the gateway to Spanish conquests of the Caribbean and Central America, the place from which Cortez sailed to Mexico, Balboa set out for Panama and Velázquez ventured to Cuba. In 1586, Sir Francis Drake plundered and sacked the city.

Five centuries later, Santo Domingo is one of the largest Caribbean cities, a bustling metropolis of more than 2 million people, located along the country's southern shore. In the heart of the capital, along the banks of the Rio Ozama, is the historic Zona Colonial, a neighbourhood of cobblestone streets and medieval architecture. Declared a World Heritage Site by UNESCO in 1990, the 12-block district has been lovingly and meticulously restored.

Nearly every major structure in the Zona Colonial is a 'first' of one sort or another. The Cathedral of Santa Maria la Menor, with its ochre coral-stone façade and priceless silver altar, was the first cathedral in the New World (1514). The Monasterio de San Francisco was the first monastery (1512), while the nearby Dominican Convent was both the first nunnery (1510) and the first place of higher learning (1538). Perched at the confluence of harbour and river, Fortaleza Ozama was the first European fortress (1503), while the Spanish Renaissance-influenced Alcázar de Colón,

replete with Moorish arches, was the first European-style palace (1510). Restoration has brought new life to Zona Colonial. It now boasts a flourish of cultural institutions, Creole eateries, music clubs and craft boutiques that draw both locals and overseas visitors. In so many ways, the neighbourhood is once again the heart and soul of Santo Domingo.

horseback rides + humpback whales

The D.R.'s holiday coast stretches nearly 320 km (200 miles) along the north shore, from Punta Cana at the island's eastern extreme to Monte Cristi near the Haitian frontier. Each beach seems to have its specialty. Cabarete, with its steady breeze, is a hangout for the international sailboarding and kite-surfing community. Divers tend to cluster in Sosua, which lies near excellent scuba spots like the Pyramids and Three Rocks. Samaná is for nature lovers while the Puerto Plata area is more family-friendly. The flashy Punta Cana is for those who do not have to ask the price.

Punta Cana is the paragon of posh beach experience. Visitors flit back and forth between blackjack tables at the local casinos and tee off at championship-quality golf courses. Sports fishing boats based at the resort's full-service marina ply the Mona Passage between Hispaniola and Puerto Rico for marlin, wahoo and other game fish. Horseback rides along the beach and jungle trails start from the Punta Cana equestrian centre, but you would have to drive one hour to La Romana to take polo lessons or watch international matches at the famous Casa de Campo.

Further west along the north coast is the Samaná peninsula. During the winter months, thousands of humpback whales gather in Samaná Bay and the nearby Silver Shoals, which is now a marine sanctuary. On the south side of the bay lies Los Haitises National Park with its wild limestone outcrops, mangrove swamps and dense rainforest.

the amber coast

The resort area of Puerto Plata lies at the heart of the Amber Coast, so-called because of the amber in the mountains behind the shore. Dominican amber is among the finest in the world. Some ancient amber pieces enclose prehistoric insects, leaves and feathers, and have been studied by scientists. The city's Dominican Amber Museum, lodged in an old Spanish colonial villa, displays several outstanding examples.

Amber is mined in three different parts of the D.R., but the oldest, hardest and most valuable, comes from the Sierra La Cumbre between Puerto Plata and Santiago. Formed by sap from the ancient hymenaea tree, amber from this region is about 40 million years old, and lies buried in alluvial deposits. The Taino, who lived on Hispaniola before the European conquest, worked amber into fine jewellery. Ironically, beads made of Baltic amber were one of the items Columbus brought on the *Santa Maria* to trade with whomever he should happen upon in his exploration. Amber was more or less ignored in the D.R. until the 20th century, when it was used in scientific research and when it became a sought-after jewel. The export of amber with enclosed insects is forbidden without permission from the government, but amber jewellery is easily available in hotels and boutiques along the Amber Coast.

With its own international airport and direct flights from both Europe and North America, the Amber Coast is thoroughly self-sufficient. Most of the resorts are tucked along the coast to the east of Puerto Plata, with the largest selection around Playa Dorada and Sosua with their white-sand strands. Founded by Jewish refugees from Germany and Austria during the Nazi era, Sosua has developed into a funky little town where small shops and thatched-roof cafés cater to a young, hip beach crowd.

THIS PAGE (FROM TOP): Dominican beaches are renowned for their fine sand and turquoise waters; amber, with enclosed prehistoric insects, is transformed into distinctive jewellery.

OPPOSITE (FROM LEFT): Santo Domingo's stout Fortaleza Ozama overlooks the Rio Ozama; thousands of humpback whales migrate through Dominican waters each winter.

dominican highlands

Far away from the coast, the Dominican Republic is dominated by three huge mountain ranges that run east–west across the country. The largest of these, the hulking Cordillera Central, culminates in the 3,175-m (10,417-ft) Pico Duarte. It is the Caribbean's highest mountain and is a popular venue for both backpack and donkey treks. With its groves of indigenous Hispaniolan pines and a temperate climate that can leave frost on higher peaks, the highlands offer quite a contrast from the country's Caribbean coast. Youthful legs and boundless energy may lead to single-day conquests of Pico Duarte, but the recommended time is three days in the company of a local guide. The first person in recorded history to reach the peak was Sir Robert Schomburgk, a British consul, who made the climb in 1851.

Tucked in the southern mountains, about 160 km (100 miles) east of Santo Domingo, is one of the country's more intriguing towns—Altos de Chavón. It is an art colony where Dominican painters, sculptors, woodworkers and weavers create, and then sell, their works. The colony's cobblestone streets and wrought-iron balconies may fool the visitor into thinking that Altos de Chavón is a historic colony. In fact, the colony was founded fairly recently, in 1975, as a place for artistic inspiration and cultural exchange.

For visitors who delight in local arts and crafts, Altos is a dream come true. It has dozens of galleries and workshops which intermingle with sidewalk cafés and flower-draped courtyards. Many of the works here reflect Dominican myths and legends, while other works seek to express a pan-Caribbean consciousness. Classes and workshops in everything from dance and music to clay and silk-screen—are taught at the local art academy. The village amphitheatre, launched in 1982 with a concert by Frank Sinatra and Carlos Santana, presents a year-round slate of music, dance and drama events. There is no place quite like Altos, on this island, or anywhere else in the Caribbean.

THIS PAGE : The art colony of Altos de Chavón, constructed almost entirely of stone, sits on a bluff above the Rio Chavón.
OPPOSITE: Colourful roadside art is a ubiquitous sight on the island.

...a place for artistic inspiration and cultural exchange.

Casa Colonial Beach + Spa

It's official—Casa Colonial Beach & Spa is the Dominican Republic's new vogue address. The *Condé Nast* Hot List includes this luxurious resort as one of the 'Best Hotels in the World', and celebrity guests such as actor Steven Bauer couldn't agree more.

The gracious service and über-chic style of this boutique resort have not gone unnoticed, and it soars above the competition

as the only Small Luxury Hotels of the World member on this tropical island-paradise. It is a world away from other resorts for which the Republic was initially renowned.

Designed by architect Sarah Garcia, the elegant and urbane Casa Colonial has 50 apartment-sized suites, each exuding an upscale ambience. The successful synthesis of modern décor and old-world charm is evident throughout in the stunning details.

Stylish Italian marble floors reflect minimalistic mahogany furnishings, and ornate wrought-iron work casts its shadow against white stucco and classical columns. The hotel's orchid-drenched beauty oozes a romantic allure with candles, the preferred source of lighting. And exhibited throughout are semi-precious stones, colourful Indian crafts, healing plants and the works of Cisneros, a successful Dominican artist.

...successful synthesis of modern décor and old-world charm...

A warm, enlivening sense of family, of place, of beauty and of harmony permeates the Casa Colonial Beach & Spa. From the delicate hand-embroidered touches in the suites to the mindful inclusion of local materials and philosophies in its interior design, it is obvious that this beautifully balanced atmosphere is not accidental. With such care taken over the resort's aesthetics, it is not difficult to imagine just how much attention is lavished upon its guests.

Gourmets will adore the mouth-watering creations produced by the inspired chefs of Lucia, the Casa Colonial's art gallery-esque dining room and cocktail bar. Indeed, the entire property's charm lies in the indigenous and international art pieces at every turn.

The resort's superbly equipped Bagua Spa offers unique indigenous therapies such as cacao cocooning alongside pampering Vichy showers and couple's massages. When equilibrium and clarity have been attained, snuggle into your silken Frette linen and sink into your very own Caribbean dream.

For sun, sand, sea and the vital fourth element—world-class golf—Casa Colonial Beach & Spa resort's location is faultless, on the island's north coast of Playa Dorada. Sun-bleached shores, aquamarine waters and exhilarating sporting options are never more than a pebble's throw away.

FACTS		
	ROOMS	junior suites • one-bedroom suites • deluxe suites • master suites • penthouse • presidential suite
	FOOD	Lucia: Asian fusion • Veranda: breakfast and lunch
	DRINK	lobby lounge & bar • pool bar
	FEATURES	Bagua Spa • rooftop infinity-edge pool • 4 jacuzzis • fitness room
	BUSINESS	meeting room
	NEARBY	Playa Dorada Golf Course
	CONTACT	PO Box 22, Playa Dorada, Puerto Plata, Dominican Republic • telephone: +1809.320 3232 • facsimile: +1809.320 3131 • email: reservascc@vhhr.com • website: www.casacolonialhotel.com

Sivory Punta Cana

With a hallmark emphasis on impeccable service and sublime gourmet dining, Sivory brings a whole new level of chic to Punta Cana, the upscale beach resort area at the eastern end of the Dominican Republic.

From Penelope Cruz and Oscar de la Renta to techno-whiz Moby and the Oscar-nominated Jake Gyllenhaal, more and more celebrities are discovering the exotic charm of Punta Cana. With its secluded location, exquisite natural surroundings and exclusive beach, Sivory—a distinguished Small Luxury

Hotel of the World—is patent-made for those who like their paradise with a large dose of privacy. And with a winning two-to-one staff to guest ratio, only the most exemplary service is guaranteed. The eclectic concierge can also set you up with every sort of activity from 18 holes of golf and horseback riding down the champagne-coloured coast to whale watching and swimming with dolphins.

Sivory's 55 suites feature custom-made Indonesian and European furnishings, and are each decked out with the latest in vacation technology—wide-screen satellite television, high-speed Internet and DVD player—as well as a personal wine cooler stocked with well-aged vintages from the hotel's top-brass wine cellar. And in keeping with Sivory's renowned intrinsic romance, each suite comes complete with a terrace with twin chaise lounges, a double shower and a bathtub for two.

THIS PAGE (FROM TOP): Nestled in its own idyllic ribbon of palm-lined beach in the posh resort strand of Punta Cana, the infinity-edge pool looks out across vast sky, fine sand and azure waters; the oceanfront junior suite is thoroughly spoiling with your own private stretch of sand, sea and plunge pool.

OPPOSITE (FROM TOP): The deluxe junior suite is a plush affair; Sivory's romantic style sees that each suite offers a tub for two.

The centre's signature treatments range from revitalizing deep muscle tissue massage and aromatherapy to other indulgences such as hydrotherapy and a Vitamin Cocktail Facial with red algae and marine plankton.

Sivory's great natural asset is its private powder-fine beach stretching nearly 400 m (1312 ft) along the waterfront. Snorkel its translucent aquamarine waters, or explore the shoreline in a kayak or sailboat. Among the other recreational amenities are an exquisite infinity-edge pool and a putting green.

What really sets Sivory apart, however, is its Art Cuisine, which takes the stage at its three superb gourmet restaurants. Culinary sophistication reaches a peak at Gourmond, where the nouvelle French dishes are treats for both the eyes and the palate. Innovative Asian fusion is the specialty at Tau, where the intimate setting accommodates just eight tables. At Laveranda, fine Mediterranean fare is served at a breezy seaside terrace. All three restaurants draw from a wine cellar stocked with more than 8,000 bottles of the best vintage from around the globe.

The resort's Aquarea Spa & Wellness Centre is a luxurious full-service oasis which includes whirlpools, jacuzzis, saunas, steam rooms, a wide range of therapeutic showers, a gym, beauty parlour and relaxation area.

FACTS		
ROOMS	55 suites	
FOOD	Laveranda: Mediterranean • Gourmond: French • Tau: Asian fusion • Myos: light meals	
DRINK	Cigar Lounge • Blu • Sybbar	
FEATURES	Aquarea Spa & Wellness Centre • infinity-edge pool • beach • water sports	
BUSINESS	conference rooms • audiovisual equipment • Wi-Fi connection	
NEARBY	Altos de Chavón artist colony • Los Haitises National Park • Samaná Peninsula • Dolphin Island • golf • horseback riding • casino	
CONTACT	Sivory Beach, Uvero Alto, Punta Cana, Dominican Republic • telephone: +1809.552 0500 • facsimile: +1809.552 8686 • email: reservations@sivorypuntacana.com • website: www.sivorypuntacana.com	

PHOTOGRAPHS COURTESY OF SIVORY PUNTA CANA.

Victorian House

The Caribbean is one of the world's most celebrated tourist magnets but, while some of the destinations in the region are long-established and well-known, newer ones are always emerging onto the scene. One of these gems is the largely undiscovered and unspoilt northern coast of Hispaniola.

Quite why it has taken so long for this region to be relished by the travelling public is something of a mystery. Certainly, the first 'tourist' to the region—the great seafarer Christopher Columbus himself—had no doubts as to the merits of this breathtaking waterfront. He immediately declared it "the fairest land under heaven" when he landed there in 1492, and promptly went on to establish himself as governor. It wasn't until recently, however, that a newer generation of explorers began to rediscover its virtues; and for those tempted to follow in their footsteps, there is no better place to stay than at Victorian House, a charming, Old World-style boutique hotel in Sosúa.

Just a short 10-minute drive from Puerto Plata's international airport, Victorian House is perched high on a cliff overlooking the spectacular beauty of Sosúa Beach and Bay. Formerly a turn-of-the-century plantation house in the Victorian gingerbread style, the original, well preserved building has been beautifully conserved and expanded upon so that the renovated hotel now comprises 50 suites. Combining Caribbean colonial features with contemporary elements, each

THIS PAGE (FROM TOP): The hotel's seaward grounds extend onto a long deck over the water lined with thatched lounging spots; here, guests can dine right at the very edge of the Caribbean; Victorian House takes its name from the era in which the gingerbread style originated before it was exported to the West Indies.

OPPOSITE (FROM LEFT): From the restaurants to the suites, the hotel exudes elegance and romance.

elegantly appointed suite enjoys a splendid sea view and comes fully-equipped with all the amenities expected of a quality resort.

When it comes to food and drink, guests at Victorian House are invited to share the dining facilities of its next-door sister hotel, Sosúa Bay Hotel, only a short shuttle ride away. Between the two, their five restaurants offer diners a plenitude of options. La Bahia serves American breakfasts, casual lunches and an atmospheric dinner by candlelight;

El Patio, light lunches and snacks as well as à la carte Caribbean delicacies for dinner. Sabatini's Italian gourmet cuisine is hugely popular; Marco Polo specializes in exotic dishes from the Far East; and L'Etoile d'Or offers an innovative New World menu. For post-dinner cocktails, El Patio, La Cascada and the Terrace Bar at Victorian House each offers a full range of international drinks and house concoctions, and most evenings are graced by lively stage shows.

Working on the philosophy, 'Treat others as you would like to be treated yourself', the staff at Victorian House pride themselves on their immaculate service and will be only too pleased to organize any of the numerous water sports and activities for which both the hotel and the surrounding area are rapidly becoming more popular. The quaint town of Sosúa offers a host of local delights too, providing visitors with the opportunity to see and experience the 'real' Caribbean.

PHOTOGRAPHS COURTESY OF STARZ RESORTS.

FACTS		
ROOMS	50 suites
FOOD	La Bahia: breakfast, lunch and dinner • El Patio: light lunches and snacks • Sabatini: Italian gourmet cuisine • Marco Polo: Far Eastern cuisine • L'Etoile d'Or: innovative New World cuisine
DRINK	El Patio • La Cascada Bar • Terrace Bar
FEATURES	scuba diving • snorkelling • water sports • supervised kid's club
BUSINESS	conference facilities
NEARBY	Sosúa town
CONTACT	Calle Dr Alejo Martinez 1, El Batey, Sosúa, Puerto Plata, Dominican Republic • telephone: +1809.571 4000 • facsimile: +1809.571 4545 • email: info@starzresorts.com • website: www.starzresorts.com

paradise islands

Currently a sun-splashed British territory, the Turks and Caicos Islands have been attracting visitors for more than 500 years. Ponce de León passed through the Turks on his quest for the fountain of youth and there is strong evidence that Columbus had his first landfall here rather than San Salvador. Pirates knew the archipelago for its excellent hideouts that made passing ships easy pickings. And for one brief shining moment in modern times, the Turks hit the headlines as the place where astronauts John Glenn and later Scott Carpenter splashed down after their historic earth orbits in 1962.

Nowadays it would be hard to find a more peaceful corner of the Caribbean. The colony embraces 40 islands and hundreds of tiny cays. The much larger Caicos are separated from the tiny Turks by the broad (and very deep) Columbus Passage. The Caicos derive their name from the Lucayan term 'caya hico' ('chain of islands'), which is exactly what they are. The Turks, on the other hand, were named after the red-topped Turk's head or fez cactus. The cactus, along with a lobster and conch shell, is depicted on the territorial flag.

island belongers + ripsaw winin'

The colony's 20,000-strong population is made up of descendants of African slaves, Bermudan salt rakers and royalists fleeing the American Revolution, plus a small group of overseas retirees who find the TCI's low-stress lifestyle and beachfront homes much to their liking. Those born here call themselves 'Belongers' and they endow these islands with a strong sense of history; preserving a very unique Afro-Caribbean culture.

Despite its small population, the islands have evolved a number of unique traditions, including their own music form—the ripsaw—a sort of local calypso played with metal handsaw, goat-skin drum and acoustic guitar. A number of dances revolve around ripsaw, including the rather decadent winin' with its hip swaying and wild gyrations. Ripsaw is one of the mainstays of the annual Junkanoo Carnival before Lent, but on any given night you can hear it on isolated beaches and local music clubs.

PAGE 72: Surfers at sunset.

THIS PAGE (FROM TOP): Boardwalk leading to the beach at Grace Bay on Providenciales; the rock iguana looks menacing, but is actually timid.

OPPOSITE: Conch shells and conch cuisine have become endearing symbols of these islands.

caicos dining: conch + everything else

The local cuisine is heavily grounded in seafood, with conch as the national dish. Conch is served in many different ways—curried, frittered, chowdered and cracked (steamed). The chefs in Providenciales have even concocted what is perhaps best described as 'nouvelle conch'—sushi and ceviche made from this protein-rich seafood. The conch takes centre stage at the annual Conch Festival at Blue Hills on Providenciales, which has evolved into one of the TCI's biggest events. The festival, which takes place in November, includes a 'conch-etition' amongst local chefs to determine the best chowder, salad and specialty dish, as well as conch shucking and blowing competitions, and the crowning of Princess Conch.

Other favourites include grits made from corn and deep-fried Johnny cakes, as well as rice and peas, which is actually a zesty mix of steamed rice and kidney beans flavoured with coconut, pigtail or salted beef. While Grand Turk has its fair share of waterfront eateries, Providenciales dominates the dining scene with more than 50 restaurants, cafés and delicatessens, some of them amongst the finest in the Caribbean. The range of cuisine available on Providenciales is truly staggering—French, Italian, Cuban, Dominican, Japanese, Jamaican, Indian and Mexican. While many of the best restaurants are resort-based, the number of chic independent eateries is increasing. Restaurants to note include Coyaba on Penn Road, where the chef whips up dishes like Caribbean mustard-encrusted French-trimmed rack of lamb and char-grilled wahoo steak in a curry sauce with tropical fruit chutney.

capital affairs in grand turk

Administrative affairs are run from Cockburn Town on Grand Turk, a place that seems caught in a time warp with its British colonial architecture, genteel manners and wild horses grazing the dunes. Taking pride of place along the waterfront is the picturesque Turk's Head Inn, built in 1850. It was once the residence of the American consul, who

was also a local salt baron. The inn has seen its fair share of luminaries over the years; Queen Elizabeth reputedly slept here on a royal visit to Grand Turk in 1966.

Salt may have been the island's money-spinner in years gone by—and was even referred to as 'white gold'—but nowadays the economy is driven by financial services and scuba diving. While financial institutions can be seen on any casual stroll through town, underwater treasures await those who would rather swim. Just beyond the placidly anchored yachts, about a hundred metres offshore, the reef plunges 2,000 m (7,000 ft). This majestic coral wall is one of the Caribbean's leading dive destinations and the main reason why scuba enthusiasts flock to Cockburn Town. Dive sites include the Black Forest (where black corals grow in profusion), the Library (a favourite site for night diving) and the Tunnels (where manta rays can be seen in the summer).

provo's blue-blood awakening

Despite its rather regal name, Grand Turk is neither the most populous nor most developed of the Turks and Caicos islands. That honour belongs to Providenciales, or 'Provo', the only island in the archipelago with direct air connections to Miami, Nassau and New York.

Provo was once home to French castaways and secluded cotton plantations, and not much else. In the 1960s, the nearly uninhabited island was discovered by a group of blue-blooded American families (including the DuPonts and Roosevelts) seeking their own special place in the Caribbean. Pooling their considerable resources, they built an airstrip, a yacht harbour and exclusive seaside bungalows, thinking the rest of the world would leave them in peace.

But what they had really done was to open Provo to the world; once word of drop-dead gorgeous beaches and aquamarine bays leaked, the rush was on.

Forty years on, Provo has grown from drowsy island into a paradise of hip resorts, championship golf courses, gourmet eateries and chic boutiques. And plenty of celebrities. Supermodel Cindy Crawford and actor Bruce Willis are among those who purportedly own houses on Provo. You never know whom you might find sipping a beer at Danny Bouys or dancing the night away at the Gecko Grille.

stunning natural attractions

Provo's 19-km (12-mile) beach at Grace Bay is considered one of the world's top strands. Flanked by top resorts, Grace Bay is long enough to accommodate those who just want to be left alone in the sun, and people who take their sun with a large dose of action: paragliding, kayaking or water-skiing. For those who snorkel, White House Reef is located in the middle of the bay. A four-wheel-drive vehicle (or a good pair of shoes) will get you to secluded strands like Northwest Point.

Provo is a diving mecca. Among its scuba spots are Sandbore Channel, the West Caicos Walls and the Molasses Reef, where treasure hunters discovered the remains of the oldest European shipwreck ever discovered in the Caribbean. This early 16th-century galleon now rests in the National Museum in Cockburn Town.

succulent molluscs + swimming holes

Provo has the world's only conch plantation, where the molluscs are raised for sale to restaurants around the world. The island's numerous coves and inlets are ripe for kayaking and fishing, while the pancake flat terrain is ideal for biking. For those who need an adrenaline fix, there is a place called The Hole—a limestone chimney with a saltwater swimming hole at the bottom that can only be reached by shimmying down a rope.

THIS PAGE (FROM LEFT): Grace Bay, often cited as one of the best beaches in the world; a huge Nassau grouper lurks in the rich reefs around Provo.

OPPOSITE (FROM TOP): The mysterious Conch Bar Cave on Middle Caicos, where ancient artefacts may be found; Provo boasts the world's only conch farm.

Island visitors may also stumble upon relics of local history. At Cheshire Hall there are plenty of ruins, such as the remains of a late 18th-century house that functioned as the centrepiece of a cotton plantation founded by Thomas Stubbs, a British royalist. Around the crest of Sapodilla Hill, overlooking Provo's south shore, are rocks bearing graffiti and inscriptions made by bygone pirates and shipwrecked sailors.

beyond provo

Wedged between Grand Turk and Provo are the low-lying Caicos islands. Given their similar names—Middle Caicos, West Caicos, South Caicos, and so on—it is understandably confusing for newcomers. However, each island has its charm. While they remain largely lost in time, they will no doubt be developed in future as Provo reaches its ecological limit. Posh resorts are already on the drawing board, including West Caicos Reserve on a previously uninhabited island of the same name. It is set to include a boutique hotel, luxury villas and a full-service marina.

middle caicos: underground treasures

Middle Caicos is the largest island in the archipelago. However, only 300 residents live on the island. Many are descendents of survivors of the slave ship *Gambia*, which hit a nearby reef in 1842 on its way from West Africa to Cuba. Bambarra, the island's largest settlement, was named after a tribe that lives along the Niger River in West Africa.

Islanders cling to a narrow band along the north coast, where rolling dunes and limestone outcrops give Middle Caicos a trifle elevation. Beneath these limestone ridges lie the island's main attraction—caverns that can be explored on foot. The largest cavern is Conch Bar Cave. Lucayan artefacts have been found there. Archaeologists speculate that the Lucayans used the cave as a place of worship, and as a refuge during hurricanes. The cave has plenty of

natural treasures—bats, land crabs, strange rock formations, and underground tidepools that reflect the bizarre geology. At the far end of the tunnel, more than a kilometre from the entrance, the trail peters out into saltwater.

north + south: secluded beaches

North Caicos once had an agricultural community that shipped vegetables to the rest of the archipelago and fine cotton in wooden sloops to America's eastern seaboard. Locally grown tomatoes and cucumbers are still available, and are delicious. But nowadays, the island's emphasis is on outdoor adventure. Birdwatchers flock to see the rare West Indian flamingos on the tidal flats near the island's southern tip while fishermen try to hook tarpon and bonefish. The 11-km (7-mile) beach at Whitby on the north shore is for sunseekers and for those who crave to be far from the madding crowd.

South Caicos is the homeport for TCI's small but thriving commercial fishing industry, which ships conch and lobster overseas. The island is also home to a marine research station that draws oceanographers seeking to study the rich waters and the humpback whales that migrate through the Turks and Caicos channels during the winter months.

salt cay: ancient salinas + shipwrecks

Salt Cay is a tiny island that was originally settled by Bermudan salt rakers who built the windmills and salinas that dot the landscape. They lived in sturdy homes, many of them are still in use, fashioned from ship timbers and limestone blocks.

Visitors come to Salt Cay for the empty beaches and the marvellous diving, including the wreck of the British warship *Endymion*, which ran aground off the island's southern tip in 1790. There is a never-ending parade of nature—the humpback whales in winter, the manta rays and sea turtles in summer, the mating of the nurse sharks in spring and the blooming of the Turk's head cactus in the fall. And if there is one classic Salt Cay moment, it is drinking rum punch and winin' the night away while someone 'rips' tunes with a screwdriver on a handsaw. Quintessential Caribbean.

THIS PAGE (FROM TOP): Ruins of a windmill in a disused salt pond; close-up of the Turk's head cactus that has lent its name to these islands.
OPPOSITE: A manta majestically glides through the waters.

...for those who crave to be far from the madding crowd.

Amanyara

This delicate sounding name translates into 'a peaceful place', which is exactly just where the idyllic and heavenly resort of Amanyara is to be found. Dramatically positioned on the edge of a 2,030-hectare (5,000-acre) nature reserve on Providenciales—a gem in the string of sparkling island pearls that form a geological extension of the Bahamas Bank —Amanyara truly is an earthly paradise.

The romantic surroundings of this elegant resort are graced with powder-fine beaches and dramatic iron-shore coves featuring natural rock bridges. Those not content with the island's stunning coastline

THIS PAGE (FROM LEFT): Amanyara's open-concept design allows its architecture and guests to fully embrace the elements—one first steps in to the soul-stirring sight of a symmetric pond touching the horizon of vast sky, its calm waters bearing the reflection of white clouds and mellow trees; indoors, the interior of each private pavilion is kept simple and airy, with spaces partitioned by unobtrusive wooden screens.

OPPOSITE: Built on a rocky edge along the unspoilt west coast of Providenciales' Northwest Point, this is a veritable paragon of peace, beauty and seclusion.

can register with the hotel's Dive Centre to explore the world's third largest reef system in the adjacent Northwest Point Marine National Park. This diving hot-spot has scooped accolades from esteemed dive journals, including 'Best Big Fish Sighting' and 'Healthiest Marine Environment'.

With such a phenomenal location as backdrop, Amanyara's design team was, at the outset, faced with a serious challenge to create an impressive, yet sensitive and harmonious work of architecture and design —a task in which they have proven to excel themselves. Some 40 cloistered timber-shingled pavilions are dotted throughout the resort's grounds, each offering shaded sun-decks and easy access to nearby rock formations via elevated pathways. Interior materials and colourways are pure and uncluttered, conveying the simplicity inherent in the Caribbean way of life.

Languorous, beautifully linen-laid king-size beds are de rigueur in the bright, airy bedrooms of each private pavilion. Slumber to the soothing music emanating either from the in-room entertainment system, or from the sea itself. The bathrooms eschew hi-tech gadgetry, proving instead classic free-standing baths waiting to be filled with opulent essential oils as a glass of chilled champagne mists over in your hand.

The expansive free-form pool reflects the cloudless blue of the skies, offering uninterrupted views out to the horizon. It is the perfect place for a refreshing dip to banish that jet lag. If a professional touch is required, the healing hands of Amanyara's therapists specialize in various massage and relaxation techniques from around the world, and will even impart their fingertip wisdom in the comfort of your own pavilion.

Mealtimes are quite often the most memorable elements of a vacation, and the culinary provisions of Amanyara's bars and restaurants are second to none. Dining options include colourful specialties such as Asian- and Mediterranean-inspired dishes, with an emphasis on freshly-caught seafood. Afterwards, stroll to the Bar, where you will be mesmerized by the unusual roof soaring in circles overhead. Be it for an oceanfront dining experience, a romantic getaway, a water sports extravaganza or simply a well-earned holiday, Amanyara is undoubtedly one of the most peaceful and breathtaking corners of the Turks and Caicos in which to escape.

FACTS		
	ROOMS	40 private pavilions • 2 villas
	FOOD	The Restaurant: Asian and Mediterranean • Beach Club: light meals
	DRINK	The Bar
	FEATURES	Dive Centre • Beach Club • water sports • scuba diving • snorkelling • pool • fitness centre • flood-lit clay tennis courts • massage and beauty treatments • library • screening room • boutique
	NEARBY	Malcolm's Beach • Northwest Point Marine National Park • Caicos Conch Farm • Providenciales Golf Club • plantation ruins • rock carvings at Sapodilla Hill
	CONTACT	Northwest Point, Providenciales, Turks and Caicos Islands • telephone: +65.6887 3337 (central reservations) • facsimile: +1649.941 8132 • email: amanyara@amanresorts.com • website: www.amanresorts.com

PHOTOGRAPHS COURTESY OF AMANRESORTS.

Grace Bay Club

Recently named the world's number-one beach, the disarming beauty of Grace Bay and its powder-fine sands line the northern shores of Providenciales. Part of the shoal of shimmering islands treading water around one of the largest and most spectacular reef systems in the world, Grace Bay Beach has found its way into the hearts of industrial authorities the likes of *Condé Nast Traveler's* 'Gold List' and *Travel + Leisure* magazine's 'Top 500' and 'World's Best' awards.

Like its namesake location, the petite and sophisticated resort of Grace Bay Club has acquired a faithful following for its genuine, attentive service and understated stylishness. Nestled in the very heart of Providenciales, the resort is delicately framed by towering coconut palm trees, brilliant bougainvillea and fragrant jasmine. The Club's considerable acreage makes it the lowest density resort on the entire island and, as a distinctly upscale destination, Grace Bay Club is, unsurprisingly, one of the Small Luxury Hotels of the World.

Housed in the resort's original boutique building is The Hotel at Grace Bay Club, comprising 21 suites. A recent refurbishment —overseen by well renowned designer Larry Foster—has seen the already stylish décor of the interiors and public spaces reach a whole new plateau of chic. The energizing colour palette is designed to harmonize with nature's own wisdom, with combinations subtly creating atmospheres which are either cool and refreshing, calm and serene, or hot and spicy. Featured in the architecture are terracotta-tiled roofs, archways and shaded courtyards with fountains—charming touches reminiscent of Mediterranean elegance.

Hand-selected furniture adorns each suite and is a celebration of vibrant eclecticism. Rattan and wicker chairs from the Philippines, armoires from Guatemala, rugs from Turkey

and Spain, and pottery from Mexico set the colourful scene. While the soul-stirring ocean views from the suites should be enough to grip your attention, flat-screen television, DVD facilities and Wi-Fi Internet are a button's touch away. When the balmy tropical clime necessitates a cooling shower, luxuriate in exclusive Elemis bath products and thick, Egyptian cotton wraparound towels.

Metres away from the couples-only Hotel are The Villas at Grace Bay Club, a new addition of 38 suites and four sensational penthouses to match some of the world's finest luxury suites. For absolute privacy and ultra-indulgence, each of the Villa Penthouses covers the length and breadth of an entire floor. Simply divine are their solid wood kitchens, Bose entertainment systems, outdoor jacuzzis and media rooms. As a finishing touch, the custom furniture and fittings derive from Italy and the United States, from iconic labels such as Michael Thomas, Palecek, Hallmark, Walters Wicker, and Bonacina.

As the first all-suite luxury resort to be established in the Turks and Caicos Islands, Grace Bay Club also holds a monopoly on cutting-edge culinary experiences. With experience at France's top Michelin-starred restaurants, Head Chef Eric Brunel runs the principal restaurant, Anacaona. Sample his Caribbean-South-Pacific fusion in one of the beachfront 'seating pods'. For light meals, The Lounge offers delicacies such as Ceviche of Turks & Caicos Baby Conch with Smoked Plantain and a Ginger-and-Teriyaki Sauce, served al fresco under sail-like awnings.

Golf enthusiasts will adore the nearby Provo Golf Course, an illustrious 18-hole Karl Litten-inspired championship course. And golf widows—or widowers for that matter—will adore Grace Bay Club's expansive Anani Spa & Fitness Centre, which features authentic Caribbean treatments and massages.

PHOTOGRAPHS COURTESY OF GRACE BAY CLUB.

FACTS

ROOMS	The Hotel (couples only): 21 suites • The Villas (family-friendly): 38 suites and 4 penthouses
FOOD	Anacaona: Euro-Caribbean cuisine • The Grill: seafood and meat specialities
DRINK	Captain's Bar • The Lounge
FEATURES	Anani Spa & Fitness Centre • 2 floodlit tennis courts • 2 freshwater pools • 2 jacuzzis • water sports • Hobie Cats • snorkelling • library • Kid's Town programme
BUSINESS	business centre • Wi-Fi access
NEARBY	Provo Golf Course • catamaran excursions • eco-tours • day-trip to Cuba
CONTACT	PO Box 128, 1 Grace Bay Circle Road, Providenciales, Turks and Caicos Islands • telephone: +1649.946 5757 • facsimile: +1649.946 5758 • email: info@gracebayclub.com • website: www.gracebayclub.com

The Palms

Located at the centre of world-renowned Grace Bay Beach in Providenciales, The Palms is a 5-hectare (12-acre) paradise accessible via a coral stone gateway and tree-lined boulevard. Its casually elegant plantation house also conceals an interior garden, cloistered exclusive boutiques and a centrepiece classical fountain.

Each of the Palm's 72 uber-luxurious two and three-bedroom suites can be subdivided into one-bedroom suites and a luxury guest room if desired. They are elegantly furnished with marble floors, vaulted ceilings and top-notch, custom-made mahogany furniture. State-of-the-art gadgetry includes Wi-Fi Internet and flat-screen TVs while bathrooms are equally impressive with hydro massage tubs. The velvety softness of top-notch Egyptian bed linens also invites a good night's sleep. And as you yacht-spot from your exclusive terrace, let the Caribbean trade winds dry your hair au naturel after a shower.

Expect the Penthouse accommodation to ratchet up the luxury quotient, given its own outdoor garden shower, jacuzzi and personal butler service. Guests will be spoilt for choice as far as sensory pleasures are

Guests will be spoilt for choice as far as sensory pleasures are concerned.

concerned. Whether you're taking a dip in the $1.8-million infinity pool, or perhaps surfing the Internet by the pool, or simply escaping into the cobalt blue of Grace Bay Beach which is only a stone's throw away, you know the experience will be an indelible one.

The Spa at The Palms is undoubtedly the highlight of the resort. Designed by Angel Stewart of Ventanas al Paraiso fame, this world-class destination is made up of eight hand-cut coral stone treatment rooms where guests will be pampered with exquisite Temple Spa products from England. In the same vein, guests can also experience total relaxation when they opt for its unique, heated waterbeds.

Families travelling with kids will be pleased to know that there's a Conch Kritters Club at The Palms, tailored specifically for children from four to 12 years of age. It offers many types of programmes with beach, pool and art activities that will keep the kids busy while their parents take time out to pursue their own hobbies. Babysitting services are also available.

The subject of food hardly strays far from the radar of guests as they get to enjoy tropical fusion cuisine at Parallel23, one of the island's most revered restaurants featuring a state-of-the-art open kitchen. For soup, salads, catch of the day, pizza and fresh gourmet sandwiches, swim up to the bar or a table at Plunge restaurant with its unique sunken dining room. These epicurean pleasures will undoubtedly leave you hungry for more.

After a unique and bespoke vacation spent at The Palms, the only thought in one's mind will probably be the name of one of The Spa's blissful treatments—'I'll Be Back'.

PHOTOGRAPHS COURTESY THE PALMS.

FACTS

ROOMS	72 suites
FOOD	Parallel23: tropical fusion • Plunge Bar Restaurant: Asian-inspired tapas
FEATURES	art gallery • tennis court • boutiques • high-speed Internet access • snorkelling • kayaking • Kid's Club • spa
NEARBY	scuba diving • 18-hole championship course and driving range
CONTACT	The Palms, Providenciales, Turks and Caicos Islands • telephone: +1649.946 8666 • facsimile: +1649.946 5188 • email: info@thepalmstc.com • website: www.thepalmstc.com

Parrot Cay

Privacy promised, paradise discovered. That is what guests can expect at the beguiling island resort of Parrot Cay. Ringed by a silken thread of sand, it is nestled near the principal Turks and Caicos islands. In a place where the tide informs the time, visitors will soon forget the world they've left behind as the body clock unwinds and finds its natural rhythm.

More than half of Parrot Cay's 60 luxuriously appointed rooms are graced with exquisite tropical garden views, best appreciated from their sun-bleached white verandahs. The Beach Villas feature airy and light rooms with private plunge pools, and

butler service for good measure. The larger properties have full-sized pools. All are tantalizingly close to the crushed porcelain sands of Parrot Cay's mesmerizing beaches.

Each stylish and climate-controlled guest room has a four-poster bed, draped with breeze-ruffled voile. Wooden furniture and naturally woven materials perch atop cooling tiled floors, and bathrooms brim with delectable Como Shambhala products.

Larger family groups or those celebrating special occasions might like to ensconce themselves in The Residence, a secluded satellite resort unto itself. A brief buggy ride from the main resort, its five luxury pads are arranged around their very own pristine bays. Imagine lingering over a blazing sunset with no interruptions except the hypnotic lapping of ocean waves.

Vestiges of normal life are also apparent in the suites. There are entertainment systems

and modern telecommunications, but this resort is definitely not meant for lunchtime laptop warriors. In fact, it is a haven designed to erase work-day worries, inviting its discerning guests into the realm of the carefree. To this end, the eye-catching infinity-edge pool and friendly staff at the laid-back Beach Bar will soon swing your attention back to what's important on this holiday—you.

With complimentary activities from tennis to daily yoga sessions, an adrenaline rush is only a moment away. A day trip may be enjoyed playing a round of championship golf on the nearby island of Providenciales. Or for high-end self-indulgence, be prepared to get pampered at the multi-award winning Como Shambhala holistic retreat, where massage and panoramic views of the wetlands go hand in hand.

When the stomach seeks attention, guests can sate their desires to the hilt at the Terrace Restaurant with a Mediterranean influence. Alternatively, diners with a hankering for a generous dash of signature Caribbean cuisines can check out the Lotus Restaurant, a crowd favourite.

Parrot Cay encapsulates the essence of the Caribbean. Unique and stylish, it boasts culinary creativity and exotic views. If this island wore an expression, it would have been a dreamy, satisfied Caribbean smile.

THIS PAGE: A serene atmosphere beckons invitingly with airy rooms and private pools.

OPPOSITE (CLOCKWISE FROM TOP LEFT): Soak in a hot bath with luxurious Como Shambhala products; access the Internet in comfort; a four-poster bed sets the mood for a night of romance.

PHOTOGRAPHS COURTESY OF PARROT CAY.

FACTS

ROOMS	60 rooms, suites, beach houses and villas
FOOD	Terrace Restaurant and Bar: Mediterranean • Lotus: Caribbean
DRINK	beach bar
FEATURES	Como Shambhala retreat • gym • infinity-edge swiming pool • 2 tennis courts • library • yoga retreats • pilates classes
NEARBY	Iguana Island • Sun Dollar Cay • reef snorkelling • sunset cruises
CONTACT	PO Box 164, Providenciales, Turks and Caicos Islands • telephone: +1649 946 7788 • facsimile: +1649 946 7393 • email: res@parrotcay.como.bz • website: www.parrotcay.como.bz

Turks + Caicos Club

The Turks & Caicos Club is an unassuming colonial-style hideaway nestled amid lush landscaping on Providenciales and lapped by the turquoise waters of the Caribbean. This new, privately-owned resort has rapidly acquired a reputation as a 'luxury home away from home', receiving high praises through word of mouth and a bonanza of acclaim from the international press. Located on the sugar-fine sands of Grace Bay—named 'World's Best Beach' at the 2005 World Travel Awards—this gated sanctuary of exclusivity sits ideally next to Provo's most astonishingly beautiful snorkelling reef. It comes as no surprise that this young, ultra-exclusive 21-suite oceanfront resort is quickly stacking up the accolades.

Highly recommended by *Condé Nast Johansens* for the last four years running and hailed as one of *Travel + Leisure's* '50 Most Romantic Retreats', the secret is out about the Turks & Caicos Club, which is impressing everyone from seasoned Caribbean veterans to the first-time visitor who comes to luxuriate in every second spent in this exotic, laid-back retreat. With 19 km (12 miles) of perfection extending in either direction in the guise of Grace Bay Beach's soft white sands, the Turks & Caicos Club lives luxury, breathes romance and sleeps in inimitable style.

THIS PAGE (CLOCKWISE FROM LEFT): The Club's stylish and beautiful four-poster beds are simply divine; the 21 suites, with their safari-themed interior and furnishings, are adored by everyone from travel writers to stylists; view of the inviting freshwater pool lined with palms, parasols, sunloungers, a gazebo and, not too far away, the Pool Bar.

OPPOSITE: The Turks & Caicos Club is renowned for its sophisticated charm and European elegance. Built in the colonial Caribbean style, the architecture is perfectly adapted for the tropical clime, with traditional 'Z' shutters and open verandahs throughout.

The Club's extensive array of activities ranges from relaxing spa treatments to skin-tingling adventures at sea with Hobie Cat sailboats, fishing, windsurfing and kayaking. Explore the multi-coloured depths of the sea—and the third largest coral reef system in the world—by scuba diving or snorkelling. On land, enjoy a romantic gourmet picnic on the beach or ride off into the sunset on horseback. For the sportive, take an eco-tour or tee off at the nearby 18-hole championship golf course.

Back at the Club, each spacious one- or two-bedroom suite features custom-made rattan furnishings, a gourmet kitchen, elegant four-poster beds draped in delicate netting, and a generously-sized private balcony which overlooks the Caribbean. Providing for guests' absolute comfort and convenience is a whole host of luxuries including twice-a-day maid service and sumptuous bath amenities. Each suite is installed with cable television and a DVD player, private safes and climate control. Wireless Internet is available in designated areas of the hotel. This is the perfect retreat for a special romantic escape, an intimate wedding or a family getaway.

For smoothies, sorbets and ice-crushed cocktails in the heat of the day, head straight for the Pool Bar. In the cool evening, saunter to Simba Restaurant & Bar. The restaurant's award-winning head chef weaves a fine Caribbean thread through his signature dishes, which feature native delicacies with imaginative gourmet flair. The service too, is unforgettably impeccable and seamless.

An exemplary five-star hotel, the Turks & Caicos Club lives to exceed your every expectation. And though the resort occupies a tranquil spot on the quiet end of Grace Bay Beach, sequestered from the main buzz of the island, the Club is fast becoming one of the most well-known and loved on Provo. The secret is definitely out.

FACTS

ROOMS	21 one- or two-bedroom suites
FOOD	Simba Restaurant & Bar
DRINK	Pool Bar
FEATURES	reef snorkelling • fitness centre • freshwater pool • beach • water sports • sunset sails • small book library • private dining
NEARBY	golf • deep-sea, bone and bottom fishing • scuba diving • horseback riding • eco-tours • conch farm tours
CONTACT	West Grace Bay Beach, West Grace Bay, Providenciales, Turks & Caicos Islands • telephone: +1649.946 5800 • facsimile: +1649.946 5858 • email: info@turksandcaicosclub.com • website: www.turksandcaicosclub.com

PHOTOGRAPHS COURTESY OF TURKS + CAICOS CLUB.

The Somerset on Grace Bay

Overlooking the celebrated pristine beauty of Grace Bay on Providenciales, The Somerset dovetails classical luxury with a brand of playful innovation in an urbane environment where anything is possible. Blending island charm with a dash of the unexpected, the accommodations and amenities are lavish, and the expert staff so professional as to be deemed a collection of personal concierges.

This newly launched development boasts a dynamic 'residence-resort' formula which balances the requirements of the discerning travel sophisticate with the needs of an up-scale resident community. For its master plan, The Somerset's acclaimed principal architects have stippled the verdant, landscaped estate with hues of Tuscany and elements of Europe while rooting the architecture and design in the stylistic purity of the Turks and Caicos.

The plush accommodations include 54 apartment-sized suites. Divided between four Estate Houses are 16 residential suites, each occupying an entire floor and replete with a private, jacuzzi-outfitted wraparound terrace. The most sumptuous of the Estate Houses are the penthouse suites, each spread over two floors connected by a sweeping staircase that leads to expansive rooms and baths. For travelling guests, the Stirling House comprises 24 luxury suites and exclusive penthouses

with rooftop terraces for vantage views. For absolute privacy and heightened exclusivity, choose from a selection of 10 breathtaking English Cottages, each naturally complete with a well-manicured garden.

However, it is outdoors really, that The Somerset's inventive individuality comes into its own. Through the heart of this oceanfront abode flows a spectacular progression of pools, fountains and waterfalls; and melding into the Atlantic is a showpiece infinity-edge pool outfitted with an underwater stereo system. Like a true grown-up's wonderland, The Somerset offers an eclectic variety of leisure activities such as its 'Extreme Croquet', a beach variation of the proper sport. You can also matriculate at the singular 'Sandcastle University' to receive personal instruction from the Somerset staff trained by Guinness world record holder, Mark Mason. The Somerset's imaginative twist of convention points to an irreverence for tradition that only the most well bred resorts can pull off successfully.

If the more familiar territory of a golf link or tennis court is preferred, Karl Litton's Provo Golf & Country Club is a shuttle ride away. The sportive can also head for a one-on-one workout session with a personal trainer at The Somerset's on-site fitness centre. For the more adventurous, not far removed from the property are iconic Caribbean dive spots as well as opportunities for some of the region's best sailing and deep-sea fishing.

When it comes to gastronomic satisfaction, the ultimate experience which shouldn't be missed is the chance to invite a local chef to craft conch delicacies in your own suite. For formal dining, the signature restaurant is a 'local meets global' culinary explosion. Its cathedral-vaulted interior opens out onto a beautiful outdoor extension which invites the moonlight to fall onto the colourful canopied beds and satisfied diners beneath the stars.

PHOTOGRAPHS COURTESY OF THE SOMERSET ON GRACE BAY.

FACTS

ROOMS	Estate Houses: 16 suites • Stirling House: 24 suites • 10 English Cottages
FOOD	Restaurant O'Soliel: fusion of Caribbean and international cuisines • tailored en-suite meals by a local chef • grocery shopping on request
DRINK	Pool Bar • Pearl Lounge
FEATURES	a cross-current lap pool and infinity-edge pool (outfitted with underwater music) • fountains • waterfalls • croquet court • fitness centre • mountain bikes • en-suite treatments and massages • The Kids' Tower • boutique
NEARBY	Provo Golf & Country Club • water sports
CONTACT	Princess Drive, Grace Bay Road, Providenciales, Turks & Caicos Islands • telephone: +1649.946 5900 • facsimile: +1649.946 5944 • email: kwhitt@thesomerset.com • website: www.thesomerset.com

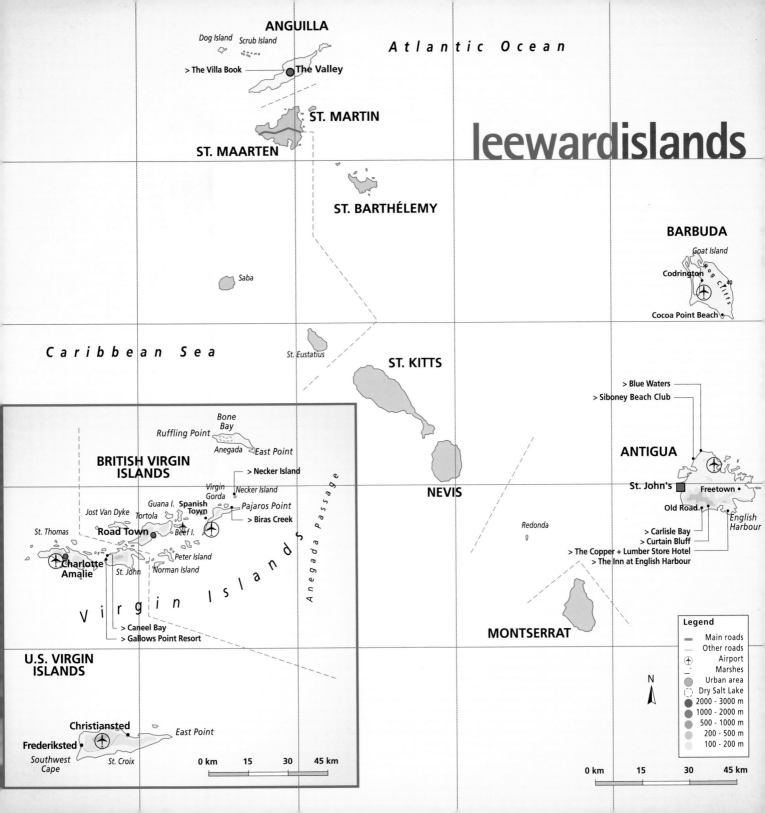

ANGUILLA

Dog Island *Scrub Island*

Atlantic Ocean

> The Villa Book ● **The Valley**

ST. MARTIN

ST. MAARTEN

leewardislands

ST. BARTHÉLEMY

BARBUDA

Goat Island

Codrington

Saba

Cocoa Point Beach

C a r i b b e a n   S e a

St. Eustatius

ST. KITTS

> Blue Waters
> Siboney Beach Club

ANTIGUA

St. John's ■ **Freetown** •

NEVIS

Old Road •

English Harbour

Redonda

> Carlisle Bay
> Curtain Bluff
> The Copper + Lumber Store Hotel
> The Inn at English Harbour

Bone Bay

Ruffling Point

BRITISH VIRGIN ISLANDS

Anegada *East Point*

> Necker Island

Virgin Gorda

Necker Island

Guana I. **Spanish Town**

> Pajaros Point

Jost Van Dyke

Tortola

> Biras Creek

Road Town ●

Beef I.

St. Thomas

Peter Island

○ **Charlotte Amalie**

St. John

Norman Island

V i r g i n   I s l a n d s

A n e g a d a   P a s s a g e

MONTSERRAT

> Caneel Bay
> Gallows Point Resort

U.S. VIRGIN ISLANDS

Christiansted

East Point

Frederiksted

Southwest Cape   *St. Croix*

0 km   15   30   45 km

Legend

— Main roads
— Other roads
✈ Airport
Marshes
● Urban area
○ Dry Salt Lake
● 2000 - 3000 m
● 1000 - 2000 m
● 500 - 1000 m
200 - 500 m
100 - 200 m

N

0 km   15   30   45 km

an arc of islands

The Leeward Islands of the Lesser Antilles, located on the eastern corner of the Caribbean, may be viewed as a geographical arc that links the large islands of the Greater Antilles with the scattered Windward Islands and South America. The Leeward Islands lie placidly between Puerto Rico and Guadeloupe. The Leewards comprises hundreds of little islands—more islands, in fact, than anywhere else in the region. The outer Leeward Islands (such as Antigua and Anguilla) are sandy and low-lying, built on limestone foundations that betray their ancient coral reef origins. The inner islands (such as St. Kitts and Montserrat) are mostly volcanic, rugged formations with rich, dark soil and black-sand beaches.

In the past, islanders on the Leewards made a living from sugarcane. Nowadays, tourism is the prime cash crop. With chic boutique hotels and swank private-island resorts, the tourism industry here is decidedly upmarket. With their sheltered waters and short passages, the Leewards is a great place for boating. Cruise ships also frequent the ritzy ports of call, where duty-free shopping and gourmet dining are among the shore-leave treats. Booming tourism, as well as subsidies from the various colonial governments that still administer the majority of these islands, has transformed the Leewards into one of the more affluent parts of the Caribbean. The Leeward Islands generally are blessed with a higher standard of living and have few of the acute social problems that plague other islands in the Caribbean.

island colonies

Despite the name, there is actually plenty of breeze on the Leeward Islands. As a matter of fact, the name is a bit of a misnomer. The Leeward Islands are actually not much in the lee of anything and are just as likely to get smacked by hurricanes as other islands in the Caribbean. The islands just happen to be slightly further west of the Atlantic trade winds than the Windward Islands.

PAGE 94: Divers off Virgin Gorda, British Virgin Islands.

THIS PAGE: Sailing in the Sir Francis Drake Channel, British Virgin Islands.

OPPOSITE: The historic English Harbour in Antigua is always full of yachts.

Unlike the Windwards, which changed hands between rival European powers many times, the Leewards were settled very early by their colonial masters. When islands did change hands—the western Virgins from the Danes to the Americans, St. Barthélemy from the Swedes to the French—it was often under peaceful circumstances. The British islands were tied together as a colonial federation for nearly 300 years with their own distinct postage stamps, cricket team and territorial flag that featured the Union Jack along with clipper ships and a pineapple. In the early 1980s, two independent nations—Antigua and Barbuda, and St. Kitts and Nevis—emerged. Most of the other islands, too small to become viable nations, have remained colonies.

british virgins: the pirate legacy

The British Virgin Islands (or BVI, as locals call their homeland) inspired the most celebrated Caribbean yarn of all time—*Treasure Island* by Robert Louis Stevenson— based on real-life larceny and pirate adventure. After a Spanish treasure galleon

wrecked on the Carolina coast in 1750, two American sea captains absconded with the spoils. Seeking shelter in what is now the British Virgin Islands, the Americans were swindled by a certain Captain Norman, who buried the loot on a desert island that now bears his name. Norman and the American captains were later caught by vengeful Spaniards. They were made to 'walk the plank' for refusing to spill the beans on the treasure's location.

Blackbeard was the most famous pirate to haunt these waters, although he probably left behind more bodies than buried treasure. When 15 of his men staged a mutiny during a passage through the Virgins, Blackbeard opted for an especially cruel punishment: he left them stranded on a tiny desert island called Dead Man's Chest with nothing but a bottle of rum for sustenance and a cutlass to settle their differences. The episode was immortalized in a seafaring song: 'Fifteen men on a dead man's chest, yo ho ho and a bottle of rum!'

Real treasure hunting is now frowned upon by the local authorities, but the sandy beaches, turquoise water and various maritime escapades still draw many people to the British Virgins. There are more than 40 islands in the chain, ranging from massive hunks like Tortola, to uninhabited cays that provide the perfect setting for a desert island adventure.

Columbus came across these islands on his second voyage to the New World. He christened the three largest islands—Tortola, Virgin Gorda and Anegada—and then

sailed off to other shores. Over the next two centuries, the Spanish, French and Dutch disputed jurisdiction over the islands until the British staked a lasting claim in 1672. Besides cricket and images of the Queen, the most conspicuous sign of British influence today is the strong affinity for boats; yachts in particular. Locals claim that the BVI is the yacht-charter capital of the world. And when you catch sight of the hundreds of masts along the Road Town waterfront, you know that this boast is not very far from the truth.

british virgins: sailing adventure

The BVI is just what the doctor ordered for anyone who loves to sail, or for those who daydream of life beneath the mast. Several sailing schools based in Road Town offer weeklong courses during which budding yachtsmen can learn the ropes from experienced local sailors. Once the basics are mastered, it is easy to navigate around BVI because the islands lie in such close proximity to each other. The waters are almost always calm, especially along Sir Francis Drake Channel, which is bounded by islands to its north and south, and festooned with pearly beaches and sapphire bays. For sailors with more experience, the open waters of the Atlantic to the north of Tortola beckon. During winter, the swells kick up waves large enough to attract surfers, especially at Apple Bay on the northeast coast of Tortola.

THIS PAGE (FROM TOP): Virgin Gorda looked like a reclining pregnant woman to Columbus; colourful buildings grace the waterfront on Tortola.

OPPOSITE: Shafts of light dancing on clear waters greet explorers who wade in the breathtaking Baths of Virgin Gorda.

Tortola has other hot spots. Brewer's Bay is said to harbour more species of tropical fish than anywhere else in the Caribbean while Cane Garden Bay offers one of the most beautiful beaches, as well as BVI's finest food in its waterfront cafés.

On the island of Virgin Gorda, The Baths is a popular anchorage that is surrounded by huge granite boulders, many of them as high as two-storey buildings. Depending on the tide, sightseers can either snorkel or walk among the rocks; and then duck into the beachfront café for a well-deserved cool drink afterwards. Columbus named the island Virgin Gorda, meaning 'Fat Virgin', because the outline of the island reminded him of a reclining pregnant woman. Her 'belly' is now the Virgin Gorda Peak National Park that has hiking trails to vistas that offer 360-degree views of the island.

To the north is Anegada. As the only coral atoll in the BVI, its lack of topography is a striking contrast to the rugged mountains on Tortola and the other major islands in the chain. Anegada's treacherous reef has claimed over 300 ships—more than any other island in the Caribbean. Needless to say, the diving experience is astounding.

u.s. virgins: shopping + partying

Originally occupied by Denmark, the U.S. Virgin Islands was purchased by the Americans in 1917 for a paltry $25 million in gold. Nearly a hundred years down the road, the U.S. Virgins now have excellent shopping malls, awesome adventure sports facilities and bustling waterfronts.

St. Thomas is one of the great marketplaces in the Caribbean with its dazzling array of luxury goods. The town of Charlotte Amalie is also one of the world's most popular cruise ship stops. From crystal and haute couture to gourmet chocolates and 30-year-old cognac, the list of what you can buy in the boutiques along Main Street and the air-conditioned malls of Charlotte Amalie is truly amazing.

Carnival on St. Thomas is a rowdy mix of Caribbean and American elements. The April shindig includes everything from calypso singers and stilt walkers to high school marching bands. Unlike other carnivals, it takes place after Easter rather than before Lent. The historic sights on the island include the Beracha Veshalom Vegmiluth Hasidim, which is the oldest synagogue (built in 1831) in continuous use in the entire U.S. It is also one of the most exquisite structures in the Leeward chain.

u.s. virgins: vintage wines + margaritaville

St. Croix retains much of its bygone Danish ambience. The landscape is littered with the ruins of more than a hundred sugar mills. The major towns, Frederiksted and Christiansted, are still full of pastel colonial buildings. The cuisine here is also a throwback to Danish days. The island prides itself with Mediterranean-style bistros and Old World cafés, serving what many consider to be the best food in the U.S. Virgins. Bacchus offers the largest wine selection (including prime vintages from California, New Zealand and Australia). The restaurant Savant has an intriguing menu that offers a tantalizing blend of Thai, Mexican and Caribbean flavours in a très romantic courtyard setting. But this largest island of all the Virgins also has its natural attractions, such as the lush West End Rainforest and the well-marked snorkel trails of Buck Island Reef National Monument off the island's north shore.

THIS PAGE: Ruins of the Annaberg Sugar Mill on St. John.
OPPOSITE (FROM TOP): Colourful buildings on St. Croix; snorkelling at Buck Island Reef National Monument.

St. John is thoroughly wild and rugged, a legacy of American tycoon families that ran much of the island as their own private resort and then bequeathed it to the U.S. National Park Service. Around two-thirds of St. John is now protected within the confines of the Virgin Islands National Park, where you can camp on the beach within sight (and earshot) of the waves and the offshore reefs. Some of the best bays and beaches can only be reached by foot or kayak. The landscape in the area has not changed all that much since the Taino inhabited St. John.

Cruz Bay is the only thing resembling a town on St. John, but despite its Lilliputian size, there are lots of things to do to keep visitors amused. Among the offbeat shops in the town's Mongoose Junction area is the Best of Both Worlds, where the paintings, sculptures, jewelleries and glassworks of more than a hundred Caribbean artists are displayed for sale. The trans-Caribbean yachting crowd hangs out at Skinny Legs in Coral Bay, where live bands enhance the 'margaritaville' languor.

THIS PAGE (FROM LEFT): *The males of the Magnificent Frigatebird, one of the species of birds in Barbuda, have red-orange throat patches that are inflated during courtship displays; an example of some of the finest beach strands in Antigua.*

OPPOSITE (FROM TOP): *Visitors sip tea amidst the ruins of a bath-house in Nelson's Dockyard; fruits for sale along a street on St. John's, Antigua.*

antigua: beaches + boats

The tiny independent state of Antigua and Barbuda boasts that it has a beach for every day of the year—365 places to dig your toes into the sand. Antigua has some fine strands, ranging from the long white-sand stretch at Dickenson Bay with all its water sports and outdoor eateries, to the isolated coves of the Five Islands Peninsula where you can take it all off and where the waves are often big enough to surf. Barbuda (a 20-minute flight to the north) has what could be the most stunning beach in the entire Caribbean—a long and luxurious pink-sand strand that curves around the island's southwest coast. The island is sparsely populated and largely undeveloped. It is a mosaic of teal-coloured lagoons, salt marshes and sandy scrub where frigatebirds, pelicans, egrets and more than 170 other bird species are known to dwell.

As headquarters of the British Caribbean fleet for more than 200 years, English Harbour on Antigua's south coast is brimming with history. Horatio Nelson and Prince William Henry (the future King William IV) were posted here as young sea captains, and by all accounts, got up to quite a bit of high jinx with the lasses. The past is brought back to life at Nelson's Dockyard National Park, where museum exhibits and historic ships mingle with waterfront cafés, shops and modern boating facilities. English Harbour has become a focal point for yachties. Both bareboat and crewed yachts are available for charter all year round. Antigua's annual spring Sailing Week is both a showcase for marine hardware and a thinly veiled excuse to party.

antigua: st. john's + cricket games

On the northwest part of the island, St. John's offers a popular port-of-call for Caribbean cruise ships. The buildings here are painted with cheerful bright colours. The Museum of Antigua and Barbuda (located in an old British colonial courthouse) offers hundreds of hands-on displays on local history, culture and nature. The best place to grab a brew along the waterfront is the Redcliffe Tavern, where an ice-cold Wadadli goes down mighty well with flying fish and chips.

Antiguans love cricket. The prevailing mood of half the citizenry is often determined by how well the Leeward Islands or West Indies teams are doing in any given test match. Many cricket legends hail from Antigua, including the remarkable Viv Richards, one of the best batsmen of all time. Cricket aficionados can revel in a new high-tech stadium built (and named after Sir Vivian) for the 2007 World Cup as well as the West Indies Cricket Hall of Fame at the Sticky Wicket Club near the airport.

anguilla: chic beaches

'Noble and beauteous, she stands midst the sea…' The Anguillan anthem is the only one in the Caribbean that must be played with steel drums. Anguilla is a self-governing member of the United Kingdom. During the early days of autonomy, locals had little more than lobster fishing to pay the bills. But the authorities quickly steered Anguilla towards the two pillars of modern Caribbean economics—tourism and banking.

Anguilla has become one of the region's trendiest destinations over the past decade. Though still quiet and secluded, it is considered by many to be 'super chic'. The three dozen beaches that ring this slender isle are nearly all spectacular, especially the 3-km (2-mile) white-sand strand at Shoal Bay. Anguilla has gained a reputation for excellent food, thanks in no small part to the presence of 70 restaurants and a gourmet cooking school with visiting celebrity chef instructors and its own hydroponic farm. The Valley is the island's commercial and administrative hub, but Island Harbour on the north shore is far more interesting with its active fishing village and picturesque waterfront. Catch a boat to a private island eatery called Gorgeous Scilly Cay, where the beer is ice-cold, the lobster is fresh from the sea and the sunsets are beyond description.

The remains of *El Buen Consejo*, a Spanish galleon that wrecked in 1772, is the highlight of Stony Bay Marine Park and Archaeological Preserve off the island's northeast coast. Lying in only 9 m (30 ft) of water, the site is ideal for both snorkellers and rookie divers. Anguilla's flat terrain is easy to explore on horseback. You can ride through the island's interior or splash through the surf on your trusty steed.

THIS PAGE (FROM TOP): Antiguans young and old love a game of cricket in the afternoons; mornings are for horseback rides on white-sand beaches.

OPPOSITE: Gorgeous Scilly Cay restaurant boasts a stunning view of turquoise waters.

'Noble and beauteous, she stands midst the sea...'

The Villa Book

Selecting a holiday destination can sometimes be a daunting prospect. There are literally thousands of places to choose from and making the right decision is often a hit-and-miss affair, more dependent on luck than judgement. Mistakes are not only costly, but they also create a sense of disappointment that lingers in the memory long after the holiday is over. For this reason, it can be both helpful and comforting to have a well-established and reliable agency provide a shortlist of those properties best suited to your requirements and, as a consequence, most likely to live up to your expectations conceived before your trip.

One such agency is The Villa Book, a property rental company run by some of the most experienced individuals in the business. Based on a close working relationship with owners and local agents, the staff at The Villa Book take pride in knowing all there is to know about their properties, and in being able to cater to individual requirements, whether it's a romantic getaway you're after, or a larger villa to suit an extended family or group of friends.

With hundreds of properties on three continents, the staff at The Villa Book are never short of options and recommendations for customers, but they are particularly strong when it comes to destinations in the Caribbean. Their properties in the region include villas in Barbados, St. Lucia, Nevis, St. Martin, St. Barts, the British Virgin Islands, Tobago, the Turks and Caicos, and, last but not least, Anguilla.

Just over 5 km (3 miles) wide by 26 km (16 miles) long, Anguilla is bordered by magnificent white sand beaches to be found anywhere in the Caribbean, and The Villa Book has beachfront properties all over the island accommodating anything between two and 16 guests each.

Three of the most alluring ones can be found in the Little Harbour Estate, a stunning property ideally located in a small secluded cove on the south coast of the island.

Villa Turquaz has three large double bedrooms, two garden suites, a cosy TV and children's room, and comes with a fully equipped gymnasium. Indigo is a three-bedroom house that perfectly captures the living style of the Caribbean, and Little Indigo is a lovely annex with two double rooms.

Although quite self-contained, these properties are adjacent to one another and can be rented together to cater to larger groups of visitors. All three are beautifully furnished with a blend of antique and modern furniture, and equipped with amenities including hi-fi, cable television, DVD and video players. In addition, each comes with its own swimming pool and access to a private beach, and all enjoy spectacular views of St. Martin and St. Barts. A maid service is included in the price and more staff can be provided if notice is served in advance.

THIS PAGE: Quiet reflection and relaxation would be ideal in this villa in Little Harbour Estate. OPPOSITE (CLOCKWISE FROM TOP): A garden suite that captures the living style of the Caribbean; the lush foliage provides a respite from the cares of life; an afternoon spent dipping in the private pool of this villa can be a therapeutic experience.

FACTS

FEATURES	all types of accommodations to suit various needs • private chefs
BUSINESS	villa rental
CONTACT	The Villa Book, 12 Venetian House, 47 Warrington Crescent, London W9 1EJ • telephone: +44.845.500 2000 • facsimile: +44.845.500 2001 • email: info@thevillabook.com • website: www.thevillabook.com

PHOTOGRAPHS COURTESY OF THE VILLA BOOK.

Blue Waters

THIS PAGE: *Blue Waters' hallmark sophistication and meticulous attention to its guests is apparent in the resort's overall design and style. Here, a view of the main pool within its central grounds.*

OPPOSITE (FROM TOP): *The Tea Terrace; view of the award-winning villa from above, sprawling across a tiny peninsula that makes the western tip of Soldiers Bay.*

Blue Waters in Antigua is the last word in Caribbean chic. Renowned for its lavish accommodations and impeccable service ethos, which are highly complimented by international celebrities from musician Paul Young to footballer Robbie Fowler, this is a swanky luxury resort where the glamorous and well-heeled head to in Antigua.

Nestling in a private bay on the island's less developed northern coast, Blue Waters' graceful villa buildings repose on pristine shores lapped by the warm, shimmering waters of the Caribbean. The 40-year-old, family-owned resort is personally managed by its perceptive owners, who take great effort in creating a distinguished property

which is constantly refurbished with the times and appointed to the very highest standards in hospitality. It comes as no surprise then, that Blue Waters has garnered for itself a sea of prestigious accolades, which include the World Travel Award for 'Antigua's Best Hotel' (2003) and a nomination by *Condé Nast Johansens* as the 'Most Outstanding Caribbean Resort' of 2005.

Undoubtedly, the main highlight behind Blue Waters' award-winning repute are its luxurious accommodations, which comprise 77 elegantly appointed rooms, suites and private villas set in 6 hectares (14 acres) of lush tropical gardens where hummingbirds dart between delicate hibiscus and brilliant bougainvillea. Ranging from superior rooms to hillside and beachfront suites, each option features expansive, light-infused living areas, breathtaking garden or sea views, private balconies, climate-control and spacious en-

suite bathrooms. Installed in each guestroom are telephones, satellite television, minibars and myriad little indulgences to make guests' stay a flawless and thoroughly relaxing one.

For an unforgettable experience, opt for a private villa. The villas are removed from the main buildings for optimum privacy and each has been strategically positioned amid the property's grounds to offer sensational panoramic views over the shifting seascape. From cliff-top vantage points to those serenely cloistered behind beautiful veils of flora, the

villas and their intimate, romantic settings make for the perfect honeymoon paradise.

Blue Waters' true pièce de resistance, however, is Rock Cottage, the resort's finest lodging on offer—and one of the world's most exclusive waterfront villas. Perched on its own cliff-top promontory which forms the western tip of Soldiers Bay, this first-class escape has been hailed one of *Harpers & Queen's* '150 Best Places on Earth' as well as 'Antigua and Barbuda's Leading Villa' at the World Travel Awards (2004). With its

own private and guarded entrance, five expansive bedrooms, a plunge pool looking out to the sea, a spacious sun patio and a dedicated chef, Rock Cottage is a world of total privacy and personalized pampering. And then, offering its occupants the complete freedom of exploring the island at any time is a 7-m (24-ft) power boat available for hire, so guests can escape, James Bond style, for an adventure around the coasts of Antigua and neighbouring Barbuda.

Guests of Rock Cottage also have easy access to the hotel's facilities, which include three pools, each providing an uninterrupted

vista of the Caribbean. From a large pool flanked by sunloungers to a more secluded version with its own sundeck, jacuzzi and bar, everyone will find their bathing niche.

Guilt-free culinary indulgence is a great vacation highlight for many travellers; and Blue Waters offers two unmatched venues in which to treat yourself to some high-style wining and dining. The table d'hôte Palm restaurant is open throughout the day and offers a variety of dining options. Breakfast and lunch may be enjoyed in the open-sided plantation building, or on its sun drenched terraces. Evenings will prove to be the most memorable however, accompanied by live Caribbean music and an excellent wine list.

For occasions warranting the height of sophistication, Vyviens' soigné, neo-colonial setting and impressive fusion cuisine offer the finest in ambience, service and gastronomic satisfaction. The noteworthy à la carte menu

THIS PAGE (FROM LEFT): Blue Waters' Rock Cottage is a cut above the rest. The exclusive villa boasts a private plunge pool overlooking the sea and, seen here not far below in the water, a power boat which guests of the villa can hire any time of the day; view of the pool and pool bar.
OPPOSITE: Inside Rock Cottage, the airy, expansive lounge area.

features fresh seafood alongside American- and European-inspired dishes, and the staff here will pre-empt your every desire.

Bar lovers too will be spoiled for choice. The beach bar cools the water babies; the pool bar, the sun-bronzed; and Pelican Bar, named after the birds which soar over Blue Waters' bay, is located within the hotel, well stocked with everything from cold beers and branded spirits to superb house concoctions and colourful, crushed-ice classics. Once a week, Pelican Bar hosts the Hotel Manager's Cocktail Party, offering a dazzlingly convivial atmosphere and even, perhaps, the chance to mingle with celebrities staying at the resort.

In between cooling cocktails, sample the resort's extensive leisure menu. Courtesy of its unrivalled location, Blue Waters boasts two beaches exclusive to the resort; something which is practically unheard of in Antigua. Maximize your little piece of paradise by taking to the azure ocean for windsurfing, kayaking and sailing trips. Come up with your own Wimbledon game strategy at the tennis court, or go for a workout in the fully equipped fitness centre. At the end of a day's exertion, plump for some five-star pampering at the resort's spa and beauty salon and indulge in the treatments and massages.

Naturally, the resort's idyllic location and expert staff make it a top choice for holding weddings and special events. From chilled champagne and suites filled with the aroma of freshly cut flowers, Blue Waters creates its own urbane style and definition of romance.

FACTS

ROOMS	superior rooms • hillside and beachfront suites • private villas • Rock Cottage
FOOD	The Palm: Caribbean cuisine • Vyviens: contemporary fusion cuisine
DRINK	Pelican Bar • beach bar • pool bar
FEATURES	private bay • 2 beaches • 3 pools • jacuzzi • fitness centre • tennis court • spa • beauty salon • water sports • weddings
NEARBY	St. John's • day-trip to Barbuda
CONTACT	Boon Point, Soldiers Bay, Antigua • telephone: +44.870.360 1245 • facsimile: +44.870.360 1246 • email: bluewaters@threesixtyhotels.com • website: www.bluewaters.net

Carlisle Bay

THIS PAGE (FROM TOP): *An Ocean Suite that radiates luxurious comfort and simple elegance; Carlisle Bay's torch-lit entrance; Indigo on the Beach provides an indelible dining experience.*

OPPOSITE (FROM LEFT): *The Library is a must for book lovers; embark on an epicurean adventure at East restaurant.*

Perhaps nowhere else on Antigua is the allure of the Caribbean as potent as that of Carlisle Bay. Named 'Hotel of the Year' in 2005 by UK's *Tatler Travel Guide*, Carlisle Bay embraces a contemporary purity that sits in stark yet pleasing contrast to the undulating hills and paradisaical shores of the Antiguan south coast.

The melding of the au courant and classic savoir-faire engenders the hallmark of Carlisle Bay. Clean lines and cool, sophisticated spaces create an atmosphere that welcomes and refreshes. The dark, polished wood and neutral tones provide a canvas for the artistry of photographs adorning its walls.

As you stroll through the airy walkways, the soft caress of the balmy ocean breeze, filtering through large colonial plantation shutters, soothes away all your cares. The suites of Carlisle Bay, furnished in crisp, cotton linen and silk features, are uncluttered spaces of elegant simplicity. Well-chosen extras include DVD/CD players, Gaggia expresso machines, fibre-optic reading lamps and luxurious daybeds.

Amenities at Carlisle Bay are anything but sparse. Indulge your cinematic whims in the state-of-the-art private screening room with its plush Italian-leather seating, while the literary selection in the Library provides for ideal poolside reading.

...the epitome of what a hotel should be: style, sophistication and service with a smile.

If programmes of a more physical nature appeal to you, Carlisle Bay has a plethora of land and sea activities to fulfil that desire. Likewise, the sybaritic indulgences at The Blue Spa, with its six luxurious treatment rooms, plunge pool, and juice bar, will leave you rejuvenated and ready to savour the epicurean pleasures that Carlisle Bay has in store for you.

Ultimately it's all about thoughtful service, relaxation and fabulous food. Indigo on the Beach offers delicious healthy grills, seafood and salads and breathtaking ocean views, whilst East restaurant serves exciting Asian food in a stunning contemporary setting. Both restaurants can be enjoyed in cool comfort; there are no fussy dress codes at Carlisle Bay.

A private candlelit dinner served on the jetty, with the soft murmur of the sea beneath and the distant shimmer of a starry Antiguan sky, will set hearts aflutter. After which, guests can head to the Pavilion Bar where strains of live jazz and piano music float up to the double vaulted roof and create a feet-tapping atmosphere.

As a member of The Leading Small Hotels of the World, Carlisle Bay is the epitome of what a hotel should be: style, sophistication and service with a smile.

FACTS

ROOMS	80 suites
FOOD	East: Asian • Indigo on the Beach: healthy grills, seafood and salads
DRINK	Indigo on the Beach Bar • Pavilion Bar • The Jetty Bar
FEATURES	gift shop • library • The Blue Spa • Blue Spa Gymnasium • yoga and pilates • 9 tennis courts • water sports • Cool Kids Club
BUSINESS	The Carlisle Room • The Screening Room
NEARBY	Nelson's Dockyard • English Harbour
CONTACT	Carlisle Bay, Old Road, St. Mary's, Antigua • telephone: +1268.484 0000 • facsimile: +1268.484 0001 • email: info@carlisle-bay.com • website: www.carlisle-bay.com

The Copper + Lumber Store Hotel

Quite apart from the fact that the modest Copper & Lumber Store probably has one of the most intriguing names for any hotel in the Caribbean, this understated and little-known gem is an incredibly charming and fascinating place to base your stay in Antigua; a cosy waterfront abode in the middle of Nelson's Dockyard complex at English Harbour.

The Copper & Lumber is also one of the few hotels in the region that is housed in an authentic historic monument—a two-storey wooden structure built as part of the dock-yard's facilities under the watchful eye of Captain Horatio Nelson, commander of the British Navy's vaunted Leeward Island Squadron in the late-18th century. As the name suggests, the original building served as a storehouse for supplies of copper and lumber reserved for maritime chores.

Set around a central courtyard, each of the 14 suites and studios is named after a ship which Nelson commanded during his long and distinguished career. Noted as one of the finest illustrations of Georgian architecture in the West Indies, they feature walls and arches of weathered brick, hand-hewn wooden beams and brass fittings that hark back to a romantic bygone age. All are decorated with genuine antiques and period furnishings in tones of ivory, cinnamon and mahogany, steamer trunks, four-poster canopy beds, old sailing prints and faux gas lamps

THIS PAGE (FROM TOP): The inn exudes period elegance throughout from the Wardroom restaurant; the bedrooms, with antique beds resting under old brick arches; to the cosy reception area.

OPPOSITE: The courtyard and restaurant. Built in 1783 as a storage facility for the British naval base's copper and lumber reserves, the building is one of the West Indies' few standing historic architectural landmarks and a fine instance of Georgian symmetry and proportion.

which evoke a nostalgic air of old English chivalry and elegance. A meticulous process of restoration and refurbishment has ensured the provision of 21st-century comforts such as television, kitchenettes and modern bathrooms while carefully making certain that the modern installations complement the original Georgian style and period authenticity.

Opening onto a courtyard cloaked in cascades of bougainvillea, the atmospheric Wardroom restaurant serves a tantalizing combination of international and Caribbean favourites. The menu runs heavily towards seafood specialties such as smoked salmon and grilled lobster, but you can also tuck into old English dishes like lamb chops with mint sauce. Those craving a more casual meal can head into the nearby Mainbrace pub for steak and kidney pie, fish and chips or an unforgettable pint of amber nectar.

The Copper & Lumber's location in the very heart of Nelson's Dockyard makes it the perfect base for exploring the national park as well as various historical exhibits, theme restaurants and specialty shops. Guests can also go on guided historical walks around Antigua or pick up a map at the front desk and walk to nearby Pigeon Beach, or hike to Shirley Heights Lookout, Fort Berkeley and Dows Hill Centre to view its multimedia show on the island's rich culture and history.

Although the Copper & Lumber doesn't boast its own beach, guests are accorded full privileges at the Galleon Beach Club on the opposite side of English Harbour, where a white-sand beach and a full range of water sports are available. The front desk can also make arrangements for sailing, golf, tennis and squash at nearby facilities.

FACTS		
	ROOMS	14 suites and studios
	FOOD	Wardroom restaurant: international and Caribbean cuisine
	DRINK	Mainbrace pub
	FEATURES	Galleon Beach Club • weddings
	BUSINESS	Internet access • facilities for corporate functions
	NEARBY	golf • tennis • full-service marina • Pigeon Beach • Admiral's House Museum • Officer's Quarters • Shirley Heights Lookout • Dows Hill Interpretation Centre
	CONTACT	Nelson's Dockyard, English Harbour, Antigua • telephone: +1268.460 1058 • facsimile: +1268.460 1529 • email: : clhotel@candw.ag • website: www.copperandlumberhotel.com

PHOTOGRAPHS COURTESY OF THE COPPER + LUMBER STORE HOTEL.

Curtain Bluff

Poised effortlessly between two sparkling bays, Curtain Bluff brings a magical touch of class to Antigua's secluded southwest shore; an all-inclusive resort known for its elegant manner and country club ambience. One of the first upscale abodes to be established in the Leeward Islands, Curtain Bluff has been around since the days when JFK was in the White House and Chubby Checker ruled the music charts. Yet it never seems to age, as refreshing today as it was 40 years ago as the new kid on the block. Possessing a rare timelessness, the resort has enchanted a loyal following that charts generations.

Drawing true inspiration from its name, Curtain Bluff sprawls across a lush peninsula like muslin cloth draped across the tranquil landscape; a spectacular sight from land or sea. The resort's airy 'great house'—where guests gather to dine, drink and chat—luxuriates amid breezy tropical gardens in the middle of the petite peninsula. A stream

THIS PAGE (FROM TOP): Not your average balcony, the Terrace Suite verandah is a lavish al fresco living area replete with its own whirlpool, loungers and exquisite Antiguan scenery; renowned for its architecture and spaciousness, its fine wine cellar and continental cuisine as well as a talent for innovation with the times, Curtain Bluff has earned a faithful following of guests who have been coming to stay for decades.

OPPOSITE: The Terrace Suite bedroom, with a private verandah overlooking the tree-lined beach.

of dazzling white bungalows gaze out from coconut palms on the edge of a white-sand beach, climbing slowly toward the top of a cliff wedged between the twin bays—like dabs of brilliant white paint against a glossy emerald and aquamarine canvas.

The 40 junior suites—with their posh marble and granite bathrooms and tropical wicker décor—have always been the most popular. But the new Grace and Morris Bay suites are even more lavish, with separate, spacious living and sleeping quarters, rustic furnishings (including four-poster beds) and sunny, expansive balconies complete with private whirlpools that overlook the water.

Food and drink have long been among Curtain Bluff's star attractions. The restaurant's exceptional continental cuisine is renowned for its incredibly fresh ingredients (most of them are flown in each day) and creative presentation—a veritable feast for both the eyes and palate. The resort's wine cellar is touted to be the best in the Caribbean, with

more than 25,000 well-aged bottles, many of them chosen personally by long-time resort owner Howard Hulford.

In addition to offering a wide choice of water activities, Curtain Bluff is a well-loved centre for racquet sports, being the only resort on Antigua equipped with both tennis

and squash courts. The hotel also hosts the annual Antigua Tennis Week, which affords casual players and beginners a chance to rub (tennis) elbows with some of the legends of the game. Also all part of the fun and thrills are amateur tournaments, pro doubles exhibitions and strategy clinics.

PHOTOGRAPHS COURTESY OF CURTAIN BLUFF.

FACTS		
ROOMS	Grace and Morris Bay Suites • Terrace Room • 18 executive deluxe rooms • 40 junior suites • 1 executive suite	
FOOD	Garden Pavilion: continental cuisine • Beach Club: light lunches	
DRINK	wine cellar	
FEATURES	fitness centre • tennis and squash courts • pool • 2 beaches • water sports • sailing • scuba diving • snorkelling • croquet • playground • library	
BUSINESS	conference room	
NEARBY	English Harbour • Nelson's Dockyard • Fig Tree Drive • Shirley Heights Lookout	
CONTACT	PO Box 288, Old Road, Antigua • telephone: +1268.462 8400 • facsimile: +1268.462 8409 • email: curtainbluff@curtainbluff.com • website: www.curtainbluff.com	

The Inn at English Harbour

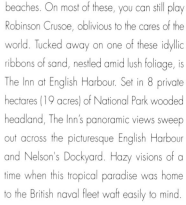

Richard Burton loved getting married. He also loved world-class honeymoons. It was only fitting then, that he spent two of them here at The Inn at English Harbour, Antigua. This colourful island on the northern edge of the West Indies is famed for its 365 pristine beaches. On most of these, you can still play Robinson Crusoe, oblivious to the cares of the world. Tucked away on one of these idyllic ribbons of sand, nestled amid lush foliage, is The Inn at English Harbour. Set in 8 private hectares (19 acres) of National Park wooded headland, The Inn's panoramic views sweep out across the picturesque English Harbour and Nelson's Dockyard. Hazy visions of a time when this tropical paradise was home to the British naval fleet waft easily to mind.

From a sun-filled beachfront suite or airy cottage perched high over the Harbour, be hypnotized as sleek yachts glide in and out of their moorings. The Inn's elegant suites are perfect vantage points from which to watch Caribbean life unfold beneath. Charmingly appointed with ceiling fans and a private verandah, several of these quaint, luxurious hideaways are scattered with Caribbean and British antiques. The Inn's plush suites naturally exude a genteel sense of history and dignity, deepened by their teak four-poster beds and hand-painted armoires.

In spite of the feel of historic weight here, the classic Inn is neither formal nor starchy. It is refined, yet unpretentious; professional, yet wonderfully friendly. Sip a rum punch in the wood-beamed Stone Bar, with its traditional fieldstone walls, fresh-white furnishings and 19th-century maps. Peruse the fine wine list as rich in choice as the area is in history.

...a rich sense of history and dignity...

At dusk, experience the unforgettable with a candlelit dinner beneath a breath-stealing Antiguan sky at the Terrace Restaurant, famed for intuitive service and reputed to be the finest restaurant in Antigua. Innovative dishes mingle tropical highlights with freshly caught fruits de mer, accompanied by an oak-aged bottle from the perfect vintage—only the very finest for the discriminating traveller here at The Inn.

THIS PAGE (FROM TOP): The Inn's lounge is to be found in the aptly named Stone Bar, a rustic wood-beamed parlour with walls of fieldstone and historic maps; the deluxe suite wraps its guests in the charming atmosphere of living in an old plantation house.

OPPOSITE: View of the English Harbour and The Inn's grey-shingled beachfront extension from its original hilltop terrace.

Yet, it is in its vibrant present that some of The Inn's most impressive offerings are to be found. A state-of-the-art fitness centre and two floodlit tennis courts await the active, with the waving fronds of wind-teased palms your only audience. The adventurous will take to the dazzling clear waters at the private beach's edge, where windsurfing, sunfish sailing and kayaking will soon become second nature, and excellent scuba diving is mere moments away. Massage therapists will be waiting on your return, promising a blissful session that will lift those spirits in readiness for evening.

FACTS

ROOMS	6 hillside ocean view rooms • 4 standard beach rooms • 16 beachfront junior suites • 8 beachfront deluxe suites
FOOD	Terrace Restaurant • Waterfront Restaurant
DRINK	Stone Bar • Beach Bar
FEATURES	fitness centre • 2 floodlit tennis courts • infinity-edge pool • beach • water sports • snorkelling • boating • complimentary water taxi to Nelson's Dockyard
NEARBY	VC Bird International Airport (20 minutes by car) • St. John's
CONTACT	Freeman's Bay, English Harbour, Antigua • telephone: +1268.460 1014 • facsimile: +1268.460 1603 • email: theinn@candw.ag • website: www.theinn.ag

PHOTOGRAPHS COURTESY OF THE INN AT ENGLISH HARBOUR.

Siboney Beach Club

Antigua's Siboney Beach Club epitomizes the ultimate Caribbean escape amidst a carefully cultivated mini-jungle on Dickenson Bay. At Siboney, guests can expect the ultimate in relaxation.

Meticulously planned by the experienced hotel staff, guests will be able to indulge in a unique and tailor-made holiday experience. Themes range from romantic and intimate to action-packed and energetic.

Couples looking for that perfect backdrop to hold their dream wedding will be charmed by Siboney's special package whereby they can choose to exchange vows on the white sand or in the hotel's verdant garden.

For those seeking seclusion and comfort—incognito celebrities are not uncommon—the bijou suite hotel provides discretion and privacy. With a freshwater pool shielded by towering palms and skirted by the riotous colours of tropical flowers, guests can comfortably snooze in hammocks stretched between palms, and remain oblivious to everything, removed from the hurly-burly of the world outside.

Meals at the award-winning Coconut Grove Restaurant are a veritable feast for the senses. Perched right at the water's edge on Dickenson Bay, the key attraction at one of Antigua's finest gourmet restaurants is its inspired Euro-Caribbean menu. It is not surprising that Fodor rates it as 'outstanding'. Sample the Lobster Bisque or Marinated Conch Salad with Mango for a true taste of the Tropics.

...the bijou suite hotel provides discretion and privacy.

Each of Siboney's 12 stylish suites features a bedroom, a bathroom and a separate living area with a private terrace. Guests can catch glimpses of the cobalt ocean through lush foliage from their private balcony. For snacks and drinks, there are kitchenettes hidden behind louvred doors.

In addition, each of these impeccably furnished hideaways is decorated with eye-catching tropical prints with well-placed sofas, armchairs and easy chairs.

Bedrooms offer the option of air conditioning or natural cross ventilation, courtesy of the trade winds. For therapeutic treatments, call Min Yang or Barbara, and they will come to your suite, bringing their finely honed spa skills.

At Siboney, feel at ease to do nothing more strenuous than sip delicious rum punch all afternoon. Alternatively, there are sporting, cultural or ecological adventures to keep you engaged. For example, you may join guided walks to Greencastle Hill or Christian Valley, or weave through the brilliant colours of reefs and uninhabited islands on a private sailing charter. Nature lovers will also be able to marvel at hummingbirds, snowy egrets and sandpipers which populate its lagoon.

For world-weary travellers who want to experience the finest of what the West Indies has to offer, Siboney is indeed the perfect getaway.

THIS PAGE (FROM LEFT): *Impeccably furnished, each suite features rattan and rich tropical fabrics; guests can relax by the freshwater pool.*
OPPOSITE: *Balconies afford glimpses of the Caribbean Sea through the lush foliage.*

FACTS		
	ROOMS	12 suites
	FOOD	Coconut Grove Restaurant: Euro-Caribbean
	DRINK	beach bar
	FEATURES	private terraces • library
	NEARBY	Christian Valley • Greencastle Hill • Dams at Body Ponds and Wallings • Sting Ray City • Barbuda island
	CONTACT	PO Box 222, St. John's, Antigua • telephone: +1268.462 0806 • facsimile: +1268.462 3356 • email: siboney@candw.ag • website: www.siboneybeachclub.com

PHOTOGRAPHS COURTESY OF SIBONEY BEACH CLUB.

Biras Creek

Getting away from it all has never been as blissful as at the secluded paradise of Biras Creek. Named one of *Travel + Leisure's* 'Top Ten Caribbean Resorts', this inspiring retreat is nestled snugly between two sloping hills, guardians of Virgin Gorda's North Sound. The waters here are so well protected and exclusive that its private marina can only be reached by an unforgettable boat journey, which hugs the contours of one of the British Virgin Islands' most breathtaking coastlines.

Biras Creek is tucked away on the coast, framed on three sides by turquoise ocean. A member of the prestigious Relais & Chateaux group, the resort's 31 suites are decorated in uplifting Caribbean tones and radiate a feel of rustic chic. Five of the resort's suites are interconnected and housed within cottages, which are dotted among the lush landscape of the island's 57-hectare (140-acre) nature reserve, criss-crossed by hiking and walking trails.

The cottages are quaintly tucked behind tree-draped entrances mere metres from the water's edge, and each suite boasts a private verandah offering panoramic views of Virgin Gorda's shimmery aquamarine waters and implausibly white, sandy beaches. The resort's two Grand Suites feature terracotta floors and hand-painted fabrics, and in the Premier Suite, specially-designed rattan and teak furnishings. Their extravagant bathrooms include outdoor garden showers and free-standing bathtubs.

All the resort's suites offer CD players, delightful Balinese-style cotton kimonos and the complimentary use of bicycles for leisurely nights in or adventurous trips out. This is a remote, television-free zone where you can truly be faraway from the world outside—the very heart of Biras Creek's charm.

And as if its location wasn't enough to make you want to linger here forever, Biras Creek's fine dining and gourmet offerings are second to none. The restaurant is dramatically sited in a hilltop fortress with open-air stonework and an elegant bar. The stunning open-walled views extend out across the untouched beauty of North Sound and the chefs take inspiration from land and sea, with Five-Spice Duck Salad and appetizing principal dishes like Grilled Grouper with Herby Couscous on an ever-changing menu. The desserts are

THIS PAGE (FROM TOP): One of Biras Creek's exclusive Ocean Suites; the lower waterfront dining area; a party of lounge chairs on the terrace of the Arawak Pavilion awaits dusk for a spectacular sunset over the North Sound.

OPPOSITE: Biras Creek stands atop raised palm-dotted landscape like a tiny tropical kingdom on a distant island—protected on land by two hills, the resort is sequestered on all remaining sides by a Caribbean bay, the Sound, and the Atlantic Ocean.

enticingly unique, and include Chilled Green-Apple Parfait or even sorbet selections served with Chilled Cantaloupe Soup.

To work off such culinary indulgences, revel in the gorgeous, sun-warmed outdoor pool, toning spa therapies, or in the extensive range of water sports—from Hobie Cats and Sunfish sailboats to kayaking and snorkelling. For something extra special, take a private helicopter trip or navigate a Boston Whaler to a neighbouring island for the experience of a lifetime. Honeymooners should know that *The Daily Telegraph* has hailed Biras Creek one of 2006's 'Top Romantic Escapes'. What better way to celebrate new beginnings than from a private, sunset yacht charter across the sail-flecked sea? After all, this is the first port of call for lovers of the real Caribbean.

FACTS		
	ROOMS	20 Ocean Suites • 8 Garden Suites • 2 Grand Suites • Premier Suite
	FOOD	hilltop restaurant • waterfront restaurant
	DRINK	Terrace Bar
	FEATURES	spa • snooker room • 2 flood-lit tennis courts • pool • beach • water sports • sailing • scuba diving • snorkelling • garden walk • hiking
	NEARBY	The Baths • Copper Mine Point • Frenchman's Cay • JR O'Neal Botanic Gardens • national parks • day-trip to Anegada • shopping and golf on St. Thomas • St. Croix
	CONTACT	Virgin Gorda, British Virgin Islands • telephone: +1284.494 3555 • facsimile: +1284.494 3557 • email: gm@biras.com • website: www.biras.com

PHOTOGRAPHS COURTESY OF BIRAS CREEK.

Necker Island

When Sir Richard Branson sought an idyllic personal paradise to call his home, one namesake location sprang instantly to mind—the British Virgin Islands. A 10-minute boat ride from Virgin Gorda, the astonishing beauty of Necker Island surpassed his every expectation.

Today, with incarnations from family retreat to honeymoon haven and private party venue, the entire reef-fringed island is at the sole disposal of jet-setting guests. Its exclusive Balinese-themed accommodations are designed for a capacity of 26 to 28, and rooms can be reserved singly during Celebration Weeks. At other times, the only other guests present will be those friends you have chosen to share the island with, so the sable-soft beaches, shimmering seascapes and turquoise waters will be for your eyes only.

Necker Island's central point is The Great House—a tall, airy Balinese-inspired villa with hypnotic views of neighbouring islands. Its eight double rooms are stylishly furnished with dreamy cream fabrics and honeyed woods for a tranquil, mellow atmosphere. The Master Suite houses a sumptuous jacuzzi, a home entertainment system and a sensational open-air bathroom worthy of a James Bond movie.

Sequestered amid bright-hued foliage in the middle of the island is the villa of Bali Lo, overlooking a freshwater pool and daybeds. For heightened exclusivity, the thatched, multi-tiered retreats of Bali Hi and Bali Cliff are perched on a precipice for a bird's eye view of the island, perfect for couples and for contemplating the breathtaking landscape in the villas' own private meditation rooms.

THIS PAGE (FROM TOP): Overlooking the island's west coast is Bali Cliff, with views of Turtle Beach from the villa's breezy verandah; Necker's beach barbeques are the favourite dinner option; simply divine is the Master Suite at the top of The Great House.

OPPOSITE: A thin palm-lined strip separates the sea from the Beach Pavilion's free-form infinity pool. Here, you'll find a swim-up bar, rocks for sunbathing, a waterfall and a breath-stealing panorama of Necker's turquoise seascape.

...the entire reef-fringed island is at the sole disposal of jet-setting guests...

The Beach Pavilion is where the state-of-the-art kitchen is to be found, and Necker's expert chefs revel in producing fine food, accompanied by the finest of wines. From lobster to a traditional roast, everything is prepared from only the freshest and most aromatic ingredients available.

'Living al fresco' is Necker's maxim, and on offer throughout this singular island is an unimaginable multitude of outdoor dining options amid its magnetizing Caribbean scenery. Enjoy a barbeque on the sand at the ocean's edge, or pluck sushi from a floating buffet as you relax in the infinity-edge pool. Making yourself at home here is actively encouraged, so enjoy being waited on hand and foot, or help yourself to a midnight snack. Take it into the Great Room for a game of pool, a tinkle of the ivories or a doze in one of the balcony's hammocks. This is an island where guests make their own options—Necker's management and staff are prepared for virtually anything to fulfill your requests for personalized arrangements (and this extends to special occasions and celebrations).

Fitness enthusiasts too will benefit from Necker's open-plan philosophy, with cooling trade winds passing through the open-walled gym to keep temperatures down. Professionally coached tennis, fishing trips and a plethora of water sports are available, with the tranquillity and specialized therapists of Bali Leha spa waiting to ease away the aches at day's end.

FACTS		
	ROOMS	The Great House (8 double rooms and a Master Suite) • 5 private Bali Houses • maximum capacity of 26–28 guests
	FOOD	The Great House • Beach Pavilion • Sunset Point • beach barbeques • sushi canoe
	DRINK	The Great House • swim-up bar at the beach pool
	FEATURES	Bali Leha spa • infinity pool at The Main House • beach pool (featuring a waterfall and a swim-up bar) • 2 flood-lit tennis courts • gym • full size snooker table • island walks • Hobie Cats • extensive range of water sports • snorkelling
	NEARBY	helicopter transfers • island hopping • scuba diving • bone fishing • deep sea fishing
	CONTACT	PO Box 1091, The Valley, Virgin Gorda, British Virgin Islands • telephone: +44.208.600 0430 • facsimile: +44.208.600 0431 • email: enquiries@limitededition.virgin.co.uk • website: www.virgin.com/necker

PHOTOGRAPHS COURTESY OF VIRGIN LIMITED EDITION.

Caneel Bay

THIS PAGE (FROM TOP): *The Wine Room at Turtle Bay Estate House; clad in an informal yet elegant mélange of traditional materials and hand-crafted furniture, each guestroom features a balcony or patio that opens onto panoramic views of lush tropical gardens or lengths of pristine white sand.*

OPPOSITE: *Undoubtedly one of the most imaginative and atmospheric dining experiences in the Caribbean, The Equator's 'Dinner in the Ruins' is set amid the glowing torch-lit coral walls and Danish stone of Caneel Bay's own sugar mill ruins.*

If refined beauty and rediscovering a sense of self are priorities when choosing an idyllic retreat, look no further beyond the sanctuary of Caneel Bay on the island of St. John, a turquoise-edged paradise amid the verdant beauty of the US Virgin Islands. Centre of its very own 70-hectare (170-acre) estate, this genteel property is lapped on all sides by the blue of the Caribbean and the riotous greenery of the Virgin Islands National Park.

In both a geographic and psychological sense, Caneel Bay is a world away from the stresses of daily life, the tingle of rum on the tongue placing you firmly in the heart of the

Caribbean. Atypical—and quite unbelievably so—of this day and age, the resort is free from telephones and other hi-tech diversions. This total immersion into serenity makes it all the more easy to remember that you're on holiday. There's even a different beach for every day of the week—Honeymoon Beach, Hawksnest Beach, Turtle Bay Beach, Paradise Beach…and the list goes on.

And as if the destination wasn't exclusive enough, Caneel Bay also plays host to unique culinary experiences unavailable on any other island. Take your beloved for an intoxicatingly romantic dinner at The Equator, a restaurant set atop the resort's own 18th-century sugar mill ruins overlooking the bay, open to ever-changing skies and lit by shadow-throwing torch lights. Crispy and succulent Carib-Asian

Prestige indeed.

cuisine is rarely savoured in such atmosphere. Wine lovers will especially adore Turtle Bay Estate House, a restaurant converted from an 18th-century plantation house. Set within here is The Wine Room, house to nearly 1,000 exemplary bottles in the Caribbean's only temperature-controlled wine room.

Caneel Bay is a flagship for Rosewood Hotels & Resorts' mindful attention to elegant detail and unparalleled, personalized service. Thoughtful interior design in the 166 airy guestrooms and cottages allows balmy trade winds to pass through. Bathrooms hewn from native rock give the impression of showering beneath a hot spring au natural, and hand-crafted wooden furniture sits comfortably on tiled floors. Such soigné interiors, coupled with views of fragrant gardens and shifting seas, represent the perfect marriage of styles.

Of course, no trip to the Caribbean would be complete without revelling in that quintessential island activity—water sports. Book a sailing charter, or snorkel above multi-

hued shoals of fish. If the workout you require is more metaphysical, fine-tune your mental and spiritual well-being in the tranquil and welcoming environment of Caneel Bay's Self Centre. Perched high on a bluff overlooking

Sir Francis Drake Channel, the Self Centre's therapeutic programme is led by educator and best-selling author Dr Deepak Chopra. Prestige indeed. On all levels, Caneel Bay really is the place to rise above it all.

FACTS		
	ROOMS	166 guestrooms and cottages
	FOOD	Turtle Bay Estate House: fusion of classical and innovative American cuisine • The Equator: Carib-Asian cuisine • Caneel Beach Terrace: lunch buffet
	DRINK	Caneel Bay Bar • Sunset Terrace • The Wine Room (wine tasting and private dinners)
	FEATURES	The Self Centre • fitness centre • tennis • pool • water sports • scuba diving • snorkelling • fishing • boat charters • massages • babysitting • children's programmes
	BUSINESS	audiovisual equipment
	NEARBY	Little Dix Bay • sugar plantation remains • pre-Columbian Amerindian relics
	CONTACT	PO Box 720, Cruz Bay, St. John, US Virgin Islands 00831-0720 • telephone: +1340.776 6111 • facsimile: +1340.693 8280 • email: caneel@rosewoodhotels.com • website: www.rosewoodhotels.com

Gallows Point Resort

Sprawling across its very own peninsula and a mere stone's throw away from the tiny village of Cruz Bay, Gallows Point offers that rare St. John combination of tropical seclusion and urban delight. For those who like to take their solitude with just a dash of lively town bustle, this is an excellent place to base a stay on the island—you can while away the morning on a quiet beach, shop your way through town in the afternoon and, come evening, dance the night away.

One of St. John's newer resorts, Gallows Point's privileged waterfront location affords splendid panoramic views of neighbouring St. Thomas and embraces 60 suites which are distributed across 15 two-storey cottages arrayed around the palm-shaded shoreline. The elegant architecture is a modern take on traditional Caribbean—each sand-coloured cottage has been designed like a miniature plantation house, with sweeping staircases, wooden shutters, jalousie doors, fan-shaped fenestration, airy verandahs and sloping roofs. Interiors are decked out with wicker furniture and pastel fabrics with tropical accents, as well as full kitchens, electronic entertainment centres and central air-conditioning.

The selection of suites includes upper level units which feature loft bedrooms and suites on the ground floor which have sunken living rooms and spacious showers. The sea-view suites offer vistas of St. Thomas—especially stunning after dusk when the island sparkles with lights—while the harbourside units overlook yachts anchored in Cruz Bay.

The cottages come fully equipped with deck chairs for lounging on your own private verandah, and ice-coolers in anticipation of the drives around St. John in search of the perfect white strand. One of the nearest is Honeymoon Beach, on the northern side of Cruz Bay, where the gentle spotted eagle rays will eat right out of your hand. A short drive up the same coast are other national park beaches, including the popular Maho Bay Beach, Cinnamon Bay with its nature trails and water sports outfitters, and Trunk Bay with its underwater snorkel trail.

St. John Adventures Unlimited at the resort can organize a full range of outdoor activities including sailing, windsurfing, sea kayaking, sport fishing, powerboating, scuba diving and, back on the island terrain, hiking and

...that rare St John combination of tropical seclusion and urban delight.

mountain biking. Superb dive spots such as Dever's Bay and Stephen's Cay are no more than a 10-minute boat ride from Cruz Bay.

Those who choose to stay closer to home can keep in touch with the world through the complimentary wireless Internet or luxuriate in the pool back at the resort. Contemplate the view out across the sea here, or cosy up to your beloved in a hammock on the beach.

Likewise, many guests opt to dine in here rather than shuffle into Cruz Bay. Gallows Point's philosophy of offering laid-back, home-style living and a friendly atmosphere means guests have the choice of either preparing their own feast in the suite kitchen or grilling fresh seafood at the barbeque area, where they can gather to mingle and watch the sun sink over distant St. Thomas.

THIS PAGE: Offering a clear gaze out across the Caribbean from its own tiny peninsula, yet mere metres from town, Gallows Point is perched on one of the most superb locations in St. John.

OPPOSITE (FROM LEFT): View across to St. Thomas from the pool; tall jalousie doors and expansive verandahs afford tranquil views of passing ships.

FACTS		
	ROOMS	60 suites
	FOOD	barbeque facility
	DRINK	lounge
	FEATURES	pool • beach • spa treatments • St. John Adventures Unlimited (organizes outdoor activities including water sports, scuba diving, snorkelling, hiking and mountain biking)
	NEARBY	Cruz Bay • Virgin Islands National Park • Mongoose Junction mall • Wharfside Village mall • Elaine Lone Sprauve Library & Museum • St. Thomas
	CONTACT	PO Box 58, Bay Street, St. John, US Virgin Islands • telephone: +1340.776.6434 • facsimile: +1340.776.6520 • email: information@gallowspointresort.com • website: www.gallowspointresort.com

PHOTOGRAPHS COURTESY OF GALLOWS POINT RESORT.

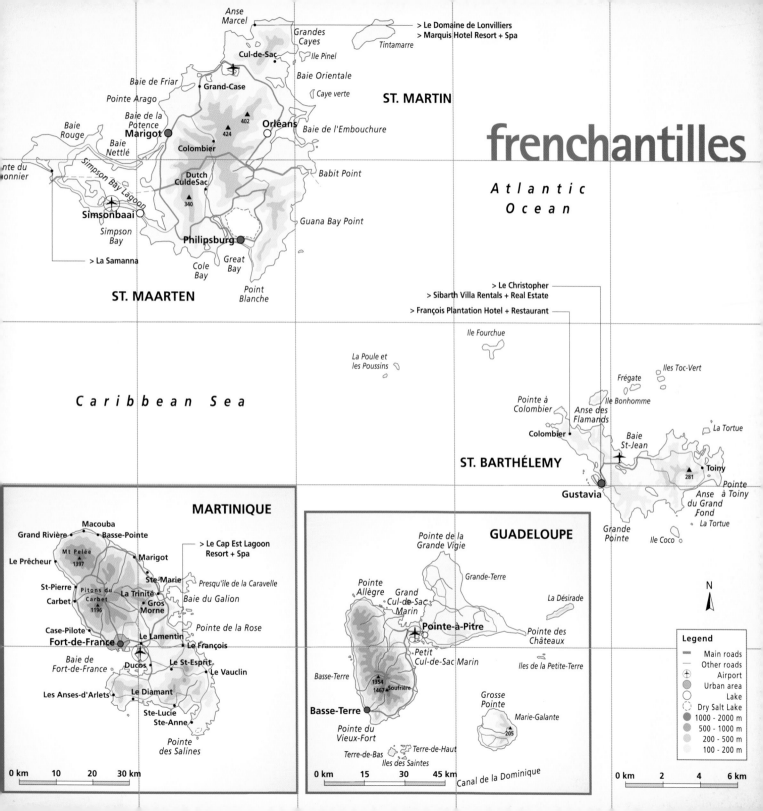

frenchantilles

ST. MARTIN

Anse Marcel
Grandes Cayes
Ile Pinel
Tintamarre
Cul-de-Sac
> Le Domaine de Lonvilliers
> Marquis Hotel Resort + Spa
Baie de Friar
Grand-Case
Pointe Arago
402
Baie de la Potence
424
Orléans
Marigot
Colombier
Baie Orientale
Caye verte
Baie de l'Embouchure
Baie Rouge
Baie Nettlé
Dutch CuldeSac
Babit Point
Simpson Bay Lagoon
340
nte du onnier
Simsonbaai
Guana Bay Point
Simpson Bay
Philipsburg
> La Samanna
Cole Bay
Great Bay
ST. MAARTEN
Point Blanche

Atlantic Ocean

Caribbean Sea

> Le Christopher
> Sibarth Villa Rentals + Real Estate
> François Plantation Hotel + Restaurant

Ile Fourchue
La Poule et les Poussins
Iles Toc-Vert
Frégate
Pointe à Colombier
Ile Bonhomme
Anse des Flamands
La Tortue
Colombier
Baie St-Jean
ST. BARTHÉLEMY
281
Toiny
Gustavia
Pointe à Toiny
Anse du Grand Fond
Grande Pointe
Ile Coco
La Tortue

MARTINIQUE

Macouba
Grand Rivière
Basse-Pointe
Mt Pelée
1397
Marigot
> Le Cap Est Lagoon Resort + Spa
Le Prêcheur
Ste-Marie
St-Pierre
Presqu'île de la Caravelle
Pitons du Carbet
La Trinité
Baie du Galion
Carbet
1196
Gros Morne
Case-Pilote
Pointe de la Rose
Fort-de-France
Le Lamentin
Le François
Baie de Fort-de-France
Ducos
Le St-Esprit
Le Vauclin
Les Anses-d'Arlets
Le Diamant
Ste-Lucie
Ste-Anne
Pointe des Salines

| 0 km | 10 | 20 | 30 km |

GUADELOUPE

Pointe de la Grande Vigie
Pointe Allègre
Grande-Terre
Pointe
Grand Cul-de-Sac Marin
La Désirade
Pointe-à-Pitre
Pointe des Châteaux
Petit Cul-de-Sac Marin
Iles de la Petite-Terre
Basse-Terre
1354
1467
Soufrière
Grosse Pointe
Marie-Galante
Basse-Terre
205
Pointe du Vieux-Fort
Terre-de-Haut
Terre-de-Bas
Iles des Saintes
Canal de la Dominique

| 0 km | 15 | 30 | 45 km |

Legend

— Main roads
— Other roads
✈ Airport
● Urban area
○ Lake
⬡ Dry Salt Lake
1000 – 2000 m
500 – 1000 m
200 – 500 m
100 – 200 m

N

| 0 km | 2 | 4 | 6 km |

french panache

Comprising St. Barthélemy, St. Martin, Martinique and Guadeloupe, there is something deliciously different about the French Antilles: a savoir-faire and style that you do not find on other islands. Marked with red-tiled roofs and bougainvillea, outdoor cafés and chic boutiques, Citroens and Renaults rumbling around the hairpin turns; it is as if a part of the Riviera had somehow shaken loose and drifted to the far side of the Atlantic.

The French pride themselves in having more panache than anyone else, and this is just as true in the West Indies as along the Champs Elysées. The way the men flirt, the way the women walk, the way everyone dresses—even on the beach—perpetually drives home the fact that these islands are French, down to the last grain of sand.

France's Caribbean heritage runs long and deep. Both Martinique and Guadeloupe have been French possessions since 1635—just 15 years after the first permanent settlement in North America. During the time between the reign of Louis XIV and the Seven Years' War (in the 18th century), France was the dominant colonial power in the region, controlling nearly all the Windward and Leeward Islands.

PAGE 132: *Children in costume for Guadeloupe's annual Baie Mahault Carnival.*

THIS PAGE (FROM TOP): *The steeple of St. Louis Cathedral, built in 1878, towers above the old town in Fort-de-France, Martinique; a striking restaurant façade in Marigot, St. Martin.*

OPPOSITE: *Poised above the north shore of St. Martin are the ruins of Fort St. Louis, built in 1767.*

keeping the french heritage alive

Even after being passed to other colonial masters, the 'French-ness' of islands such as Montserrat and St. Croix was not extinguished. They still have French place names, and the language and cuisine also carry unmistakable French overtones.

Much of the cultural heritage of the French Antilles can be traced to its African and colonial history. An important part of this heritage is the beguine, which is both a dance and a musical form. The dance is best described as a slow rumba, while the sound—a mingling of ancient African rhythms and French peasant music—is sometimes likened to New Orleans jazz. It was actually an American composer, Cole Porter, who took the beguine beyond the French Antilles in the 1930s.

Despite their 'Old World' ambience, the French Antilles are among the most modern of the Caribbean isles. As fully-fledged overseas departments—with a status not unlike that of Hawaii within the United States—the four French islands find themselves flush with overseas investments and an economy linked to the European Union. The modern airports, sleek superhighways, efficient medical and education systems—and the fact that Antilles athletes can play on the French national and Olympic sports teams—are among the benefits of close association with the mother country.

st. barts: hip hangout

Compared to the other French Antilles, St. Barts (or St. Barthélemy, to use its proper name) marches to the beat of a different drum. Perched at the northern tip of the Leeward chain, far too dry and rocky for sugarcane, the island never developed the plantation society that so dominated islands such as Martinique. Most Bartians trace their roots either to the feisty Norman and Breton fishermen and farmers who settled here 400 years ago, or to the Scandinavian pioneers who landed during St. Bart's century-long tenure as the only Swedish colony in the Caribbean. In addition to speaking an archaic variety of French, the typical Bartian is much more likely to have blond hair and blue eyes than dreadlocks and ebony skin.

Once an exclusive retreat for billionaires—the Rockefellers at one end, the Rothschilds at the other—the island was later discovered by Hollywood stars such as Tom Cruise, Uma Thurman and Natalie Portman, who all crave the Bartian blend of privacy and casual chic. The place is a tad less elitist these days, but is hip as ever. You never know who might be sitting next to you at the outdoor café.

Lacking the gorgeous scenery of other Caribbean isles, St. Barts wins you over with ambience. 'An atmosphere of esoteric tranquillity' is how one French writer describes the island. Most visitors get the feeling of being far removed from the rest of the world while still being close to all their favourite creature comforts like gourmet cuisine—one of the island's trump cards. French, Caribbean and Mediterranean flavours are served at more than 50 eateries. Top-shelf shopping can be found especially along the Quai de la République in Gustavia, a quaint little port town that retains its bygone Swedish name. Shoppers can buy wine at bargain-basement prices, as well as the latest Parisian frocks before they are even seen in New York or L.A. Other than the crumbling remains of Fort Karl, Gustavia retains very little of its Scandinavian days. The surroundings are actually more reminiscent of the Riviera: red-roofed houses crawling up the hillsides and yachts moored in snug harbours.

st. barts: sandy jewels + outdoor gems

St. Barts does not have a lot of beaches (only 14) but all of them are bona fide gems. With its red-roofed villas, palm-shaded promenades and outdoor cafés, the mushroom-shaped Baie de St-Jean is the spitting image of chic enclaves you find along the French Riviera. Grand Cul de Sac is more reminiscent of French Polynesia with its tranquil cove and turquoise lagoon. The remote Anse du Gouverneur unfolds as a huge expanse of white sand backed by rocky headlands. Anse de Grande Saline is for those who prefer their beaches (and partners) au naturel.

Despite its petite size, St. Barts packs a lot of punch. One can easily laze away on the beach or around the hotel pool, or fill the day with exciting action from sunrise to sunset. Visitors can learn how to sail at the St. Barts Yacht Club, or play beach volleyball. Surfers head for Lorient and Anse des Cayes on the north shore, where breakers find their first landmass after rolling all the way across the Atlantic. Divers can explore the underwater wonders of the Pain de Sucre, l'Ane Rouge or a

dozen other excellent spots in the five marine reserves that ring St. Barts. Snorkelling is also excellent, especially round Ile Petit Jean (Little John Island) at Colombier bay.

The rich, royal and famous flock to St. Barts between Christmas and Easter—'La Saison' in local parlance. The island is refreshingly uncrowded the rest of the year. This mild-mannered island lets its collective hair down during the annual Feast of St. Louis at the end of August. It is celebrated with fireworks, fishing derbies, pétanque (a game similar to lawn bowling) competitions and Norman folk dancing. Other events include the Caribbean Film Festival in April or the Fête du Vent regatta in August. Many of the resorts and restaurants are closed in the fall, when the island slips into its hurricane season hibernation.

THIS PAGE (CLOCKWISE FROM ABOVE): Beach pétanque is popular on all the French isles; buildings with gabled roofs and a miniature windmill adorn a village in St. Maarten; the French and the Dutch share this captivating island.

OPPOSITE (FROM TOP): Fort St. Louis overlooks the Marigot waterfront on St. Martin; Orient Beach on St. Martin really does seem far away from the rest of the world.

st. martin: double delight

A 20-minute hop to the northwest of St. Barts is St. Martin. It is an island with the unique distinction of being the world's smallest territory that is shared by two sovereign nations. The result of an extraordinary diplomatic arrangement in 1648, the northern half is French (St. Martin) while the south is Dutch (St. Maarten). The territory was divvied up by having a Dutch official and a French official walk in opposite directions along the shore until they met up again. The line between their starting and ending points became the border, although since the advent of the European Union, it is hard to determine where the frontier lies. The locals claim the food is better on the French side, while the shopping is tops in the Dutch zone. The fun never seems to stop on either side; the island is renowned as 'party central' and the nightlife is probably unsurpassed in the Caribbean. The nightlife is a heady blend of Euro-style discos like the Q Club (with its 'fibre optic walls' and revolving DJ booth) and waterfront bars like the Calmos Café at Grand Case. Gambling establishments here include one with an ancient Roman theme, another that specializes in sports betting, and one where 'tux and tails' is the preferred attire.

BIENVENUE EN PARTIE FRANÇAISE
WELCOME TO THE FRENCH SIDE

st. martin: beaches for all seasons

There are about 37 strands to choose from, ranging from beaches that are deserted to others where it can be hard to find a vacant patch on Saturday afternoons, especially during the high season. Adrenaline junkies flock to Orient Bay (Baie Orientale) to water ski, kite-surf or parasail. The south end of Orient is the island's sole clothing-optional beach. Those who crave privacy hike to Baie Longue or cruise to Ilet Pinel for a day of snorkelling and sun worship.

With its boutiques and bistros, Marigot is the hippest hangout on the French side, a chic seaside village where you can also anchor your yacht or sail to nearby Anguilla. Yet Marigot is much more than that, as the village is also a hub of island history. Perched above the waterfront is an old French fort that offers stunning views of both the town and Anguilla in the distance. And just down the shore is the petite but noteworthy St. Martin Museum, with artefacts from both pre-Columbian and early colonial days.

martinique: paris of the west indies

Martinique is the southernmost of the French Antilles. It is the birthplace of Empress Josephine (Napoleon's wife) and is the island that inspired post-Impressionist master Paul Gauguin long before his celebrated sojourn in Tahiti. For centuries, this island was the political and social hub of the French Caribbean with its sprawling habitations (plantations) run by migrant aristocrats who strived to recreate Versailles court life.

By the early 20th century, St-Pierre, located on the northwest coast, had evolved into the chicest city in the Caribbean: a glimmering metropolis which has been dubbed the 'Paris of the West Indies'. Ladies in fancy dresses and men in top hats once promenaded up the waterfront, admiring the sailing ships and steamers anchored offshore. Even in those days, St-Pierre was cutting edge, with telephone service, electric tramlines and moving-picture cinemas. It also had a most decadent carnival—a bacchanalian romp with satanic undertones that was scandalous even by French standards.

But it all ended in May of 1902 when the most horrific disaster in Caribbean history struck St-Pierre—the eruption of nearby Mt. Pelée volcano. The massive pyroclastic flow of hot ash, rock and poisonous gas destroyed the city (and every ship in the harbour) within minutes. There was only one survivor, a drunk confined in the city jail. Self-righteous onlookers attributed the cataclysm to divine retribution for the town's evil ways.

martinique: duty-free + carnival devils

Fort-de-France, further down the west coast, became the island's new capital and is remembered by movie buffs as the place where Humphrey Bogart courted Lauren Bacall—and smuggled French resistance fighters—in the film version of Ernest Hemingway's To Have and Have Not. Nowadays, the city is the port of arrival for the thousands of visitors who come to Martinique by airplane and cruise ship. A huge tricolour flutters above a stout French fort along a waterfront where naval vessels share anchorage with sleek trans-Atlantic yachts and inter-island ferries.

Vendors hawk local arts and crafts in La Savane park. But the real shopping is in the narrow streets beyond, where duty-free boutiques and department stores dispense luxury goods imported from France: perfume, watches, shoes, jewellery, wine and gourmet deli foods are sold at a fraction of what you might pay in Paris.

Like its fiendish forerunner at the foot of Mt. Pelée, the devils come marching in when Fort-de-France revs into carnival mode during a pre-Lent celebration called Vaval that is dedicated to Satan. The carnival slithers across five days of unashamedly wicked street parties and parades during which it is often hard to tell the girls from the boys—many of the locals are in drag. The carnival includes gender-bending mock weddings where the men are dressed as hookers or pregnant brides, while the women are their reluctant grooms. Vaval culminates on Ash Wednesday with a drunken dance of the she-devils around La Savane, during which they burn an effigy of Satan to mark the death of the year's merriment. Not for the faint of heart … or the firm of morals.

martinique: gourmet coast

The remainder of Martinque is rather sedate by comparison. The landscape is a mosaic of plantations, mountains and white-sand strands. The resorts and holiday homes are mainly in the south, scattered around Les Trois-llets (with its bustling marina and country club) and the beaches at Les Salines. This being French terrain, anyone wearing anything more than a bikini bottom to the beach is definitely considered a prude.

The blustery Atlantic coast is only just emerging as a holiday destination and is gradually earning a reputation as the best place to dine in the French Antilles. Luring chefs from Michelin three-star restaurants in Paris, Le Bélem at Cap Est has crafted a menu of Franco-Caribbean delights like conch raviolis with sautéed morels and pastilla of duck with foie gras. The restaurant's wine tower offers more than a thousand bottles of fine French libation. This part of the island also produces the best rum, in particular the flavoursome rhum agricole distilled at the historic Habitation Clément in Le François.

In the far north, the forested slopes of Mt. Pelée (which is best scaled with a local guide) and the 'wild coast' between Grand-Rivière and Le Prêcheur that can only be traversed by foot or boat, gives visitors the impression of being in a different world altogether. Despite its seclusion, a good deal of local history unfolded at Le Prêcheur. It was here that the last of the island's Carib Amerindians flung themselves into the sea rather than surrender to the French. It was also the place the Marquise de Maintenon (second wife of Louis XIV) was born into the plantation aristocracy that dominated Martinique until well after the French Revolution.

guadeloupe: mother nature's child

The butterfly-shaped Guadeloupe is actually composed of different land masses—two hulking islands called Grand-Terre and Basse-Terre, the teardrop-shaped Marie-Galante, and a tiny archipelago called the Iles des Saintes. With around 450,000 people, this is the most populous region of the French Antilles, and probably the most unassuming. The people here pride themselves on hard work and talent. Some idea of the importance of this territory to the French is the fact that they relinquished Canada in order to maintain control over Guadeloupe at the end of the Seven Years' War (1763).

In Pointe-à-Pitre, the largest city, boutiques take a backseat to factories and cargo-laden docks. The territory's only 'tourist strip' is around the south end of Grand-Terre where there are hotels, dance clubs and seafood eateries. Beyond this, Guadeloupe is largely a place of secluded beaches, fishing villages and sugarcane fields.

Guadeloupe is a place where Mother Nature continues to hold her own against the forces of modernity. This is especially true on Basse-Terre, which is dominated by tropical forest and volcanic peaks. More than a third of the island is given over to national parks and forest reserves, with trails that meander to secluded waterfalls and isolated hot springs. The Route de la Traversée—one of the most spectacular highways in the Caribbean—cuts across Basse-Terre through the heart of the rainforest, which is especially fragrant during the summer months when the flamboyant trees are in bloom.

THIS PAGE (CLOCKWISE FROM ABOVE): An outdoor café menu along the Anse d'Arlets in Martinique; Martinique is known for its rum; bananas ready for shipping at Plantation Leyritz on Martinique's northeast coast.
OPPOSITE: Steam emitting from the summit of La Soufrière volcano on Guadeloupe, a dormant giant that still rumbles.

...where Mother Nature continues to hold her own...

Le Christopher

Boasting a legendary barman, the most extravagant oceanfront pool in St. Barts and affordable first-rate services and amenities, Le Christopher has a head start in the quest to become the island's top boutique hotel.

A scenic drive from the island's capital of Gustavia, Le Christopher nestles at the foot of a hill embraced by a sheltered bay and luscious tropical gardens. With spellbinding views of cloudless skies, turquoise waters and porcelain sands, the hotel offers some of the best seats on the island for the sun's stunning dusk performances. Beach lovers will adore the celebrated beauty of nearby Salines and the handful of other exclusive beaches in the vicinity. And with neighbour St. Martin visible on the heat-hazed horizon from mattressed poolside sunbeds, this understated haven of style and serenity will leave you wondering why you hadn't discovered it sooner.

Le Christopher's success in combining top-notch facilities and services with bona fide friendliness is often attributed to independent ownership. The hotel is personally managed by the proprietor himself, guaranteeing an intimate ambience and a touch of homespun hospitality which gives the hotel its genial character and which makes it so ideal for families, couples and honeymooners alike.

The idyllic, oceanfront accommodations comprise 39 rooms, a Family Suite and an executive Aloès Suite. All are air-conditioned and complete with Wi-Fi access, telephones and entertainment systems. The cosy, warmly

lit rooms feature private outdoor patios or terraces, most with teak loungers in which to enjoy a good book, a cool nightcap or simply the pleasure of your own company. Adding an earthy, peaceful feel to the rooms are natural furnishings of teak, mahogany, weaves and rattans. The elegant interiors are enhanced by views of hypnotic seascapes, and by the emerald-greens and colour-bursts of a glossy, verdant tropical garden.

Infused with island colours and elements, the common spaces too are well thought-out in décor, artfully lit with candles and lamps. Taïno restaurant picks up these themes; its romantic shore-side setting allows the sands to tickle your feet as the menu tantalizes your taste buds. The cuisine has a distinct French-Asian twist, and fresh seafood is a definite highlight. Sample the Fresh Skewered Black Tiger Prawns or the chef's spectacular duo of Tahitian Mahi Mahi and Tuna with Coconut and Lime, then top it all off with a perfectly proportioned Caribbean Crème Brûlée.

For guests wishing to burn off that brûlée, Le Christopher runs regular yoga and pilates classes. Alternatively, opt for a workout in St. Barts' largest and most well-equipped fitness centre. On request, tennis and horse riding can also be arranged for you nearby. With the sea lapping all sides, water sports are the obvious day-time highlight and diving, deep-sea fishing and excursions by boat or helicopter to other islands are all extremely popular diversions. After sunset, head to the lively piano bar for after-dinner drinks and settle in for yet another evening of culinary satisfaction and live musical entertainment. Guests will also not want to miss the chance of sipping the cocktail of a lifetime, whipped up by the island's most famous barman at Mango's thatch-roofed pool bar.

FACTS		
	ROOMS	41 ocean-view rooms and suites
	FOOD	Taïno: fusion French and Asian cuisine • Mango restaurant • children's menu available
	DRINK	piano bar and lounge • Mango pool bar
	FEATURES	freshwater infinity pool • fitness centre • tennis • water sports • sailing • plane, helicopter and boat excursions • horse riding • massages and beauty services
	BUSINESS	laptop hire • Wi-Fi access
	NEARBY	Gustavia
	CONTACT	Pointe Milou, 97133 St. Barthélemy, French West Indies • telephone: +590.590 276 363 • facsimile: +590.590 279 292 • email: lechristopher@wanadoo.fr • website: www.hotelchristopherstbarth.com

PHOTOGRAPHS COURTESY OF LE CHRISTOPHER.

François Plantation Hotel + Restaurant

Named after Christopher Columbus' brother Bartolomeo, St. Barts is a small, rocky island of volcanic origins and remarkable beauty. The island once teemed with pirates, among whom berthed the notorious Monbars, who is said to be the inspiration behind Hergé's Rackham the Red and JM Barrie's Captain Hook. Today, St. Barts has metamorphosed into a hideaway for multi-millionaires, its hilly landscape dotted with upscale hotels, resorts and pastel-coloured celebrity villas.

Perched atop a hill overlooking the Baie des Flamands, far away from the buzz of the central tourist districts, François Plantation fits St. Barts' exclusivity profile to a tee, with its distinguished and well-earned reputation for sybaritic living and dining.

The accommodations of this renowned four-star hotel comprise 12 cosy mahogany and sky-coloured cottages, each specially designed and situated for the utmost privacy and tranquillity. Of these, four are skirted by brilliant tropical flowers and infused with the scent of jasmine blossoming in the gardens outside. The other eight cottages occupy an exclusive hilltop location, offering splendid views of the cobalt sea. Incorporated in the elegant, colonial-style interiors are boat wood floors, resonant mahogany furnishings and queen-size beds. The bathrooms are luxurious affairs, clad in white marble and featuring double basins and showers.

François Plantation's pièce de résistance, however, is the Villa Plantation, located on the highest point of the property. This haven of exclusivity is replete with one expansive

THIS PAGE (FROM TOP): Luxuriant tropical plants accentuate the elegance of the cottages; François Plantation is legendary for its Mediterranean-inspired cuisine and wine list.

OPPOSITE (FROM LEFT): Gaze upon the scenic Baie des Flamands and Pointe Milou from the strategically sited pool; cottages at François Plantation are designed for the utmost privacy and tranquillity.

bedroom, leather furniture, a private pool, a fully-equipped kitchen and a modern home entertainment system. From the spacious sun-deck, admire breathtaking sunset views over the Baie des Flamands and Pointe Milou.

If the ivory sands below don't tempt you, sink into the depths of the unusual grey-tinted pool or meditate on its teak deck. Or, relax in your climate-controlled cottage with the retinue of music, television and Internet gadgetry.

For divine gastronomic delights, guests will surely revel in absolute satisfaction here,

for François Plantation is quite possibly the very best French restaurant on St. Barts. François Plantation is owned by a professional winemaker and keen oenophile, so it comes as no surprise that the wine list—put together by Pascal Martin, one of the island's top sommeliers—is as sublime as the seascape glimmering from the dining verandah.

With such exceptional vintage offerings, six-course meals to accompany tastings are a must, especially when the gourmet cuisine excels in every sphere. To start off the day, viennoiseries and lavish cooked breakfasts are served with fresh organic fruit juices. For dinner, the inspired evening menu is unrivalled; guests can even sign up for cookery classes with the master himself. François Plantation has itself perfected the art of matching ambrosial wine and cuisine with seamless service and gracious lodgings. For a classy Caribbean experience with an epicurean French twist, look no further.

FACTS		
	ROOMS	12 garden- and ocean-view cottages • Villa Plantation
	FOOD	François Plantation: French cuisine
	DRINK	wine list selected by Pascal Martin
	FEATURES	pool • cigar room • wine tasting • cookery classes
	BUSINESS	conference and event organisation
	NEARBY	St. Jean airport • Inter-Ocean Museum • Gustavia • water sports
	CONTACT	Colombier, 97133 St. Barthélemy, French West Indies • telephone: +590.590 298 022 • facsimile: +590.590 276 126 • email: info@francois-plantation.com • website: www.francois-plantation.com

PHOTOGRAPHS COURTESY OF FRANÇOIS PLANTATION HOTEL + RESTAURANT.

Sibarth Villa Rentals + Real Estate

THIS PAGE (FROM TOP): *A highly recommended private villa with a view of shimmering water; four bedrooms adorned with plush linen and uncluttered, elegant bathroom vanities.*

OPPOSITE: *With a spectacular ocean view from the terrace of this villa SIB AOM in St. Barts, one can simply loll around, soak in the breeze, and admire the beauty of nature.*

Perhaps it was the thrill of landing on a short airstrip in a tiny plane, or the sultry sea breeze wafting from the Caribbean sea. Perhaps it was that certain je ne sais quoi inherent in the French culture of St. Barthélemy (St. Barts as it's known by the locals) or the magic that this then-unheard-of island possessed.

Or maybe it was all that and a touch of Providence which drew two young strangers from different worlds into a heady whirlwind romance that resulted in a lifelong partnership and the founding of the Sibarth Villa Rentals.

The year was 1974 and the two strangers were Brook and Roger Lacour. At the behest of her parents, Brook arrived at St. Barts for a brief island jaunt, that was where she met Roger Lacour—an entrepreneur from Guadeloupe who came to settle on St. Barts' burgeoning real estate scene, and stayed a lifetime.

The Sibarth business grew from humble beginnings. In 1975, the Lacours opened the

La Caleche boutique which not only sold beachwear but served as an informal tourism office where Roger managed their initial real estate investment and villa rental business. Brook began helping villa owners match their rentals with requests from her network of boutique clients, friends, relatives as well as business associates from the United States.

The unspoilt beauty and exclusivity of St. Barts, with its seductively charming Creole architecture, was a magnet for discerning visitors who were seeking an altogether different experience—one that would combine exquisite cuisine, pristine natural environment with an all round joie de vivre. The Lacours, in all their generosity and spirit of service, have been the facilitators of that experience up to this very day.

Nowadays, Sibarth Villa Rentals and Real Estate is an internationally renowned and efficient company providing unparalleled service in the island's real estate investment and villa rental market. From simple beach houses to luxurious estates, Sibarth offers astute clients the widest choice of properties for purchase or rental. Synonymous with Sibarth is the fully integrated, professional service offered to clients. From initial query of prices and facts right through to the final transaction, Sibarth ensures a fuss-free villa transaction experience.

Whilst Sibarth has grown in size and stature from its humble beginnings as a word-of-mouth cottage business, 30 years of success have not changed its tenements.

The Lacours remain custodians of island life rarely found elsewhere. Their love and respect for St. Barts' pristine environment and its people have undoubtedly instilled a sense of reverence, guardianship and genuine hospitality in the business.

Of the visitors that travel to St. Barts, very few leave unmoved as many return time and again, and there are those, like the Lacours, who stay for a lifetime.

FACTS

FEATURES team of 30 people dedicated to villa rentals and 8 people to real estate • unique selection of 300 properties offered for rental and for sale (villas, land, commercial listings, apartments) • full management and concierge service for rentals • full translation, legal, fiscal and administrative services for real estate purchases

BUSINESS exclusive international partnership in the US with Wimco, exclusive representative for Europe and US, and exclusive affiliate of the Christie's Great Estates network

CONTACT headquarters: La Maison Suédoise, Rue Samuel Fahlberg, 97133 St. Barthélemy, French West Indies • website: www.sibarth.com • Sibarth Villa Rentals: telephone: +590.590 298 890 • facsimile: +590.590 276 052 • email: villas@sibarth.com • Sibarth Real Estate: telephone: +590.590 298 891 • facsimile: +590.590 278 522 • email: estates@sibarth.com • branch office: Eden Rock Hotel

Le Domaine de Lonvilliers

The tropical island equivalent of the tower of Babel, St. Maarten/St. Martin is home to more than 70 nationalities and five principal languages. Charting a diverse multicultural history, its charming heritage and exquisite culinary fusions are attracting ever-more stars to this Caribbean gourmet capital.

Hidden away on the more intimate French side of the island is the exclusive but friendly and unpretentious escape of Le Domaine de Lonvilliers. Nestled in 3 hectares (8 acres) of

lush tropical vegetation, this gated safe-haven crests a 0.8 km- (half-mile-) long wave of pure white sand on St. Martin's exclusive northwest coast. From the hotel's verdant surroundings, the beautiful Anse Marcel Cove is the breathtaking sight that rewards the eye.

Newly renovated, Le Domaine exudes a quality of modern European sophistication and West Indian charm. Its elegant Creole-inspired accommodations are contemporary abodes of style and exclusivity; the spacious rooms and suites are infused with light and cheerful Caribbean colours which reflect St. Martin's vibrant ethos. Each air-conditioned guestroom boasts a private terrace area that offers stunning views over luscious gardens or the hypnotic rippling of the ocean. Even the bathrooms too are luxuriously appointed, with suite baths incorporating large, double-soaking tubs and the Deluxe and Premium suites going one notch up with separate

showers and generously-proportioned dressing rooms. The latter suites are also each fully-equipped with a large American kitchen, which makes them ideal for families.

For fine cuisine in the atmospheric setting of a beamed Creole-style house, head for La Veranda, which offers a spread of innovative continental cuisine, creative grills and ocean-fresh seafood. The restaurant's French chef tantalizes palates with his exquisite 'cuisine du monde' and serves up memorable fresh crab and lobster specialties.

As a prelude to an evening stroll along Anse Marcel's pristine sands, enjoy a cocktail at the hotel's beach bar, Ô Paradis. Once a week, the Manager's cocktail party offers an extra touch of conviviality and the chance to step out of your seclusion just for one night to mingle with the hotel's cosmopolitan guests.

Le Domaine excels too in offering extensive recreational options; and water babies will delight in the large, sun-warmed freshwater pool or in one of the hotel's two whirlpools. The hotel also sports a 12-m (40-ft) sailing boat which guests can charter to explore the neighbouring islands of Saba, St. Barts and Anguilla. After an island tour on jet-ski, enjoy a juicy fruit skewer on a lounger on the hotel's private beach. For super-stylish idling, plump for a secluded wooden cabana, where the Le Domaine's attentive staff will ensure you won't have to lift any fingers to order another drink. The indulgence and expert pampering continue in the hotel's spa, where blissful treatments and massages await.

Off-property sports and facilities—which include tennis courts, mountain biking and scuba diving—are all readily available nearby and just a concierge call away. For a more leisurely itinerary, ask to be set up with days of romantic sailing trips, horse-back riding and 18-hole golfing.

FACTS		
ROOMS	99 garden-, terrace- and ocean-view rooms • 21 deluxe and premium suites	
FOOD	La Veranda: French-Caribbean cuisine	
DRINK	Ô Paradis beach bar	
FEATURES	beach • outdoor pool • two whirlpools • children's pool • spa • fitness room • kayaking • snorkelling • speedboat, sailing boat and beach trimaran for hire	
NEARBY	golf • tennis • scuba diving • deep-sea fishing • motorized water sports • horseback riding • local museums and art galleries • restaurants	
CONTACT	Anse Marcel, 97150 St. Martin, French West Indies • telephone: +590.590 523 535 • facsimile: +590.590 291 081 • email: resa@ledomainestmartin.com • website: www.hotel-le-domaine.com	

PHOTOGRAPHS COURTESY OF LE DOMAINE DE LONVILLIERS.

Marquis Hotel Resort + Spa

Owned by a bona fide marquis whose family ancestry can be traced back to the 12th century, this is a distinctive property boasting an impressive pedigree. Perched comfortably atop a verdant hill overlooking the secluded valley of Anse Marcel, this unassuming little gem offers a truly superb personal touch provided by a small team of dedicated staff. And, far from the madding crowd, Le Marquis is a peaceful enclave as intimate and serene as you can get on one of the Caribbean's most popular islands.

From the moment you arrive to your reluctant departure, the Marquis will have quietly seduced you. This charming and petite boutique hotel is built in the Creole style with natural woods, quaint gingerbread detailing and a sheer riot of colourful paintwork. With

just 17 rooms and suites—each individually decorated and named after a Caribbean island—the Marquis also offers gorgeous panoramic views of Anse Marcel's lush surroundings and pristine white beach, all set against the dramatic backdrop of the Atlantic Ocean and the island of Anguilla.

THIS PAGE (CLOCKWISE FROM LEFT): Marquis' Bar by the pool, set in stunning colours amid lush hilly landscape and vast clear sky; one of the resort's arresting red-beamed terraces overlooking the coastline and out across the sea; the riotous effusion of colours—and these are to be found in an exhilarating assortment of tones—are a warm welcoming touch throughout the resort's grounds.

OPPOSITE: The entrance to one of the Marquis' deluxe rooms, with a charming, rustic Caribbean ambience worthy of a great Bogie and Bacall romance.

...a hidden jewel in the Caribbean where you can make your very own corner of paradise.

Nestled in a quiet tropical garden setting, the rooms and suites have the feel of a private home, with all-day room service provided by traditionally-attired staff. Sunlight ricochets off the bright walls, and the interior drips with spicy and earthy colours of the Caribbean. From cool tiled floors to the exposed beams of the ceiling, each climate-controlled room is stylishly designed for comfort, leisure and pleasure. Snooze in a yielding hammock on a private terrace or explore the gadgetry, with wireless Internet, satellite television and entertainment systems as standard.

For gastronomic satisfaction, foray into the elegant selection of fine wines cellared at the hotel, and tuck into Creole delicacies amid the festive atmosphere of the Marquis' first-class partner restaurants.

If stimulated into action by the sun-kissed sands of Anse Marcel and the beckoning blue of the Caribbean, get some adrenalin pumping with the hotel's extensive array of activities. A detailed orientation of the island is explained to guests upon their personally-welcomed arrival, and, each morning, a staff member takes time to speak with each and every guest to help plan the day—from complimentary use of the hotel's fully-equipped fitness & sports centre to signing privileges for beach chairs and access to all of Anse Marcel's exclusive restaurants and water sports. And then by night, you'll find the staff bartending by the pool, ready to listen to all your island experiences.

If your definition of 'holiday' is an escape from strenuous exertion, then a personalized in-room spa package can be tailored to your requirements. Attain a blissful state of nirvana through balneotherapy, Thai massage and Reiki sessions, all in the quiet privacy of your own exclusive suite.

Richly surrounded by the undulating green-cloaked pleats of St. Martin, the Hotel Marquis is understated; a hidden jewel in the Caribbean where you can make your very own corner of paradise.

FACTS		
	ROOMS	2 superior rooms • 13 deluxe rooms • 2 suites
	FOOD	Le Calypso: Caribbean, French and international cuisine La Locanda: Italian gourmet • La Veranda: French and Creole cuisine
	DRINK	Marquis' Bar • La Veranda's beach bar
	FEATURES	in-room spa treatments and massages • fitness & sports centre • 4 tennis courts • 2 squash courts • beach • water sports • scuba diving • deep-sea fishing • sunset cruise • horseback riding • private beach picnics
	NEARBY	international airport (35 minutes by car) • Grand Case • Marigot • Philipsburg
	CONTACT	Pigeon Pea Hill, Anse Marcel, 97150 St. Martin, French West Indies • telephone: +590.590 294 230 • facsimile: +590.590 874 633 • email: info@hotel-marquis.com • website: www.hotel-marquis.com

PHOTOGRAPHS COURTESY OF MARQUIS HOTEL RESORT + SPA.

La Samanna

The Orient Express is synonymous throughout the world for its urbane refinement and luxury. La Samanna is one of its captivating boutique hotels, and it certainly upholds this reputation with amazing finesse. A celebrity magnet and exclusive enclave, this is the World Travel Awards' selected leading hotel and spa resort (2005) on St. Martin.

Just what is it that attracts megastars like Richard Gere and style icons such as Cindy Crawford? Flawless discretion, for one thing. Adjacent cerulean lagoons and the unfurled white ribbon of Baie Longue beach are also powerful pull-factors. La Samanna boasts a picture-perfect setting on the ritzy retreat of St. Martin, nestled in 22 hectares (55 acres) of impeccably groomed beachfront estate. Its immaculate luxury lodgings and impressive intuitive service standards have garnered for itself an AAA Four Diamond rating and, with an enviable two-to-one staff-to-guest ratio, it

comes as no surprise that authorities such as *Condé Nast Traveler* and *Travel + Leisure* lovingly shower La Samanna with a plethora of prestigious awards year after year.

The lavish accommodations range from oceanfront rooms to premium three-bedroom villas and sumptuous specialty suites such as the Baie Royale which offers the most magnificent views of the sea from the hotel. Throughout the accommodations, the interior design introduces a romantic French colonial theme—just think exotic Indo-Chine —and the bathrooms feature complimentary lotions and bath amenities from L'Occitane.

Various other exquisite touches that make La Samanna a cut above the rest include its elegant Moorish-style architecture and in the guestrooms and bathrooms, intricately laid with Spanish tiles. The exteriors feature imposing columns and white-washed arches which complement the stylish interiors,

THIS PAGE (CLOCKWISE FROM TOP LEFT):
La Samanna is one of a rare breed of hotels which excels in every aspect of hospitality, leaving nothing to chance; naturally, it boasts an enviable and extensive selection of fine wining and dining options; the accommodations are lavish and offer divine views of the sea.

OPPOSITE (FROM LEFT): Elysées Spa; from its guestrooms to the lounge, the resort is bathed in exotic beauty and romance.

adorned in a colour-palette reminiscent of the French Riviera. Without question, La Samanna has created a winning style that blends contemporary sophistication, romantic allure and tropical island serenity; this is one abode where guests can marvel as a concealed television rises up from its cabinet, then slip through the sliding doors to meditate on their private sundeck.

Those who prefer to step out of their self-contained suites for relaxation and specialist pampering can head to the Caribbean's only pilates studio or Elysées Spa, where you can indulge in single treatments or an individually tailored weeklong spa package.

It goes without saying that La Samanna's natural proclivity for spoiling its guests with epicurean delights extends to the gourmet menu and wine list. Sip apéritifs at Bar Le Champagne before strolling to the signature restaurant, which *Gourmet* magazine calls the 'World's Best Hotel Dining Rooms'. Built with a romantic al fresco terrace that is set on a bluff overlooking the gorgeous inlet of Baie Longue, diners can expect gastronomic satisfaction and an ambience which are nothing short of sublime. For starters, try the Lumpfish Caviar with Soy and Sake Infusion, then inch your way through the Brown-Butter Seared Diver Scallops before you pause to mull over the tantalizing dessert selection. With sommelier-led wine tastings, a cellarful of vintages and 12,000 well-aged bottles to match the excellent cuisine, wine-lovers and oenophiles too will revel in pleasure.

Even brides-to-be too will have all their prayers answered here—the St. Tropez of the Caribbean—because La Samanna has also been named as one of the most romantic honeymoon destinations in the world.

FACTS		
	ROOMS	81 beachfront rooms, suites and villas
	FOOD	in-house restaurant: gourmet French-Caribbean cuisine • The Grill: seafood delicacies
	DRINK	Bar Le Champagne • beach bar • wine cellar
	FEATURES	Elysées Spa • fitness centre • tennis courts • pool • beach • beach cabanas • Water Sports Caban (organizes on- and off-property sea sports and charters)
	BUSINESS	Rendezvous Pavilion (equipped with conference and reception facilities)
	NEARBY	St. Barts • Anguilla • Pinel Island
	CONTACT	PO Box 4077, 97064 St. Martin, French West Indies • telephone: +590.590 876 400 • facsimile: +590.590 878 786 • email: reservations@lasamanna.com • website: www.lasamanna.com

PHOTOGRAPHS COURTESY OF LA SAMANNA.

Le Cap Est Lagoon Resort + Spa

Le Cap Est is the pinnacle of opulence on Martinique's east coast. Adored by travel writers all across the globe, the island's most voguish destination resort and spa enamours —according to *The Sunday Telegraph*—'an elite crowd in search of pampered anonymity'. So when tranquillity, relaxation, beauty and style form your primary requirements, Cap Est is the ultimate choice of the discerning.

Located near the picturesque town of François, Cap Est's well-sung stylistic success is often credited to its sophisticated mélange of Franco-Caribbean and Southeast Asian influences. The resort's 50 fashionable suites are distributed among 18 breezy, multi-hued villas, all gazing out across the breathtaking Atlantic Ocean. Bordering a lagoon whose waters positively glow with a shimmering aquamarine translucence, it's little wonder that Cap Est has single-handedly tempted the wealthy jet-setter back to Martinique.

Both at garden and balcony level, each air-conditioned suite in this member of the Relais & Châteaux collection is furnished in minimalist style and brightened by splashes of buoyant tones ranging from soft plum and light beige woods to invigorating blue and vermillion. All the suites boast a king-sized bed and the last word in technology. Plasma-screen televisions are de rigueur, as are Internet and DVD installations. Then there is

THIS PAGE (CLOCKWISE FROM LEFT): Cap Est's architectural and design fusion of Franco-Caribbean and East Indies styles is a great hit; from sea, glimpses of the resort's bright crimson roofs amid swaying palm trees give its arriving guests a titillating idea of its exclusive offerings; some of the most divine and delightful features in this all-suite, five-star luxury resort are the generously sized rooms and their wooden beds draped in a cascading fall of sheer white.

OPPOSITE: Cap Est's Lounge Bar is widely acclaimed for housing one of the most excellent cellars in Martinique. Guests can enjoy some of their finest champagnes and rums to live jazz or a steel band, as well as to an equally extensive selection of cigars.

their enviable 'maxi-bar'—an elevated form of the minibar that includes a refrigerator and even ice-cube and espresso machines. At Cap Est, heading out for coffee and calling down for ice are a thing of the past.

At Le Campêche restaurant, guests are offered the freshest lobster, served beneath elegant parasols on a sun-shaded terrace. Evening meals at the wood-framed Belém are a superb fusion of French and Carib cuisine. Feasting amid soothing paprika and cinnamon walls, romantic views of the starry Caribbean evening will be as satisfying as the exquisite dishes themselves.

France's *Bon Voyage* magazine gushes about experiencing love at first sight with Cap Est's champagne cellar, cigar list and phenomenal rum menu. Extending to more than 100 varieties, sample some of the absolute finest vintages on the island to set the mood for a night of cool jazz or steel band entertainment, and get into the spirit—and the spirits—of the Caribbean.

No contemporary Caribbean resort is complete without a lavishly equipped spa, and Cap Est's Spa by Guerlain is simply to die for. Catering for the spoiled, globetrotting spa-seeker are such sublime facilities as an exclusive Guerlain treatment cabin, a pair of massage cabins, two hydrotherapy cabins, a hammam and a Japanese pool set amid quiet and idyllic greenery. Here in serene surroundings, luxuriate with a Vichy shower, or slip into a blissful state of nirvana with a cocooning wrap or massage.

For the sportive, head straight for Cap Est's private beach. Take the morning learning to kite-surf, don a sun hat for an exhilarating afternoon of big game fishing, then cruise around the coast on a catamaran.

It came as no surprise when *The Times* recently hailed the divine Cap Est Lagoon Resort & Spa the 'hippest, classiest place' in Martinique's ritzy equivalent of Beverly Hills. And, suffice to say, an argument to counter this claim has yet to be heard.

PHOTOGRAPHS COURTESY OF LE CAP EST LAGOON RESORT + SPA.

FACTS

ROOMS	19 garden suites • 24 deluxe suites • 7 executive suites
FOOD	Le Campêche: Creole cuisine & light meals • Le Belém: fusion cuisine
DRINK	Cohi-bar • Lounge Bar
FEATURES	Spa (featuring Guerlain beauty products, a cardio-fitness room, hammam, Vichy shower, balneotherapy and hydrotherapy) • floodlit tennis court • freshwater pool • beach • water sports • kite surfing • helicopter excursions • library
BUSINESS	meeting room
NEARBY	Golf Country Club de la Martinique (featuring an 18-hole Robert Trent Jones course)
CONTACT	97240 Le François, Martinique • telephone: +596.596 548 080 • facsimile: +596.596 549 600 • email: info@capest.com • website: www.capest.com

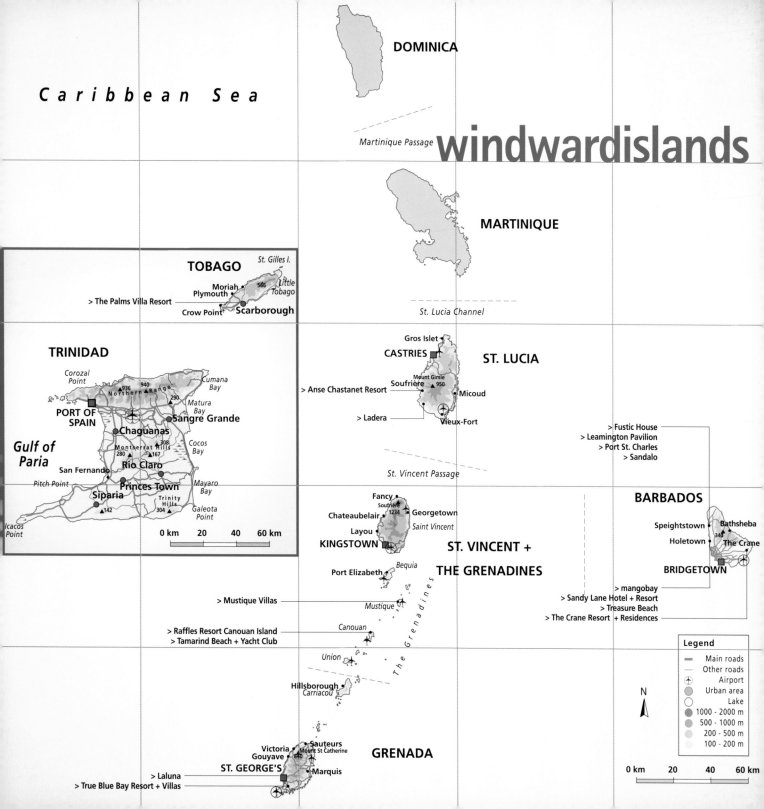

DOMINICA

Caribbean Sea

Martinique Passage

windwardislands

MARTINIQUE

St. Lucia Channel

TOBAGO

St. Gilles I.

Moriah
Plymouth
> The Palms Villa Resort
Crow Point
Little Tobago
566
Scarborough

TRINIDAD

Corozal Point
Cumana Bay
▲936 ▲940
Northern Range
290
Matura Bay
PORT OF SPAIN
Chaguanas
Sangre Grande

Gulf of Paria

Montserrat Hills
308
280▲ 167▲
Rio Claro
Cocos Bay

San Fernando
Pitch Point
Princes Town
Mayaro Bay
Siparia
▲142
Trinity Hills
304
Galeota Point

Icacos Point

0 km 20 40 60 km

CASTRIES
Gros Islet
ST. LUCIA
Mount Gimie
> Anse Chastanet Resort
Soufrière ▲950
Micoud
> Ladera
Vieux-Fort

> Fustic House
> Leamington Pavilion
> Port St. Charles
> Sandalo

St. Vincent Passage

BARBADOS

Fancy
Soufrière
Chateaubelair 1234
Georgetown
Layou *Saint Vincent*
KINGSTOWN

Speightstown
Holetown
Bathsheba
340
The Crane

BRIDGETOWN

**ST. VINCENT +
THE GRENADINES**

Port Elizabeth
Bequia

> Mustique Villas
Mustique

> mangobay
> Sandy Lane Hotel + Resort
> Treasure Beach
> The Crane Resort + Residences

> Raffles Resort Canouan Island
> Tamarind Beach + Yacht Club
Canouan

Union

The Grenadines

Hillsborough
Carriacou

Victoria
Gouyave
Sauteurs
Mount St Catherine
840
GRENADA

> Laluna
ST. GEORGE'S
Marquis
> True Blue Bay Resort + Villas

Legend

— Main roads
— Other roads
⊕ Airport
◉ Urban area
◯ Lake
■ 1000 - 2000 m
■ 500 - 1000 m
■ 200 - 500 m
■ 100 - 200 m

N

0 km 20 40 60 km

the fiesty windwards

They are called the Windward Islands because they are the Caribbean islands closest to the trade winds that bluster across the Atlantic Ocean from Africa. These zephyrs, on which thousands of slave ships once sailed, continue to whisk hurricanes towards the region. The names of the islands roll off the tongue: Trinidad and Tobago, St. Vincent and the Grenadines, St. Lucia, Dominica, Grenada and Barbados. Once ruled by the British as a federation of colonies, they are now sovereign islands.

Over the past hundred years, the Windwards have become a wellspring of great writing, a cradle of World Beat music, a birthplace of political experimentation and the training ground for some of the best athletes to ever emerge from the West Indies. St. Lucian poet and playwright Derek Walcott and much-vaunted Trinidad scribe V.S. Naipaul, both of whom have won the Nobel Prize for Literature, hail from the Windwards. These islands also gave the world musical legends like Barbados-based Eddy Grant and the Grenada-born carnival crooner, Mighty Sparrow. Among the notable athletes are Olympic gold medal sprinter Hasley Crawford and NBA basketball player Adonal Foyle, who is also an education advocate and democracy activist.

The inhabitants of these islands have always been feisty and rebellious. After Columbus reported evidence of cannibalism, the Spanish studiously avoided the Windward Islands, leaving the French and British to fight over them for several hundred years. It was on these rugged islands that the Amerindians held out the longest against the European onslaught and where the last of the Caribs remain as the only indigenous peoples left in the Caribbean.

Rising from the sea as volcanic mounts, the Windwards have long been endowed with rich, dark soil that makes them amongst the most fertile islands in the Caribbean. Active volcanoes huff and puff—and every so often erupt—within earshot of flourishing spice gardens and banana groves. Part of the enduring charm of the Windwards is the bygone island life. Farming and fishing villages continue to flourish, and the sweet sounds of Sunday hymns drift from chapels that seem as old as the hills.

PAGE 158: *Children parade on stilts in the Carnival on Trinidad.*

THIS PAGE (FROM TOP): *The Cropover Festival in Barbados has evolved from a celebration of the end of the cane harvest to an island-wide carnival; Grenada is the 'Spice Island' that also has abundant fruits.*

OPPOSITE: *The distinctive Piton peaks are located on the western coast of St. Lucia.*

THIS PAGE (FROM LEFT): *Bridgetown's buildings add colour to the historic waterfront; the British heritage endures in many ways on Barbados.*

OPPOSITE (FROM TOP): *The historic Barbados Parliament building houses the Parliament that was established in 1639; Lord Nelson overlooks the Bajan Trafalgar Square in Bridgetown.*

barbados: little england

There was a time, in the not-too-distant past, when you could set your watch by the arrival of the daily Concorde plane from London. The sleek plane used to glide low across the Caribbean on its approach to Grantley Adams International Airport. The supersonic marvel may have been retired, but the island remains a favourite with the British glitterati who flock to the posh hotels and villas along the shore.

Perhaps the epithet 'Little England of the Caribbean' is a bit of a stretch, especially considering Barbados has been independent for more than three decades, but even ardent nationalists are willing to admit that Barbados retains more British flavour than any other island in the West Indies. In Bridgetown, the island's bustling little capital, a statue of Lord Nelson looks down upon a Trafalgar Square which predates the London version by 36 years. Local policeman walk the beat in chipper British uniforms and judges preside in flowing black gowns and white wigs. Even the national holidays are drawn from colonial times. The annual Holetown Festival commemorates the landing of the first English settlers in 1627, while the island's famous Crop Over celebration derives from a bygone British festival called Harvest Home.

The British, in turn, have always held a special place in their hearts for Barbados. Over 370 years of continuous British rule, the island played host to a number of English notables including former prime ministers Anthony Eden and Winston Churchill, shipping magnate Edward Cunard and Prince Alfred (Queen Victoria's son). The current Royal Family has also left its mark on the island: numerous plaques laud recent visits by Queen Elizabeth and Prince Philip. Prince Charles has played at the Barbados Polo Club on several occasions and Prince Andrew was the very first person to tee off at the island's Royal Westmoreland golf club.

Barbados also has the unique distinction of being one of the earliest places on the planet to integrate the myriad races into the political system (Bajans elected their first

'coloured' representative in 1831) and mandate compulsory education for all citizens. Thus, it avoided many of the racial and political problems that later plagued other Caribbean islands. In fact, the social harmony that permeates Barbados is one of the first things a visitor notices. This remains the kind of place where people greet strangers with a smile and a hardy 'Good Morning!'

barbados: shaded beaches + botanic parties

Created from limestone and coral rather than volcanic upheaval, Barbados boasts more white-sand strands than anywhere else in the Windwards. Nearly everywhere you look there are fine beaches. But the über-chic resorts cluster along a stretch of the Leeward shore called the Platinum Coast. With beaches shaded by coconut palms or mahogany trees, the Platinum Coast is the epitome of tropical opulence—a mosaic of luxury spas and emerald golf links, gourmet eateries and well-manicured polo fields where the players knock back champagne, caviar and cucumber sandwiches between chukkas.

The rolling green hills of the Bajan interior are strongly reminiscent of the Scottish Highlands, although underground they are more like something from a different world with underground limestone caverns filled with stalagmites, stalactites and subterranean streams. Battery powered trams whisk visitors through a corkscrew journey into the depths of the earth at Harrison's Cave. Further south, across a wide swath of sugarcane fields, is Gun Hill and the remains of its British colonial signal station, which still affords breathtaking stem-to-stern views of Barbados.

The island's east coast could not be more different with its windswept, rocky shore that is like Cornwall, without the cold. The beaches around Bathsheba offer some of the

best surf in the Caribbean. On the bluffs above, cozy little pubs serve Guinness and flying-fish sandwiches to those who would rather watch than brave the waves. The remains of a Victorian station lie beneath a narrow-gauge railway track that has been transformed into a pleasant coastal trail. Further south, Codrington College is like a tropical Oxford, complete with Jacobean balustrades and an elegantly decorated chapel.

Another British tradition that took root in Barbados is the passion for plants. Many of the island's attractions—like Andromeda Botanic Gardens and Francia Plantation—are floral wonderlands where garden aficionados can gape at picture-perfect anthuriums and heliconias. The national horticultural society, which has won numerous gold medals at the Chelsea Flower Show in London, offers private garden tours during which the planter's punch is every bit as luscious as the landscapes.

barbados: fast horses and flying fish

One of the island's more popular urban attractions is Garrison Savannah, the home of the Barbados Turf Club. Located in Bridgetown, the six-furlong turf track harks back to 1845 when British officers stationed at the garrison began racing their steeds. The 'triple crown' of the local racing calendar includes the Sandy Lane Gold Cup (March), the Midsummer Creole Classic (July) and the Barbados Derby (August). The historic buildings in the Garrison Historic Area include the fascinating Barbados Museum in the old British military prison.

Central Bridgetown huddles around a narrow harbour called The Careenage, where schooners were turned on their sides (careened) in colonial days for repairs and maintenance. Nowadays it is a popular yacht anchorage and the fulcrum of the city's social life, where restaurants and nightclubs are spread willy-nilly along the waterfront. Although Barbados was never ruled by the French, the island was not immune to Creole influence, especially in its cuisine. Local delicacies include the rich and meaty pepper pot stew, buljol pickled codfish salad, and plantains stuffed with spicy plantation pork, both available at the legendary Waterfront Café overlooking The Careenage.

st. vincent + the grenadines

Comprising a string of 32 paradise islands that drift in the warm aquamarine waters between Grenada and St. Lucia, the Grenadines have long been seen as the Hollywood of the West Indies—the tropical stomping ground of Johnny Depp, Michael Caine, Mick Jagger and countless other movie and music stars. But at the same time, they remain amongst the most unassuming of Caribbean isles. There are places where ancient ways and means persist, and where people could not care less that a star like Orlando Bloom might be sitting at the next table. This is precisely why so many celebrities sojourn in this archipelago.

St. Vincent is the largest and most populous of the group, a precipitous island dominated by the smoking, simmering, fire-spitting cone of La Soufriere Volcano, which can be climbed in less than a day. Kingstown, the capital, sprawls over numerous hills and vales near the island's south end. Kingstown is a cruise port that cannot seem to shake its banana boat past. Its lack of development means that much of the city's exquisite colonial architecture remains intact and untouched. Many of the Georgian-style structures are fashioned from ballast brought to St. Vincent in the belly of sailing ships. Amidst all the brick and mortar are fragile treasures like the famous 'scarlet angel' of St. George's Cathedral. This magnificent stained-glass window was originally created for St. Paul's in London, but was rejected by Queen Victoria who thought all cherubs should be clad in white. Rather than destroy the delicate masterpiece, it was shipped off to one of her majesty's most far-flung colonies.

THIS PAGE: Thoroughbred race horses at the Barbados Turf Club during the annual Cockspur Gold Cup.

OPPOSITE (FROM LEFT): The eastern shore of Barbados bears the full brunt of the Atlantic waves; surfing near Bridgetown.

Around the west side of St. Vincent are black-sand beaches and cliff-flanked bays where much of the *Pirates of the Caribbean* trilogy was filmed. Those in the know can guide you to secluded coves where waterfalls plunge hundreds of feet into swimming holes. One of the few places in the West Indies where boats are still the primary means of transportation, ferries sail south from St. Vincent to the various bits and bobs that comprise the Grenadines. There is a daily service to nearby Bequia and a weekly mail boat to islands further south.

the grenadines: bequia's boat-building tradition

Bequia is one of the great sailing havens in the Caribbean. It is a popular stop on the trans-Caribbean yacht circuit and is a place where sailors tend to while away for far more days (or weeks) than originally planned. Often several hundred boats at a time seek shelter in Port Elizabeth harbour. Bars and restaurants cater to both yachties and shore-bound visitors. At waterfront hangouts like Frangipani and De Reef, the beer and banter flow from lunchtime till well after midnight, with reggae and calypso bands setting the mood for all-night revelry.

The island's rowdy reputation stretches back to bygone days, when Bequia was one of the whaling and boat-building capitals of the Caribbean. Although they only catch one whale every couple of years, whaling is legal here and the old-timers still spin tales of hunting humpbacks with harpoons launched from small wooden boats. Bequia's other forte has passed down into modern times as a thriving model-boat building business. Craftsmen build everything from windjammers and motor yachts to meticulously made miniatures of local whaling boats. Yacht owners from around the

THIS PAGE: Actor Johnny Depp escapes from phantom buccaneers in Pirates of the Caribbean: Dead Man's Chest, *which was filmed largely on the island of St. Vincent.*

OPPOSITE (FROM TOP): Bequia's skilled model-makers receive commissions from boat owners all over the world; Les Jolies Eaux Villa, once the private getaway of England's Princess Margaret, overlooks Gelliceaux Bay on Mustique.

world—including the British royal family—have commissioned models of their own boats from the waterfront workshops in Bequia. The miniatures can be made of mahogany, pine and gumwood, complete with genuine canvas sails.

the grenadines: mustique + beyond

From Bequia's eastern shore you can usually spot a hazy island in the distance—Mustique. Not that interesting at first glance, but awfully appealing upon further inspection. Mustique has been frequented by a veritable 'who's who' of British socialites and celebrities that includes Princess Margaret and *Maxim* magazine publisher Felix Dennis to David Bowie and Sir Mick Jagger (who recently paid U.S.$4 million for a second home on the island). Peppered with posh private villas and exclusive boutique hotels, Mustique is the sort of place where you do not ask the price—unless it is irrelevant.

This hip side of the Grenadines continues further south, in a string of island hideaways that stretches all the way to Grenada. Canouan is famous for its super-chic European-style casino and an 18-hole championship golf course that has been rated as one of the most challenging (and scenic) in the West Indies. All around, romantic private island resorts with rustic beachfront bungalows provide 'unplugged' pampering. One of the most southerly islands, Union Island is renowned for its swank yacht club and Tahiti-like peaks. Last but not least, are the Tobago Cays. Comprising five uninhabited islands, the Tobago Cays are located inside a horseshoe-shaped reef that is probably one of the best snorkelling sites in the world. No buildings, no people, no traffic, no worries. Just peace and quiet.

st. lucia: natural assets

St. Lucia's rising renown is due to awesome geography—white-sand beaches and aquamarine bays framed by jungle-covered peaks—and islanders who must be among the friendliest in the Caribbean. Rarely without a smile, Lucians know how to make visitors feel welcome.

Most of St. Lucia's resorts are located along the western shore, many on their own secluded bays and beaches. Anchoring the bottom end of this coast are the twin Piton peaks, the most recognizable mountains in the region. The view from the top is worth the arduous climb. Around the corner, is the steamy Soufriere 'drive-through' volcano and the surprisingly romantic Diamond Mineral Baths, where bathers can laze in a très private room in a spa commissioned by King Louis XVI more than 200 years ago.

THIS PAGE (CLOCKWISE FROM ABOVE): The 13th tee at Raffles Resort on Canouan Island, the Grenadines, offers what may be the most incredible view any golf course could offer; the Castries Saturday Market in St. Lucia is a great place to grab some bananas; Creole cuisine is common throughout the Windwards.

OPPOSITE (FROM TOP): Rodney Bay on St. Lucia is where the rowdy 'jump up' street party starts every Friday night; Tobago Cays in the Grenadines is great for diving and sailing.

st. lucia: delightful surprises

Having been French and British possessions, Lucian food is a fusion of various influences, resulting in a vibrant Creole cuisine that embraces seafood and soups, as well as curried meats. With dishes like barracuda in coconut curry sauce and sautéed calamari à la Creole, local cuisine reaches its peak in restaurants like The Coal Pot in Castries.

Lucians let their hair down on Friday nights, when 'jump ups' unfold at several spots around the island. The most famous place is Rodney Bay, where rum and reggae fuels all-night street parties, music blasts from monster-sized speakers, and honeymooning couples dance in the streets. In St. Lucia, the nights are cool and everything is nice and easy. Down along Anse-La-Raye bay, the 'jump ups' are more sedate. Here, the focus is on lip-smacking seafood grilled at waterfront stalls. The biggest party of them all unfolds each May when the St. Lucia Jazz Festival takes over the island. Top-name artists take the stage at more than a dozen venues all around the island. Among those who have played here in the past are Wynton Marsalis, Herbie Hancock, and Earth, Wind and Fire.

St. Lucia's central highlands are among the most pristine in the Caribbean with much of the rainforest protected within the confines of national parks. Nature lovers can hike or mountain bike along jungle trails in search of the rare and elusive Jacquot parrot. Offshore, St. Lucia is teeming with wildlife, boasting more than 150 species of tropical fish. Those who opt for winter visits (November to March) can watch three different types of whales including humpback, orca and sperm. Among the island's most dramatic dive sites are Superman's Flight (an underwater wall right below the Piton peaks) and the wreck of the *Lesleen M*.

trinidad + tobago: double your fun

Trinidad and Tobago is the most culturally diverse nation in the Caribbean. The blend of African, Asian, Anglo and Hispanic influences comes across in many aspects of local life, especially in its effervescent music. Although these islands are Caribbean, geologically they are more South American. In fact, some geologists believe that Tobago is actually the northeastern extreme of the Andes.

Trinidad is the larger island, but Tobago has dazzling beaches, primeval jungles and amazing dive spots. Tobago boasts the nation's most historical site—Fort King George—a stout British bastion located high above Scarborough. Erected in the 1770s, the restored fort includes the Tobago Museum which has exhibits on island history, culture and geography, and showcases works of local artists. Downhill from the fort is the Blue Crab, one of the island's better eateries. Among the café's many Asian-inspired delights are curried crab, roti pancakes and chicken grilled over coconut husks.

trinidad + tobago: carnival time

The islands are known for the annual carnival, believed to be the first in the Caribbean. Locals call it 'Mas', short for Masquerade. It has a little bit of Rio, a touch of Mardi Gras, and a lot of music made up of soca, calypso and steel-band serenades. This is carnival the way it was meant to be, not a slick commercial show, but a party of the people, a spontaneous outpouring of human emotion that plays out in flamboyant costumes, parades, dance shows, food festivals and incredible steel-band competitions. It is a giant week-long party during which everyone 'jumps wit da band … and plays da mas to da fullest'.

Originally a masquerade ball for the island's elite in the late 1700s, the event slowly evolved into an egalitarian street spectacle. Over the years, various immigrant groups have added to the party. Venezuelans created funky bovine costumes called 'cattle mas' and the Asian Indians crown their Chutney Soca

Monarch each year. More than 40 'mas camps' (carnival troupes) spend months making elaborate costumes and rehearsing their routines. Meanwhile, musicians are busy in the 'panyards' (steel-band practice areas) composing what they hope will become the next 'road march' (official carnival song).

New music debuts at 'fêtes' and thousands attend outdoor concerts in the weeks leading up to carnival. Carnival week kicks off with the finals of two nation-wide musical competitions—Panorama for steel-bands and Dimanche Gras for calypso. The party reaches fever pitch on Monday and Tuesday with masquerade parades. People come dressed as devils, burrokeets (centaurs) and feather-clad showgirls. On Tuesday night is Las Lap, the final blowout, followed by 'cool down' beach parties on Ash Wednesday.

trinidad + tobago: island soundtrack

Trinidad and Tobago is the nation that gave the world steel drums, musical instruments fashioned from 55-gallon oil drums. Anything played by an orchestra can just as easily be rendered by a steel drum band (steel-bands), although you are much more likely to hear calypso or soca. Calypso traces its roots to the first African slaves who came to the islands. Initially a medium to secretly mock slave owners, it slowly evolved into a medium for social commentary. Soca is a late 20th-century invention. It is pure party music designed to help you forget your troubles and dance the night away. But the music scene does not stop there—throughout the islands you can find at least a dozen different homegrown styles including parang (developed by Latin American settlers) and tassa (created by Asian Indian immigrants). All of these genres are alive and thriving. New music is produced all the time and is readily accessible to anyone.

Visitors to the islands can spend their days relaxing on the beach or engaging in various adventure sports. The nights can be filled with music in the local nightclubs, beachside cafés and steel-band panyards.

THIS PAGE (FROM TOP): Revellers flood the streets of Port of Spain during Trinidad's Carnival; steel drums wait silently in a panyard for the next Carnival.

OPPOSITE: Moko jumbies or stilt-walkers are an integral part of the Trinidad Carnival.

THIS PAGE (FROM LEFT): *Mace drying in the sun at the 300-year-old Belmont Estate, a working plantation that is a cultural and historical attraction in Grenada; Concord Falls in Grenada's rugged interior.*

OPPOSITE: *View of St. George from Fort George in Grenada.*

grenada: the spice isle

Long known as the Isle of Spice, Grenada's rich volcanic loam and steamy climate are ideal for producing a wide variety of products such as cinnamon, cloves, nutmeg, cocoa, vanilla and ginger. The captivating fragrance of spices that emanate from the farms or forest can be discerned throughout the island. One of the greatest joys in Grenada is being able to sample these spices in local soups, stews and ice cream that can only be described as divine. Some of these exquisite spices even make their way into the locally brewed rum.

Grenada is one of the most relaxing corners of the Caribbean. It is an island-state that has gone from political upheaval to marine and environmental tourism in little more than two decades. As the southern gateway to the Grenadines, the island sports half a dozen full-service marinas. The gorgeous nearby islands, such as Carriacou (of Grenada) and Petite Martinique (of the Grenadines), have become havens for the international yacht crowd.

Grenada is said to possess every major eco-system found in the region, from mangrove swamps and white-sand strands to dry tropical forest and cloud-shrouded woodland. Much of the interior is protected by national parks such as Grand Étang and Levera. Both of them are criss-crossed by dozens of streams and networks of footpaths. Walks can range from a brisk half-hour circuit around Grand Étang Lake to an all-day ascent of Mt. Qua Qua. Hikers often cool off with a dip (skinny or otherwise) at the secluded Seven Sisters Falls.

The more urbane side of Grenada comes to light at the 300-year-old Belmont Estate, a fully-operational nutmeg and cacao plantation that opened its doors to the public in 2002. In addition to watching (and participating) in various agricultural endeavours, visitors can walk through a museum that has antiques, photos and other colonial memorabilia, Carib artefacts and a display on Grenadan independence. Visitors can then reward themselves with a cup of delicious hot chocolate, made from beans grown, fermented and cooked within a stone's throw away.

...one of the most relaxing corners of the Caribbean.

The Crane Resort + Residences

Lying on Barbados' idyllic southeast coast with its beautiful pink sands, turquoise waters and offshore reef is Crane Beach, lauded as one of the world's most exquisite ribbons of sand. Like its celebrated namesake location, The Crane is a crown jewel of luxury hotels, occupying a privileged eyrie atop a cliff here and boasting a long, intriguing list of former guests who include the likes of the famous American cowboy, 'Wild Bill' Hickock.

The Crane is thought to be the Caribbean's oldest operating hotel. Although it officially opened its doors to guests in 1887, the style of the well preserved fenestration and casements in the original historic mansion—which stands in pristine condition and today forms the hotel's east wing—suggests that it was first built around 1790. The idea of establishing a hotel in the area came from the island's early wealthy, who were drawn to Crane Beach for its perfect bathing conditions—the seclusion, soul-stirring vistas and reinvigorating waters.

The hotel's popularity has been growing ever since. After more than two centuries in operation, a long and extensive process of expansion and refurbishment was undertaken at the beginning of the millennium, creating the present day's 16-hectare (40-acre) estate which comprises the original hotel as well as a new development of all-suite residences.

THIS PAGE (FROM TOP): The Crane's recently launched Residences; on offer for private ownership at the Residences is a selection of one- to three-bedroom suites; the best views of Crane Beach and its offshore coral reef are to be enjoyed from the clifftop pool.

OPPOSITE: Hidden on the far side south of the resort and cut into the cliff is a flight of 200-year-old steps which lead down to a historic bathing spot popular among Barbados' early elite.

Skilfully combining the Old World charm for which it became famous with the modern amenities expected of a first-rate luxury resort, the young Residences at The Crane perfectly complements the grand old classic not only in terms of architectural style but in lavishness as well. Its host of 21st-century luxuries includes everything from private open-air patios for sunbathing to the expansive clifftop pool—a showpiece framed by classic Doric columns and overlooking the shore and reef below.

The suites in the Residences are spacious, featuring king-size four-poster beds and private verandahs. Tastefully appointed with furniture designed by local artisans, they have succeeded in creating a romantic ambience that blends well with the classic and timeless air of the original hotel. The 1887 resort itself comprises 18 rooms and suites altogether. Built with coral stone walls, high ceilings and hardwood floors, the elegant period furnishings include mahogany four-poster beds and ceiling fans.

An old-time local favourite here is L'Azure restaurant, famed for its Caribbean delicacies and popular Sunday brunch. The dining room is set within coral stone walls and opens out onto a verandah overlooking the beach. For a contemporary touch, newly launched Zen offers authentic Thai and Japanese cuisine as well as tatami rooms for private parties.

Snorkelling off the nearby coral reef or a tee-off on one of Barbados' superb courses can be arranged by the warmly obliging staff, who will also be happy to offer directions to the far side south of the resort, where guests will find the flight of rocky steps leading down the cliff to the mid-18th-century bathing spot which inspired the birth of the historic hotel.

FACTS

ROOMS	1887 resort: 18 rooms and suites with garden or ocean views • private residences: junior, one, two and penthouse suites
FOOD	L'Azure: Caribbean cuisine • Zen: authentic Thai and Japanese cuisine
DRINK	pool bar
FEATURES	cliff-edge pool
NEARBY	dinner theatre shows • golf • weekly catamaran cruise • deep-sea fishing • island tours • Crane Beach • Bat Cave • Hawksbill turtle watching at Foul Bay
CONTACT	Crane, St. Philip, Barbados • telephone: +1246.423 6220 • facsimile: +1246.423 5343 • email: reservations@thecrane.com • website: www.thecrane.com

PHOTOGRAPHS COURTESY OF THE CRANE RESORT + RESIDENCES.

mangobay

THIS PAGE (CLOCKWISE FROM TOP): Revel in the warmth of the sun and cool off at the beach; be greeted by the magnificent sea view from the comfort of an Oceanfront room; the hotel pool is a popular spot for social gatherings.

OPPOSITE: An ensemble of lights at the hotel entrance sets the night ablaze.

An intimate, all-inclusive hotel, mangobay creates its very own niche on the fabled west coast of Barbados. The wide, whitewashed circular driveway wraps around an elliptical fountain whose copper-glass mosaic tiles reflect shards of patterned light. In the cool foyer, the rich Italian marble floor dramatically paves the way towards your Caribbean adventure.

mangobay takes resort living up one level (literally) with the addition of a new fourth floor. Oceanfront penthouse suites,

with their floor-to-ceiling glass enclosures, provide the ideal perch to watch the changing hues of light melt across the Caribbean sky. Expect other accessories and facilities ranging from large plasma TVs that occupy both the living room and bedroom to the wet bar and the ever popular plunge pool.

The sensual curves of the free-form pool with its clusters of coconut palms and vermilion blooms provide a languid resting

place. Nearby, amongst the bright-hued foliage is mangobay's Bar, where courteous staff serve up your choice of eclectic liquid concoctions.

mangobay's beachside restaurant is an invitation to al fresco dining. The briny sea breeze carries with it the tantalizing aromas of mangobay's culinary creations. Meanwhile, icing sugar sands and the soft ebb and flow of the Caribbean sea are a mere step away from the newly-constructed boardwalk, whose wooden frames snakes across the breadth of mangobay.

At mangobay, your time will be devoted to adventure, exploration or simple relaxation. During the day, the limpid waters of the Caribbean Sea will satisfy your aquatic pleasures and adventures—an underwater wonderland where shimmering curtains of multi-hued fish part before your very eyes. If your preference is more of a terrestrial nature, take to the surrounding hills for a scenic walking tour or indulge in a spot

of retail therapy at nearby Bridgetown that promises a host of surprises.

At night, an atmosphere of conviviality pervades the air. Dulcet piano tunes give way to the stirring melodies of live bands. With various heart-stirring entertainment and attractions each night of the week, you'll find it hard to resist altogether, especially if nightlife is your cup of tea.

mangobay is a place where barefooted elegance goes hand in hand with a blitheness of spirit and whose magic lies in the ability to woo you away from the cares of the world.

PHOTOGRAPHS COURTESY OF MANGOBAY.

FACTS		
	ROOMS	76 rooms • 2 penthouse suites
	FOOD	mangobay restaurant: international
	DRINK	mangobay bar
	FEATURES	2 pools • nearby tennis courts • water sports
	BUSINESS	guest lounge
	NEARBY	Holetown • Bridgetown
	CONTACT	Second Street, Holetown, St. James, Barbados • telephone: +1246.432 1384 • facsimile: +1246.432 5297 • email: reservations@mangobaybarbados.com • website: www.mangobaybarbados.com

Sandy Lane Hotel + Resort

The Sandy Lane Hotel in St. James is, quite simply, the top in Barbados. For jetting royalty, celebrities and business tycoons, this genteel member of the illustrious Preferred Hotels & Resorts Worldwide collection remains the ultra-luxury accommodation of choice. Synonymous with premier luxury and Caribbean glamour since its establishment, Barbados' most feted address has recently reinvented itself.

The revamped Sandy Lane gazes out from a rich mahogany grove, greeting its guests with a classical Palladian-style façade of coral stone. Through the gaps between its marble-smooth, pristine white columns, catch glimpses of the Caribbean's cerulean blue. Contemplating this scene from the backseat of a chauffeured Bentley adds an extra aura of exclusivity as you prepare to become the star of your own show at Sandy Lane.

THIS PAGE (CLOCKWISE FROM ABOVE):
You get a dawning impression of Sandy Lane's urbane exclusivity and refined beauty even before stopping off at the porte cochère; the al fresco Terrace Lounge; just perfect for private parties is the exclusive five-bedroom Villa.

OPPOSITE: View across the free-form infinity pool to the resort's world-class, ultra-luxurious Spa.

The whispered scent of tropical flowers permeates Sandy Lane's opulent interiors, from sumptuously decorated rooms to penthouse suites. Blended in the interior design are key ingredients integral to a flawless visit—style, comfort and state-of-the-art technology (in the form of the in-house NeosTV entertainment system). Hotel ennui is something from which guests never suffer at Sandy Lane. For simpler pleasures, pad across the ornate mosaic floors onto your own private terrace to marvel at the soft-edged silhouette of the hotel at twilight.

Whether you've arrived for a secret luxury holiday or an exclusive corporate gathering, the multi-faceted, all-anticipating Sandy Lane has a side created especially for you. The extensive fitness centre and free-form pool will get your hearts racing, as will the curves of the prestigious Tom Fazio-designed Country Club and Green Monkey courses, honoured to host the World Cup golf championships in 2006.

After a tee-off, slow down and relax with refreshing drinks at the Golf Clubhouse, which features an elegant restaurant and bar.

Alternatively, check yourself into a private and personalized suite at Sandy Lane's Spa. Housed in a Romanesque mansion, this is the ultimate haven for self-indulgence and ultra-pampering. Enjoy a chakra treatment or nap in the crystal laconium, then reinvigorate with a dip in the facility's singular ice cave before enjoying fresh fruit juices at The Spa Café.

Dusk is when guests reappear refreshed and transformed, palates stirred by the aromas carried on the warm sea breeze. L'Acajou and Bajan Blue restaurants perch on the very edge of the Caribbean, the spectacular panoramic views matched only by the length and breadth of their New World, Asian and haute-cuisine menus. Celebrity chefs like Ken Hom take the helm in the kitchen occasionally, thrilled to be leading a world-class team in an extraordinary and universally praised establishment. Well, naturally, one doesn't expect anything short of incomparable at the Sandy Lane.

FACTS		
ROOMS	Orchid Rooms • Luxury Orchid Suites • Ocean Rooms • Luxury Ocean Rooms • Dolphin Suites • Luxury Dolphin Suites • 2 Penthouses • 1 five-bedroom Villa	
FOOD	L'Acajou • Bajan Blue • Spa Café	
DRINK	Monkey Bar • Terrace Lounge • Beach, Pool and Golf Club bars	
FEATURES	golf: 3 championship courses and The Club House • spa • fitness centre • tennis • pool • beach • water sports • boutiques • Treehouse Club (for children)	
BUSINESS	St. James Room • Spa Room • private suites	
NEARBY	Grantley Airport (35 minutes by car)	
CONTACT	St. James, Barbados • telephone: +1246.444 2000 • facsimile: +1246.444 2222 • email: mail@sandylane.com • website: www.sandylane.com	

PHOTOGRAPHS COURTESY OF SANDY LANE HOTEL + RESORT.

Treasure Beach

As its name suggests, Treasure Beach is a trove full of glittering, hidden delights. Voted 'Caribbean Hotel of the Year' by *Caribbean World* magazine, this enticing oasis lies in St. James on western Barbados' picturesque Platinum Coast, where lush emerald gardens positively drip with high colour and murmur a warm welcome to the tranquil tropics.

A friendly privately-owned boutique hotel, Treasure Beach recently celebrated a grand re-opening after an extensive refurbishment. It now has 35 stylish suites, each beautifully appointed for the ultimate in intimacy and personalized service. Along with the cocktail

bar and dining area, these exclusive havens form a horseshoe cluster around the heart of the hotel—the temptingly cool freshwater pool.

Each light, airy suite affords a quiet view of the garden or the freshwater pool, or an unparalleled panorama across Paynes Bay's ivory sands. Ideal, though not exclusively, for honeymooners, the hotel's dreamy, charming suites lend themselves naturally to romance. Images of petal-strewn four-poster beds lying against coralstone walls and champagne for two on a cool verandah spring immediately to mind. The hotel's renowned antique-chic Hemmingway Suite has also entered a new echelon of luxury with enviable additions—spacious terraces, a walk-in shower for two and, a private plunge pool.

All the bathrooms feature Temple Spa's trendsetting lifestyle products. Favoured by celebrity fashion icons Kylie Minogue and Victoria Beckham, these niche luxuries are

...beautifully appointed for the ultimate in intimacy and personalized service.

The award-winning Al Fresco restaurant overlooks the verdant beauty of the hotel's gardens, where beautiful mature tamarind, mahogany and palm trees are silhouetted against the moon. Al Fresco's head chef is constantly innovating to produce globally-inspired dishes with fresh ingredients which are sourced locally. For after-dinner drinks, Richard's Bar next door is the ideal spot in which to muse over an impressive cocktail list, or simply to enjoy a cosy evening over a game of backgammon.

For those inclined toward more strenuous activity, Treasure Beach boasts a superb air-conditioned fitness suite, offering as well to make arrangements for tee-off times at golf courses nearby, island safaris, horseback riding, scuba diving and deep-sea fishing. Snorkel above shoals of pearlescent fish, and marvel afresh at the vibrant hues and life teeming just beneath the Caribbean's surface. If you holiday to shop, Holetown Shopping Plaza is a leisurely stroll away.

the perfect complement to Treasure Beach's newly re-designed bathrooms and soothing natural wellness philosophies.

As the final flames of sunset fade, leave the darkness outside your private balcony for the warmth of an armchair in the marble-tiled suite. Diversions such as high-speed Internet and wide-screen satellite television can fill the peaceful hour before dinner.

FACTS	**ROOMS**	35 suites
	FOOD	Al Fresco restaurant
	DRINK	Richard's Bar
	FEATURES	fitness suite • freshwater pool • beach • water sports • scuba diving • snorkelling • sailing • deep-sea fishing • hiking tours • island safaris • library • babysitting
	BUSINESS	private meeting room
	NEARBY	Grantley Adams International Airport (40 minutes by car) • Bridgetown • Holetown Shopping Plaza • Andromeda Gardens
	CONTACT	Paynes Bay, St. James, Barbados • telephone: +1246.432 1346 • facsimile: +1246.432 1094 • email: reservations@treasurebeachhotel.com • website: www.treasurebeachhotel.com

PHOTOGRAPHS COURTESY OF TREASURE BEACH.

Fustic House

Paradise does exist on earth—just north of Speightstown on the 'platinum' west coast of Barbados. Here nestles Fustic House, one of the Caribbean's most enchanting, idyllic and prestigious private estates.

A classic Caribbean 'great house' built as early as the 17th century, Fustic House came to prominence on the international jet-set circuit in the 1970s when Britain's eminent theatre designer Oliver Messel—creator of some of the most impressive resorts, hotels and private homes in the Caribbean—turned his genius to redesigning and transforming the historic plantation property. The result, as a generation of fortunate guests can testify, is as close to perfection as you're likely to find anywhere.

A beguiling combination of Old World glamour, rustic charm and modern luxury, Fustic House is set within its own 4-hectare (10-acre) garden of eden, just a short walk from the beach. The estate's pastoral gardens sprawl across a coral ridge above the quaint fishing village of Half Moon Fort, offering its privileged guests the best of both worlds— the exclusivity and intimacy of a private estate coupled with easy access to the beach.

Three separate and distinct wings house the elegant accommodations and facilities. The Great House is spread over two floors and contains the dining room and library, as well as two expansive suites which afford magnificent views out across the gardens to the sea. The newer Messel and Plantation Wings are not far removed from the Great House, and each features two suites which accommodate up to four persons in each.

Built of coral stone and hardwood, each wing is composed of airy, expansive rooms and spaces which are beautifully appointed with ethnic textiles, objets d'art and wicker

A beguiling combination of Old World glamour, rustic charm and modern luxury.

Giverny—and a spread of Barbados' finest gastronomic fare. Diners are offered a menu of exceptional fusion dishes which blend the best elements of Caribbean and International cuisines. The dishes are individually prepared by Kenroy Hunte, who is regarded as one of the best chefs on the island. The experienced and dedicated staff can arrange additional services which include relaxation and healing therapies—from reiki to hot stone and deep tissue massages—as well as golf and tennis on Barbados and day-trips to nearby islands.

and natural wood furnishings. Defining the interiors are splashes of white in the ceilings, walls and fabrics as well as soothing green accents from the pillars, louvered shutters and decorative palms. The earthy tones and leafy hues blend seamlessly into the verdant garden landscape; and wandering the meandering paths which connect the wings, one cannot help but pause at a courtyard to admire Messel's masterful melding of inside and outside to create this unifying feel of space. Much of Fustic House's magical atmosphere is conjured by the estate's elysian grounds—a veritable wonderland of lush gardens where sunlight seeps through the canopy of mature trees to cast delicate silhouettes on the lawns. To the south of the gardens, in a grotto gazing out to sea, lies another Messel masterpiece—an organically shaped rock pool carved out of the coral ridge, flowing with spring water and shaded by overhanging foliage.

Some other exquisite delights that guests will discover at Fustic House include a tranquil lily pond—reminiscent of Monet's garden at

FACTS		
	ROOMS	Great House: 2 suites • Messel and Plantation Wings: 2 suites each
	FOOD	fusion of Caribbean and international cuisines by personal chef Kenroy Hunte
	FEATURES	lagoon pool • extensive landscaped gardens and a tropical ravine • lily pond • diving platform at nearby beach • speedboat • games room • villa manager • wireless Internet access
	NEARBY	Speightstown • Holetown • beaches • golf • tennis • water sports • shopping • restaurants
	CONTACT	Bajan Services Ltd, Newton House, Battaleys, St. Peter BB26094, Barbados • telephone: +1246.422 2618 • facsimile: +1246.422 5366 • email: villas@bajanservices.com • website: www.bajanservices.com

PHOTOGRAPHS COURTESY OF BAJAN SERVICES.

Leamington Pavilion

Of all of the glamorous holiday destinations in the world, Barbados' Platinum Coast is surely one of the most alluring and desirable. Apart from enjoying the most exquisite of tropical climates, its coastline is blessed with a breathtaking combination of crystal clear waters, coral sand beaches and some of the most gilt-edged hospitality properties in the whole of the Caribbean. One such pedigree is Leamington Pavilion, which comprises an Italianate luxury pavilion and a private cottage set in idyllic, landscaped oceanfront gardens.

Originally owned by the Heinz family (of baked beans fame), the villa subsequently became the official residence of the United States Ambassador to Barbados. During this time it played host to several US presidents —including Ronald Reagan—before it was purchased by the current English owners and redesigned into a holiday home appointed to the very highest order.

Over the years, the property has undergone several dramatic transformations, most notably in the 1960s by the luminary Oliver Messel, Britain's leading theatre designer. Since then, it has further benefited from the talents of other well-known interior designers, namely Nicky Haslam, who extended and remodelled the villa in 1990, and, Heather Aguilar-Swan, who helped to oversee extensive renovations in 2005. The result is intoxicating—an elegant blend of baroque lavishness and classic opulence.

The Pavilion comprises four bedrooms, each of which is accompanied by a spacious marble-clad bathroom. Furnishings are of the

THIS PAGE (FROM TOP): The sumptuous interior furnishings possess a quality of baroque grandeur; classical churrigueresco and sophistication in the dining room; other design highlights include the delicately shaded latticework and sculpted window-shaped arches featured on the walls in this sitting area, which create a trompe l'oeil gazebo setting.

OPPOSITE: Watched over by a pair of gazebos, the pool looks out across to the glistening sea.

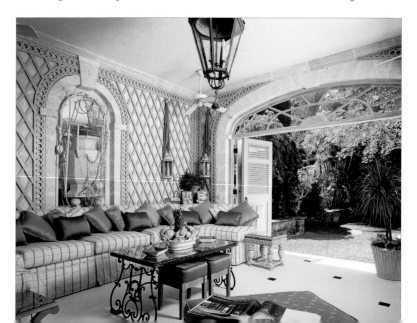

finest quality throughout, with an emphasis on antique furniture and period oil paintings. Also housed in the Pavilion are an elegant dining room as well as indoor and outdoor sitting areas that look out across a luxurious pool to the beach and sea beyond.

The Cottage, hidden within the estate's grounds on a secluded spot on the beach, may be rented together with the Pavilion, or separately. Guests renting both the Cottage and Pavilion have full access to all the latter's facilities, which include the pool and tennis court. The Cottage is, in itself, self-contained and complete with a fully-equipped kitchen, exclusive sun terrace and private entrances, which makes it an ideal honeymoon home.

Fine dining here is a sumptuous affair in more ways than gastronomic satisfaction (which is served, in grand style, on crystal and Wedgwood china). The formal dining room, presided over by classically styled statues and an elaborate chandelier, looks out to the pool and is beautifully candlelit by night.

Should Leamington's sybaritic lifestyle become the cause of a guilty conscience, the property has plenty to keep its guests fit and active. The ocean is right at your doorstep, offering endless possibilities for water sports. Leamington also boasts its own tennis court and a fitness area located in one of the outbuildings. Alternatively, a tee-off on one of the island's illustrious golf courses can be arranged by the experienced and superbly trained staff, whose services are claimed to rival those of first-rate luxury hotels.

FACTS

ROOMS	Pavilion: 4 bedrooms • Cottage: 1 bedroom
FOOD	meals and drinks may be individually tailored and served on the terrace, in the poolside gazebos or in the formal dining room
FEATURES	oceanfront • landscaped tropical gardens • swimming pool • fitness room • tennis court • wireless Internet access • villa manager
NEARBY	Speightstown • shopping • restaurants • golf • beaches • scuba diving • snorkelling • water sports
CONTACT	Bajan Services Ltd, Newton House, Battaleys, St. Peter BB26094, Barbados • telephone: +1246.422 2618 • facsimile: +1246.422 5366 • email: villas@bajanservices.com • website: www.bajanservices.com

PHOTOGRAPHS COURTESY OF BAJAN SERVICES.

Port St. Charles

Imagine exchanging the monotony of endless grey office blocks for a marina full of glistening white super yachts basking in the Caribbean sun. That sought-after experience is what guests at Port St. Charles wake up to every single morning.

Located on the stunning shoreline of St. Peter, Barbados, this luxurious beachfront development offers apartments and villas that are uniquely appointed by individual owners willing to share the peaceful privacy of their residences. Perfect for languorous weekends and lengthier holidays, these properties radiate the comforts of a real home, eschewing the impersonality of branded hotels.

Set against impressively high standards, Port St. Charles' accommodations include features such as wireless Internet, classic marble bathroom suites and fully equipped kitchens. All bedrooms have ensuite bathrooms while most accommodations have cooling plunge pools out on the deck. Top-floor apartments have cathedral ceilings with exposed beams and phenomenal views.

Lagoon-front villas are sanctuaries unto themselves. Clustered around a courtyard, each looks onto the lush foliage of a dazzling tropical garden, where an effervescent fountain flows into an intimate plunge pool.

Barbados is world-renowned for its idyllic, ocean-lapped shores, providing two principal options for beach bunnies. North Beach is a favourite with children;

THIS PAGE (FROM TOP): Expect no less than a breezy ambience in the lagoon-front villas; La Mer restaurant charms diners with its ocean view; home-owned villas exude the comfort of homes.

OPPOSITE: Located on the shoreline, Port St. Charles offers visitors marina-based accommodations with plunge pools.

the second one is a watersports nirvana in the south. With free use of equipment, avid snorkellers and kayakers can revel to their hearts' content, their parties occasionally gate-crashed by inquisitive resident turtles.

Marina communities are famously friendly places—Port St. Charles is no exception. Guests and staff at its gym, cafés or the spectacular beaches nearby have been known to mingle openly with one another, sharing tales of the ocean, sailing, fishing and fine dining.

Culinary-wise, guests will get a chance to reach new heights of indulgence at La Mer, the resort's signature restaurant. It occupies a key vantage point at the marina's edge, with uninterrupted views of seductively sleek yachts bobbing against a backdrop of sparkling water.

For chilling out, there's the Sunset Isle Pool Bar or the new Port St. Charles Club to put you in the right mood. After sharing a few exotic cocktails with fellow guests, you may be greeted by invites for fishing trips, tennis matches and gym workouts that seem to flow as smoothly as the island's premium rum.

With world-class amenities all within your reach as well as unparalleled levels of luxury, privacy and indulgence, Port St. Charles is certainly the place to stay for that elusive state of mind that you've always wanted to have—complete relaxation.

FACTS		
ROOMS	123 rooms
FOOD	La Mer Restaurant • Port St. Charles Club
DRINK	Sunset Isle Pool Bar • Port St. Charles Club
FEATURES	hairdressing and beauty salon • exercise room • 2 floodlit tennis courts • water taxi • non-motorized water sports
NEARBY	Speightstown • Holetown • shops • restaurants
CONTACT	Port St. Charles Development, Port St. Charles, St. Peter, Barbados • telephone: +1246.419 1000 • facsimile: +1246.422 7447 • email: psc.reservations@caribsurf.com • website: www.portstcharles.com

PHOTOGRAPHS COURTESY OF PORT ST. CHARLES.

Sandalo

Imagine staying in an English country manor house situated on a beautiful stretch of pure white sand in one of the most desirable and exclusive beach locations in the Caribbean. Then add an idyllic tropical garden setting, a luxurious pool looking out across lush foliage and fine sands to the sea, direct access to the beach from the manor and professional staff intent on pampering you like visiting royalty. If you've conjured these images in your mind, you'll probably find that you're thinking of a place very much like Sandalo, a magnificent property boasting an ultra-exclusive beach address on Barbados' glamorous west coast —world-renowned Gibbs Beach.

Sandalo offers the best of two different worlds. This is a successful marriage of, on one hand, the elegance and sophistication of high-end luxury and, on the other, the laid-back quality of the Caribbean lifestyle. Few places achieve the combination with such effortless grace; and Sandalo's enviable flair for blending sumptuous high-style living with barefoot simplicity may be largely attributed to the work of architect Ian Morrisson, who recently oversaw the full-scale renovation and refurbishment of this exceptional abode.

The whole place exudes an air of class. The furnishings, fittings and décor are all of an exceptionally high standard, whether it's the state-of-the-art media room fully equipped with plasma television, electronic games and

surround sound stereo, or the air-conditioned kitchen, custom designed by Joshua Jones and specially imported from the United Kingdom. Then there is the superbly trained, warmly obliging and attentive staff—among whom is an experienced butler—dedicated to ensuring that guests leave their cares at the door.

The impressive main house contains two floors, the first of which has four bedrooms, most with super-king-size beds, spacious en-suite bathrooms and private terraces which offer splendid views of the pool and sea. The fifth bedroom is to be found in Pineapple Cottage, tucked away in an intimate corner of the property. The cottage too is lavishly appointed with a super-king-size bed and en-suite bathroom, its own kitchenette and a private patio for lounging.

One of Sandalo's great attractions is its selection of dining locations, depending on the occasion—whether it's breakfast on the

...blending sumptuous high-style living with barefoot simplicity...

THIS PAGE (FROM LEFT): A blend of class and idyllic simplicity is achieved with the employment of natural and neutral tones; unforgettable dining experiences are to be had at the poolside gazebo, especially by night.

OPPOSITE (FROM LEFT): Sandalo boasts an über-exclusive address on Gibbs beach in Barbados; its back gate lies just behind the pool, behind the main house, and it will lead you straight onto your own private corner on the beach.

verandah, lunch in the poolside gazebo or a casual and hearty dinner on the barbecue terrace (fully-equipped with an ice-making machine and refrigerator for the purpose). The cuisine is accompanied by views of the gardens and sea; add a highly innovative chef who caters to diners' individual tastes, and you'll find entertaining a breeze and each meal a memorable gastronomic experience.

To work off the excesses of indulgent living, wining and dining, follow in the footsteps of celebrity guests before you and take a long walk along one of the world's most famous beaches. Sandalo's back gate opens straight out onto an isolated corner on Gibbs Beach for the utmost seclusion. The staff can also help set you up with water sports, from para-sailing to water-skiing, and sailing trips.

FACTS		
ROOMS	main house: 4 suites • Pineapple Cottage: 1 suite	
FOOD	meals and drinks may be individually tailored and served in the air-conditioned kitchen or poolside gazebo or at the barbeque terrace	
FEATURES	beach • pool • state-of-the-art media room • wireless Internet access • villa manager • chef	
NEARBY	Speightstown • Holetown • shopping • restaurants • golf • beaches • scuba diving • snorkelling • water sports	
CONTACT	Bajan Services Ltd, Newton House, Battaleys, St. Peter BB26094, Barbados • telephone: +1246.422 2618 • facsimile: +1246.422 5366 • email: villas@bajanservices.com • website: www.bajanservices.com	

PHOTOGRAPHS COURTESY OF BAJAN SERVICES.

Laluna

Secreted away on the magical Spice Island of Grenada, this intimate, alluring hideaway is nestled amid the emerald-green hills of a secluded bay on the island's jagged southwest tip. Here, its 16 thatched-roof cottages dot the beautiful hillside of Morne Rouge, peering out to the cerulean ocean from behind graceful veils of lush foliage and brilliant blossoms.

Laluna is especially adored for its privacy, mesmerizing beauty and romantic ambience. Its luxe style and enchanting Mediterranean-inspired accommodations are the creation of acclaimed designers Carmelina Santoro and Gabriella Giuntoli (the stylist behind Giorgio Armani's exclusive villa in Pantelleria, Italy). Together, they have ensured that every aspect and detail has been meticulously thought-out and appointed, from the lucent glow of the hotel's stunning showpiece freshwater pool to the cottages' exquisitely hued, textured walls, which have been rendered with a delicate impasto quality using an old Mediterranean concoction of cement infused with cinnamon, sienna and sun-kissed ochre pigments.

The cottages are built and furnished with fine materials from the Caribbean and as far away as Italy and Bali. The minimalist lines and otherworldly Indonesian elements give the enclave a peaceful, meditative quality; and the sensitive blend of warm, earthy tones and sensuously textured materials creates an aura of rustic charm and romance.

In each cottage, open-plan living areas offer a king-size bed, television, stereo and CD player. Each airy living space opens out onto a spacious verandah with a luxurious private plunge pool; and uniquely designed semi-outdoor bathrooms are appointed with signature soaps and lotions specially made by a monastery in the Italian Alps. Bamboo-roofed sundecks make idyllic outdoor lounges, their blue walls reminiscent of a cloud-dappled sky or the deep azure ocean itself; elegant Italian lamps, their rich glow reflected from the stucco-style paintwork of the walls, light draped Balinese four-poster beds.

Yet, for all its lavish lodgings and upscale designer feel, Laluna is not a slick, insincere establishment. This is an authentic and friendly abode owned by a husband-and-wife team with a genuine desire to offer every guest Mediterranean hospitality, barefoot comfort,

unforgettable romance and the Caribbean experience of a lifetime. Laluna's proprietor, Bernardo Bertucci, fills the hotel with his warm Italian enthusiasm and urbane style, which are accompanied by the charming and light-hearted touches of his wife Wendy Potter.

The intimate and congenial hospitality is to be found too in the kitchen and restaurant. Amiable chef Benedetto La Fiura effortlessly whips up Sicilian delicacies with a Caribbean twist. Sign up for his 'Taste of Laluna' course

to learn how to make authentic Italian dishes. The restaurant itself seats a cosy 48 and opens onto the beach, offering stirring views of the bay. For drinks, Sunset Bar offers large, Indonesian-style sofas beneath its thatched roof, and wine-lovers can select a fine Italian vintage from the expertly stocked cellar.

Laluna is all about an unhurried, informal attitude, so occupy a chaise longue on the secluded private beach or sip rum spiced with island-grown nutmeg in a shaded pavilion.

Amid such tranquil, aesthetic surroundings, spiritual well-being and fulfilment are naturally an integral part of the Laluna experience; and guests are encouraged to meditate on their own private verandahs or to enjoy a blissful and relaxing massage there. For the sportive, there are plenty of opportunities for boating, kayaking, scuba diving and snorkelling; and a quick word to the concierge is all it takes to set up a tennis match, round of golf, deep-sea fishing trip or island eco-tours.

PHOTOGRAPHS COURTESY OF LALUNA.

FACTS		
ROOMS	16 cottages	
FOOD	Italian cuisine with a Caribbean twist by Benedetto La Fiura	
DRINK	Sunset Bar	
FEATURES	freshwater pool • private plunge pool • fitness room • yoga • massages • mountain bikes • snorkelling • Hobie Cats • kayaking	
BUSINESS	wireless Internet	
NEARBY	golf • island eco-tours • deep-sea fishing • scuba diving • sailing trips	
CONTACT	PO Box 1500, Morne Rouge, Grenada • telephone: +1473.439 0001 • facsimile: +1473.439 0600 • email: info@laluna.com • website: www.laluna.com	

True Blue Bay Resort + Villas

True Blue Bay is one vivacious and multi-coloured—figuratively and literally—carnival of a resort. Located on the shimmery shores of Grenada in the southern reaches of the Caribbean, this is where the tropical sea meets the Atlantic Ocean. On a beautiful island saturated with sun and spice, True Blue Bay is the prize that awaits those who seek gold at the end of the rainbow.

Formerly an indigo plantation estate, the family-run resort is impeccably managed by its owners, giving it a distinctive, down-to-earth blend of homespun hospitality, exceptional friendliness and colourful Caribbean chic.

The resort teems with the effervescent hues of the Caribbean in a celebration of eternal summer. From the glossy greens of the implausibly tall palm trees to the sun-bleached spectrum of the beach cabanas, it is a veritable feast for the eyes. Unusual sculptures and symbols of the sea dot the gardens, bright walls and striking wrought-ironwork. Sweetly scented tropical flowers are scattered in warm welcome throughout the suites, whose dramatic colour schemes

THIS PAGE (CLOCKWISE FROM ABOVE): The earthy teak fittings and up-lifting colour scheme reflect the warm feel of home envisioned by the family-run resort; True Blue Restaurant is touted as one of Grenada's top three, serving Caribbean and Mexican cuisine to live island music; one of the resort's two-bedroom villas which look out onto the beach across the marina.

OPPOSITE: View of the resort's three tower suites. Perched high on a hill above the marina, the suites' private viewing balconies each comes fully equipped with rattan loungers and telescopes.

...an ambience of sparkling conviviality.

create an ambience of sparkling conviviality. Sweet-pepper reds jostle with sunny tangerine shades, bringing the glory of Grenada into each bright, airy room.

Studding the slopes and verdant lawns leading down to the marina are the resort's stylish waterfront apartments. Their delightful climate-controlled interiors are furnished with tropical materials including rattan and teak, lending the rooms a natural and harmonious feel. Though the resort offers the perfect get-away accommodation for a family holiday, it caters too for romantic escapes, with gauze-draped beds and hypnotic hammocks that beckon from patio verandahs—generous vantage points which afford unforgettable vistas over the glistening yacht-flecked bay.

Then there are the Club True Blue Villas, which have been designed for occasions warranting the ultimate in luxury. Tingle and refresh in your private jacuzzi bath tub and plunge pool, before languishing away in the grandeur of a generously sized four-poster

bed. The earthen tones and light, unfettered feel of these two-bedroom villas perfectly mirror the enviably simple and relaxing way of life in the Caribbean.

True Blue Restaurant occupies an idyllic spot, extending on decks over the water's edge. Highly acclaimed for its Caribbean and Mexican cuisine, the Grenada Tourist Board numbers it among the island's top three restaurants. The evening entertainment is as varied and vibrant as the acclaimed

cuisine, with regular live performances of jazz and Caribbean music. Dreamy days can be spent on, in or beneath True Blue Bay's iridescent surface. Kayaking, Hobie Cat sailing, windsurfing, yacht charters and deep-sea fishing trips can be organized for guests at the resort's marina, and Aquanauts Dive Centre down by the bay specializes in exhilarating diving and snorkelling trips. For a celebration of endless summer, follow the wave of happiness to True Blue Bay.

FACTS		
	ROOMS	26 standard rooms • 4 waterfront apartments • 3 tower rooms • 5 two-bedroom villas
	FOOD	True Blue Restaurant: Grenadian and Mexican cuisine • Snack Bar
	DRINK	Lounge Bar by the waterfront
	FEATURES	spa • Bay View pool • Petit Anse (infinity) pool • marina • Hobie Cats • kayaks • Aquanauts Dive Centre: courses and trips for scuba diving and snorkelling • 2 children's playgrounds • boutique • car rental
	BUSINESS	meeting room • wireless Internet
	NEARBY	yacht charters • biking trails • nature walks • restaurants • St. George's Harbour
	CONTACT	PO Box 1414, Grand Anse, St. George's, Grenada • telephone: +1473.443 8783 or 888.883 2482 (US toll-free line) • email: mail@truebluebay.com • website: www.truebluebay.com

PHOTOGRAPHS COURTESY OF TRUE BLUE BAY RESORT + VILLAS.

Anse Chastanet Resort

et on a sparkling blue bay on St. Lucia's luscious leeward coast, the magical Anse Chastanet blends that 'ends of the earth' feel many people crave in a Caribbean resort with exceptional lodging, top-notch service, myriad island activities and gourmet cuisine.

Anse Chastanet was born as a diving mecca back in the early 1980s when hardly anyone came to St. Lucia. Over the years, this Windward Islands icon has evolved into an impressive all-round destination spread across a spectacular 242-hectare (600-acre) seaside estate. The scuba diving here is still unparalled but Anse Chastanet is also, today, a special favourite among honeymooners, beachcombers, nature lovers and those who are content just whiling away in a hammock.

Rooms and suites are arrayed along the bay and a heavily wooded hillside strewn with tropical flowers. Designed by architect-owner Nick Troubetzkoy, these make some of the most unique and memorable abodes you will ever come across in the Caribbean. Fashioned from different materials, they are decorated in distinct manners with local hardwood furnishings and St. Lucian folk art. In keeping with Anse Chastanet's philosophy of total escape, all guestrooms are free from telephones, television, radio and the Internet. Some peer down on the resort's private bay and white-sand strand while others offer truly breathtaking prospects of the towering Piton Peaks—one of the most remarkable views in the whole of the Caribbean.

THIS PAGE (FROM TOP): The premium hillside rooms are strategically located, offering extraordinary panoramic views of the Pitons; the Infinity Suites are the resort's piece de resistance— each is extravagantly appointed with a private infinity-edge pool.

OPPOSITE: Nestled amid exquisite natural surroundings which exude the quality of a mystical ancient world, Anse Chastanet has a timelessness that makes you feel you have arrived at the end of the earth, at the beginning of time.

Taking Troubetzkoy's vision of 'building in harmony with nature' to a new height of sophistication are the Infinity Suites at Jade Mountain. Looking out across to the stunning Pitons from the highest point of Morne Anse Chastanet, this is a 'resort within a resort' with its own reception area and concierge. Each suite—featuring a private infinity-edge pool—is an extravagantly sweeping space which resembles a theatre set, deliberately designed without a fourth wall for unobstructed views over St. Lucia's Elysian landscape.

Perched high above the bay, Piti Piton and Treehouse restaurant offers a scrumptious blend of Creole, Mediterranean and French cooking that Anse Chastanet calls Tropical World Cuisine. The menu changes daily and many of the ingredients are grown in the resort's own herb garden and fruit orchard—or caught right offshore by local fishermen.

While scuba diving remains one of the most well loved activities at Anse Chastanet, guests will not want to miss excursions to legendary underwater sites like Superman's Flight, Fairyland and the famous wreck of the *Lesleen M.* But plenty of other water sports are available right off the beach. Or hop a ride to Anse Mamin, where the ruins of an old sugar plantation offer plenty of scope for hiking, mountain biking or a picnic on the beach. Guides offer half-day treks into the mountains behind Anse Chastanet; fascinating insights into St. Lucian nature that culminate with a walk through Soufrière village. Round things off with a yoga class in the new beachside pavilion or a soothing treatment at the resort's Kai Belté Spa, where the menu runs the gamut from shiatsu and foot reflexology to a local Creole treatment called wosh cho (hot stone).

FACTS		
ROOMS	hillside rooms • beachside rooms • two-bedroom suites • Infinity Pool Suites	
FOOD	Piti Piton & Treehouse: Caribbean, French and Mediterranean cuisine • Trou au Diable: international, Caribbean and South Asian cuisine	
DRINK	Piton Bar • Beach Bar	
FEATURES	Kai Belté Spa • beach • bay • water sports • scuba diving • hiking and mountain biking trails • art gallery	
NEARBY	Soufrière town • Piton Peaks • Mount Soufrière 'drive-through' volcano • Diamond Mineral Baths • St. Lucia National Rainforest • Anse La Raye Friday Night Jump-up	
CONTACT	PO Box 7000, Soufrière, St. Lucia • telephone: +1758.459 7000 • facsimile: +1758.459 7700 • email: ansechastanet@candw.lc • website: www.ansechastanet.com	

PHOTOGRAPHS COURTESY OF ANSE CHASTANET RESORT.

Ladera

Recently voted the Caribbean's best hotel *and* the very best in the world by readers of *Condé Nast Traveler*, Ladera astonishes in a number of ways—dramatic showpiece architecture and design, intriguing interior décor, sensational nouvelle island cuisine and seamless service that's at once highly efficient and elegantly unobtrusive.

First and foremost however is Ladera's location. Nestled 335 m (1,100 ft) above sea level amid a hillside mango grove jungle surrounded by lush, misty rainforest, the resort seems to float above St. Lucia's leeward coast, endless vistas of the verdant tropical range and cerulean Caribbean from every room and the famous Piton Peaks right outside your windows. The sort of hypnotic view that you can ponder for hours without taking your eyes off the scenery and that, to some extent, truly does take your breath away —from the high altitude if nothing else.

Since its launch in the early 1990s, this eco-lodge-style resort has earned a string of accolades for discreet, ambrosial pampering in a sublimely rustic setting. A luxury resort that attracts a loyal clientele of the wealthy and well-known from all around the globe, Harrison Ford, Raquel Welch, Bill Gates and David Bowie count among its former guests. But Ladera is also a star in its own right, having been featured on film as one of the locations for the blockbuster *Superman II*.

Spread along the ridge in linear fashion, the 19 suites and six villas are modelled on the idea of treehouse living and deliberately designed without a fourth wall, leaving each spacious sleeping area open to the sun for breathtaking, unobstructed panoramas of the Pitons, Soufrière valley and Caribbean Sea. Each guestroom features timbers, stone and tile-work, boasting their own private plunge pools and gauze-draped four-poster beds.

THIS PAGE (CLOCKWISE FROM TOP): **The infinity pool—with spellbinding views of the Pitons and cerulean sea below—is one of the most memorable in the world; Ladera exudes a stirring quality of ends-of-the-earth romance; Dasheene restaurant and Tcholit bar above the pool.**

OPPOSITE (FROM LEFT): **Each of the guestrooms are designed without a fourth wall for a unifying feel of the breathtaking landscape.**

Beauty and wellness treatments inspired by St. Lucia's volcanic origins are available at the resort's Ti Kai Posé Spa or in the privacy and comfort of your own room. Weekly art exhibits, fashion shows and woodcarving demonstrations are also Ladera institutions. For those who can actually tear themselves away from all the indulgences on the hilltop, the resort offers shuttle services to the white-sand strands at Anse Chastanet and Jalousie as well as the market and waterfront shops in nearby Soufrière town.

Furnishings range from 19th-century French colonial style to contemporary wicker, with Caribbean art strewn here and there as foils to the indoor plants.

Award-winning Dasheene restaurant offers equally expansive vistas of the spectacular St. Lucian range and an innovative blend of Continental and Creole cuisine that earns just as many kudos as the hotel. Working as a team, local chef Nigel Mitchell and English-born Orlando Satchell have created dishes one finds nowhere else in the region —Tangy Island Tamales, Lucian Lamb Curry, and Green Papaya & Pumpkin Fritters, just to name a few. High tea is served every afternoon in Ladera's vast tropical gardens.

FACTS		
ROOMS	6 villas • 19 suites	
FOOD	Dasheene: innovative Caribbean and Continental cuisine	
DRINK	Tcholit bar	
FEATURES	Ti Kai Posè Spa • pool • water sports • library • boutiques • shuttle service to and from Soufrière town and nearby beaches	
BUSINESS	computer station • private telephone room	
NEARBY	Soufrière town • Piton Peaks • Diamond Mineral Baths • Mount Soufrière 'drive-through' volcano • St. Lucia National Rainforest	
CONTACT	PO Box 225, Soufriere, St. Lucia • telephone: +1758.459 7323 • facsimile: +1758.459 5156 • email: reservations@.ladera.com • website: www.ladera.com	

PHOTOGRAPHS COURTESY OF LADERA.

Raffles Resort Canouan Island

THIS PAGE: *Aerial view of Canouan island, of which the unsparing Raffles Resort covers two-thirds mass in land and coast.*

OPPOSITE (CLOCKWISE FROM TOP LEFT): *The resort's Jim Fazio-designed Trump International Golf Course is widely touted to offer the most challenging links and inventive landscaping in the Caribbean; Raffles Villa's private pool; although recently launched, the resort is regarded as a regional paragon of immaculate service.*

The premiere New World spin-off of the legendary Raffles Hotel in Singapore, this five-star tropical resort sprawls across two-thirds of Canouan island in the gorgeous Grenadines and boasts just about anything a guest could ever desire in an exclusive island hideaway.

Set around a sparkling sapphire bay at the foot of verdant tropical mountains, the 121-hectare (300-acre) resort offers myriad luxury escapes for the discerning epicurean.

Guests can golf to their hearts' content at one of the best championship courses in the Caribbean or languish on the estate's private beaches all day; they can circumnavigate Canouan in their own catamaran of a day and gamble the night away at the resort's elegant casino. They can be pampered at the resort's elaborately conceived beach spa, or go on a dive exploration around some of the most pristine reefs in the entire Caribbean.

Like its Southeast Asian namesake, this Raffles boasts a bit of history—the ruins of a 17th-century Anglican church looming above the driveway as you approach the lobby. Originally built in Canterbury, England and shipped stone-by-stone across the Atlantic, the church was destroyed by a hurricane in 1902 and recently resurrected as the Raffles Canouan's wedding chapel.

Created by architectural maestro Luigi Vietti—also the mastermind behind the Aga Khan's posh Costa Smeralda development in Sardinia—the Raffles' 156 rooms, suites and villas are lined in sumptuous Italian textiles and hand-painted mosaic tiles. Audaciously coloured walls and Italian leather armchairs complement the Mediterranean ambience, as does the LavAzza espresso machine that one finds in every room. Yet modern touches are also pervasive and include wide-screen satellite television, Sony PlayStation and DVD

player. Given the resort's overall size and rolling terrain, each room is also equipped with an electric golf cart that guests can use to tool around the property's wide grounds.

Dabs of pastel pink, apricot and lemon against the green hillsides, the resort's suites and villas are arrayed in two tiers around a natural amphitheatre that spills down to the scenic bay. All of them feature expansive sea or garden views from private patios with palapa-style roofs woven from Venezuelan chiqui-chiqui palm fronds. The resort's flair for lavishness reaches its peak in Raffles Villa, a three-bedroom and four-bathroom beachfront retreat extravagantly complete with its own private pier, infinity pool, indoor and outdoor jacuzzis, fitness centre, cinema, loft study and, in Raffles' classic colonial style, butler service.

Besides its premier white-glove service and flawless sophistication, Raffles Canouan is perhaps most well known for offering the most challenging golfing in the Caribbean. Trump International Golf Club is an 18-hole, par-72 championship course designed by luminary Jim Fazio. The first nine holes—laid

Back at sea level, Raffles' house brand Amrita Spa blends various Eastern beauty, aromatherapy and massage treatments with yoga and meditation sessions overlooking the Caribbean. The spa's plush facilities are set around its very own beach where, crawling up a lush hillside, 10 private treatment suites sit on layered terraces connected by a solar-powered funicular lift. Each suite features a private balcony replete with a whirlpool and daybeds where guests can linger long after indulging in the spa's signature treatments.

RafflesAmrita also offers one of the most soul-stirring spa experiences to be found in the Caribbean—therapy in a pair of glass-floored treatment cabins built over the water to reveal the magical coral reef and under-water life below. Accessible only by boat, the cabins are decorated with mosaics in hues of blue to reflect the chatoyant light and colours of the island and surrounding sea. To

THIS PAGE (FROM TOP): Built above sea level and weaving through the verdant billowy landscape and water channels of Canouan, the villas offer private views of the island quite unlike anything else; indoors, the stylish furnishings include terracotta floors, tropical lattice-work and ethnic rugs.

OPPOSITE (FROM TOP): RafflesAmrita Spa's famed pair of glass-floored treatment cabins built over water and its 10 private hillside suites.

out in a semi-volcanic crater along the north side of the bay—are nothing more than a prelude to a spectacular and following nine that climb 256 m (840 ft) into the sky. The breezy 13th tee offers a mind-blowing view that stretches all the way from Grenada in the south to St. Vincent in the north. The golf club also oversees the exclusive Trump Club Privé, a swank European-style casino tucked inside the hilltop Villa Monte Carlo.

complete and complement guests' newfound feeling of well-being and rejuvenation, healthy Amrita Spa cuisine may be sampled at the resort's Godhal Beach Bar & Grill nearby.

White Alba truffles and premium-aged Parmesan cheeses are among the gourmet delicacies at La Piazza, an elegant, romantic Italian restaurant perched high above the bay. Down along the bay is Jambu's, a delicious East-West alternative that combines Oriental flavours and West Indian spices. Barracuda in Red Curry Paste and Lemongrass-encrusted Lamb Chops are just two of the tantalizing favourites. At the opposite end of the Raffles fine-dining spectrum is hilltop La Varenne, a

classic Old World restaurant where candle-light complements champagne and caviar. But on top of such singular and luxuriant facilities, Raffles Canouan is also a true-blue beach resort. While most hotels are lucky to boast one good beach, Raffles offers three white-sand strands including ultra-secluded Maho Bay on the island's north shore. For

the adventure-seeking, a full range of water sports is available, including complimentary snorkelling gear, windsurfs, Sunfish sailboats, jet-skis and pedalos. Besides scuba diving and sailing trips which can be arranged by the resort, one of the most popular day-trips is speedboating to the five tiny isles which make up the Tobago Cays.

PHOTOGRAPHS COURTESY OF MUSSA STUDIOLIVIO.IT.

FACTS

ROOMS	156 rooms, suites and villas
FOOD	La Piazza: gourmet Italian • Jambu's: trans-ethnic cuisine • La Varenne: European gourmet • Godhal Beach Bar & Grill: Caribbean-Cuban cuisine
DRINK	Bellinis • Jambu Bar • Pool Bar
FEATURES	Trump International Golf Club • Trump Club Privé • Amrita Spa • fitness centre • tennis centre • freshwater pool • 3 beaches • Sugar Palm Kid's Club
DRINK	business centre
NEARBY	Tobago Cays • Grenada • Bequia
CONTACT	Carenage Bay, Canouan Island, St. Vincent & the Grenadines • telephone: +1784.458 8000 • facsimile: +1784.458 8885 • email: info@raffles-canouanisland.com • website: www.raffles-canouanisland.com

Tamarind Beach + Yacht Club

Those in the know playfully refer to the Eastern Caribbean island of Canouan as the 'Heart of the Grenadines'. Nestled snugly among the palms in one of Canouan's sheltered west-facing bays are the understated, yet captivating and luxurious, beach-front rooms and suites of the Tamarind Beach Hotel & Yacht Club. Pampered guests will be forgiven for suspecting that the hotel's friendly Italian managers have organized the spectacular sunsets directly in front of their balconies as a personal favour. Fortunately, this serene and enviably unspoiled island attracts visitors who like to keep it that way.

In particular, for those who love to spend their vacation both on and below the water, Canouan is sheer heaven. Sailors are lured here by the island's myriad bays and coves, while divers can explore the startling colour-bursts of fish and coral thriving on the surrounding barrier reef—one of the largest in the Caribbean. If your passion involves simply relaxing on a sun-bleached ribbon of silk-white sand—accompanied by nothing but a good read—the Tamarind's quietening surrounds make the perfect sanctuary. At the same time, the hotel is an excellent base from which to explore the Grenadines by boat.

THIS PAGE (CLOCKWISE FROM TOP):
Illuminated by candle and torch at dusk, Pirates Cove bar has an enchanting sunset ambience; the hotel's deluxe suites are well designed in plan for easy access and a homely feel and, at the same time, alluring with a white-draped four-poster bed; thatched-roof Palapa restaurant opens onto a seafront terrace and a breathtaking panorama.
OPPOSITE: The Tamarind's jetty is a red-letter sight amid virtually nothing but vast sea and sky.

The hotel's 40 secluded hideaways are scattered among verdant tropical gardens like pebbles dropped onto the sand. Each air-conditioned room and suite is lined with warmly lit Brazilian walnut panelling, and subtly marries elegant Italian interior design with island-specific materials and architecture. Step outside onto your private balcony in a Frette bathrobe and contemplate the shape-shifting wonder that is the Caribbean Sea.

At the heart of this beachfront oasis lies the Palapa restaurant with its high thatched roof. It is worth taking your cocktail out into the flower-drenched beauty of the terrace to admire the stunning panoramic views from the water's glittering edge. If you have worked up an appetite on a PADI dive course, you will appreciate the hearty Italian favourites and West Indian fare on offer here. The Palapa's adventurous chefs deftly commingle the finest local ingredients with produce specially imported from Italy to deliver a delicious Mediterranean-Caribbean culinary fusion. If reapplying sun-milk was the day's most strenuous activity however, sip a cocktail or indulge in light snacks at the Pirates Cove bar nearby.

Equally difficult to refuse are the hotel's recommended itineraries: a session of hydro-biking, snorkelling or windsurfing followed by a blissful massage. Or a boat-trip through glass-clear waters along miles of pristine white beaches to the neighbouring islands of Petit Tabac, Palm Island or Mustique. Yet, beautiful though these islands undeniably may be, you will find yourself irresistibly drawn back to the haven of the Tamarind.

FACTS

ROOMS	32 beachfront rooms • 8 beachfront suites
FOOD	Palapa: Italian/Caribe cuisine • Pirates Cove: snacks
DRINK	Beach Bar
FEATURES	Dive Club • water sports • snorkelling • massages • boutiques • babysitting • sea excursions • island safaris
NEARBY	Trump International Golf Course at Raffles Resort • Mauhault beach • Mount Royal
CONTACT	Canouan Island, St. Vincent and the Grenadines • telephone: +1784.458 8044 • facsimile: +1784.458 8851 • email: info@tamarind.us • website: www.tamarindbeachhotel.com

PHOTOGRAPHS COURTESY OF TAMARIND BEACH HOTEL + YACHT CLUB.

Mustique Villas

At one time or another, we have all dreamt of leaving our everyday lives behind and escaping to a tropical island paradise—a place where we can forget about the real world and indulge in our every whim.

A flight of fancy? Not anymore—not since the British aristocrat Lord Glenconner laid eyes on the island of Mustique some 50 years ago. He immediately purchased the tiny, untapped Caribbean territory and set about transforming it into one of the world's most exclusive, beautiful and idyllic retreats—an internationally renowned

hideaway for royalty, political leaders and celebrities, and a byword for unsurpassed glamour, sophistication and elegance.

Mustique lies 29 km (18 miles) south of St. Vincent and forms part of St. Vincent & the Grenadines, a collection of exquisitely unspoiled islands in the Lesser Antilles. It measures 2.5 km (1.5 miles) by 5 km (3 miles), and encompasses 566 hectares (1,400 acres) of rolling hills and lush tropical vegetation, all fringed by stretches of white sandy beach and set in clear aquamarine waters.

There are fewer than 100 villas on Mustique, each reflecting the individual tastes and lifestyles of its owner, and 64 of them are available for rent. Ranging in size from two to nine bedrooms, they offer the discerning traveller a wide variety of design

THIS PAGE (FROM TOP): The Ocean Breeze Villa is surrounded by unmarred, gorgeous scenery; a spacious layout and high ceiling define the living room in Aurora Villa.

OPPOSITE: Flanked by coconut trees and other tropical plants, Sea Star's new beachfront pool pavilion takes pampering to a new level as guests are free to enjoy breakfast by the pool or a massage at the terrace.

styles, from Tuscan villa and French chateau to plantation house and beachfront cottage. Most have private freshwater swimming pools and all boast a group of dedicated and attentive staff including cooks, housekeepers and gardeners.

In addition to the villas, there are other outstanding options for visitors. The first is Cotton House—a newly renovated 19-room boutique hotel, scenically located on 5 hectares (13 acres) of landscaped gardens and featuring one of the Caribbean's finest restaurants, The Veranda. The second is a guesthouse called Firefly, which has four rooms and a restaurant.

Also, there's a restaurant and bar called Basil's—a Mustique landmark that sits on stilts at the water's edge. It offers drinks and casual dining, providing the ideal spot for socializing with other guests.

Despite its small size, the island has everything that's needed to keep its guests entertained, including charming spa facilities and several tennis courts as well as activities such as scuba diving, horse riding, fishing and boating. But probably the greatest attraction of Mustique is what it doesn't have—traffic, noise, pollution, crowds and crime.

The whole place has the atmosphere of an elite private club, so it's as though you're staying with friends, and it is perhaps for this reason that so many visitors find themselves coming back, year after year and decade after decade.

PHOTOGRAPHS COURTESY OF MUSTIQUE VILLAS.

FACTS

ROOMS	64 villas • 19-room boutique hotel • 4-bedroom guesthouse
FOOD	Veranda Restaurant: Caribbean • The Beach Cafe • Firefly Bar and Restaurant: Caribbean • Basil's Bar: Caribbean
DRINK	Basil's Bar • Firefly • Cotton House Hotel
FEATURES	spa • tennis courts • equestrian centre • water sports
NEARBY	St. Vincent & the Grenadines
CONTACT	The Mustique Company Ltd, PO Box 349, St. Vincent & the Grenadines • telephone: +1784.488 8000 • facsimile: +1784.488 9000 • email: villarentals@mustique-island.com • website: www.mustique-island.com

The Palms Villa Resort

Situated just minutes away from Tobago's best beaches and the eclectic attractions of Scarborough village, The Palms Villa Resort offers a cosy combination of luxury escape and home-style service in one of the island's most heavenly settings.

This 4-hectare (10-acre) estate boasts five brand-new villas. Each is a masterpiece of contemporary West Indian architecture, featuring whitewashed wooden verandahs tucked beneath striking green metallic roofs, set beautifully against lush tropical gardens. Comfortably sleeping up to six adults in three bedrooms with plenty of privacy to spare, the villas make for a perfect family holiday home or corporate getaway. Each sleeping area is accompanied by an en-suite bathroom and French doors that lead to teak balconies, allowing their occupants to take full advantage of the fresh air and verdant surroundings night and day.

Downstairs, the spacious living rooms are outfitted with 26-inch televisions, DVD players, music systems, board games and a library of books. French doors open onto a breezy, expansive verandah which overlooks a full-size private pool. The kitchens are also equipped with the latest appliances, ready for whatever a guest might want to cook up, or for home-cooked meals prepared by the housekeeper assigned to each villa. Upon prior arrangement, the front desk will stock

your fridge and pantry with your favourite foods and beverages. Poolside barbecues complete the picture of island paradise bliss.

Venturing beyond the estate's borders, the front desk can arrange all sorts of water sports and island activities, from a tee-off at one of Tobago's championship golf courses or bird watching in the western hemisphere's oldest nature reserve (established in 1764), to snorkelling off the famous Buccoo Reef with its coral gardens and chromatic tropical fish. Just down the road is Scarborough, the island's tiny capital, where you can sink your teeth into local sights like Fort King George and the village market or choose to hop a ferry over to Trinidad.

Exploring Tobago—either in a rented car or a chauffer-driven vehicle arranged by the resort—guests stumble across an endless string of stunning bays and beaches. Pigeon Point has long been considered one of the most picturesque beaches in the Caribbean, its pristine, pearly sand framed by towering coconut palms. Man O' War Bay, on the other hand, is one of the region's finest natural harbours whose shore is lined with charming fishing villages and dozens of tiny beaches. Leatherback turtles lay their eggs at the aptly named Turtle Beach on Great Courland Bay; and the black-sand strand at Bacolet Bay—where *Swiss Family Robinson* was filmed—offers a superb beach escape within a 5-minute drive of the villas.

FACTS		
	ROOMS	5 villas
	FOOD	in-villa catering and grocery shopping available upon request
	DRINK	basic overnight staples available at resort
	FEATURES	private pool • music, movie and book library • personal housekeeper
	BUSINESS	office facilities • wireless Internet
	NEARBY	golf • beaches • scuba diving • snorkelling • windsurfing • parasailing • kite surfing • boating • bird watching • rainforest treks
	CONTACT	Signal Hill, Old Road, PO Box 1070, Signal Hill, Tobago • telephone: +1868.635 1010 • facsimile: +1868.635 1011 • email: info@thepalmstobago.com • website: www.thepalmstobago.com

PHOTOGRAPHS COURTESY OF THE PALMS VILLA RESORT.

aruba+dutchantilles

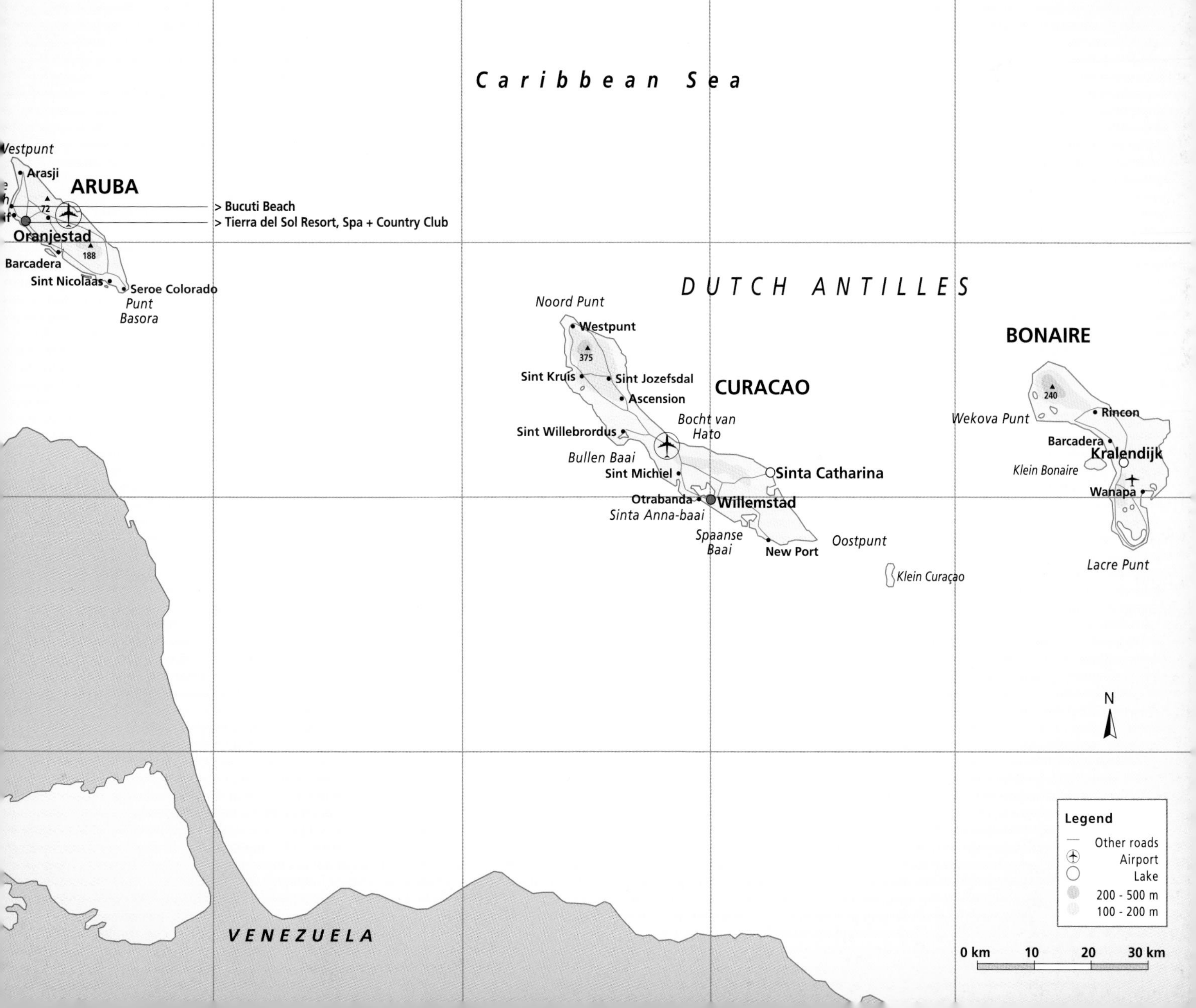

Caribbean Sea
Westpunt
Arasji
ARUBA
72
> Bucuti Beach
> Tierra del Sol Resort, Spa + Country Club
Oranjestad
188
Barcadera
Sint Nicolaas
Seroe Colorado
Punt Basora
DUTCH ANTILLES
Noord Punt
Westpunt
375
Sint Kruis
Sint Jozefsdal
Ascension
CURACAO
Bocht van Hato
Sint Willebrordus
Bullen Baai
Sint Michiel
Sinta Catharina
Otrabanda
Willemstad
Sinta Anna-baai
Spaanse Baai
New Port
Oostpunt
Klein Curaçao
BONAIRE
240
Rincon
Wekova Punt
Barcadera
Kralendijk
Klein Bonaire
Wanapa
Lacre Punt
N
VENEZUELA
Legend
Other roads
Airport
Lake
200 - 500 m
100 - 200 m
0 km
10
20
30 km

dutch roots

Three tiny Dutch islands, Aruba, Bonaire and Curaçao
(collectively called the ABCs), are located at the southern
end of the Caribbean. Despite their shared heritage (350 years of Dutch rule), each
island has developed distinct characters. Aruba is the consummate party isle, Bonaire
is the laidback beach paradise, while Curaçao is the arty enclave. This makes the
ABCs ideal for visiting on single trips or for a holiday that takes in all three.

The people of these islands come from diverse locations such as the West Indies,
Latin America and the once-vast Dutch empire—from Java, Suriname, Malacca,
Ceylon and even New Amsterdam (later, New York City). Today, islanders trace their
roots to ancestors from more than 50 nations, producing an ethnic mix that permeates
every aspect of local culture.

The islands share similar geography. Lying in a part of the Caribbean that does
not get much rain, all three of them are arid, desert-like islands. Rust-coloured soil,
rocky outcrops and cacti are integral parts of the landscape. The natural beauty of
these islands is largely preserved in national parks. Underwater, the coral reefs are
among the richest dive sites in the Caribbean. Humidity tends to be much lower here
than in other Caribbean isles and the ABCs are rarely troubled by hurricanes.

papiamento + pastechi

A unique language called Papiamento is spoken on these islands. It is a colourful and
expressive creole spoken only in the ABCs. Although its exact origins are unknown,
many scholars think that Papiamento first emerged as a pidgin used by Portuguese
slave traders to communicate with African slaves. The descendants of some of these
traders wound up in the Dutch Antilles, where the pidgin took in Dutch, Spanish and
even Arawak words, eventually evolving into Papiamento. The phrase 'Mi ta bon
danki' (meaning, 'Thank you very much') is a typical mix, with Portuguese and Dutch
words. Most ABC islanders also speak Dutch and English.

*PAGE 208: Jumping off a rocky
cliff in Curaçao.*

*THIS PAGE: Thatched huts provide
much-needed shade along the
shores of Aruba, one of the
Caribbean's more arid islands.*

*OPPOSITE: The gabled roofs,
colourful façades and boats
along the Punda waterfront
make Curaçao look like the
'Amsterdam of the Tropics'.*

Drawing inspiration from similar origins, the local cuisine might as well be called Papiamento. Dutch influence comes across in dishes rich with cheese such as savoury pies filled with cheese and meat (pastechi) or hunks of baked gouda stuffed with meat or fish (keshi yena). One of the most distinctive dishes is funchi, a side dish made from cornmeal mush that is often served during breakfast. As one might expect, seafood plays a prominent role in ABC cuisine. Local desserts include the bolo pretu, a wedding and holiday cake that can be prepared with as many as six types of liquor.

Given the cultural diversity, eating in the ABCs is an international affair with cuisine from around the world and restaurants in the most romantic settings. Hidden inside an old plantation house, Gasparito offers Aruba's best traditional dining and doubles as a gallery of local folk art. At the stylish Astrolab Observatory restaurant in Curaçao, diners can enjoy escabeche of red mullet with goat cheese polenta or red snapper with artichoke pesto while admiring art in the adjacent Kurá Hulanda sculpture garden.

aruba: sun, sand + shipwrecks

Aruba is the epitome of Caribbean fun in the sun. It is an island that combines white-sand beaches and rowdy nightlife, duty-free shopping and adrenaline-pumping sports. With around a million visitors per year, Aruba is now the top tourist destination in the southwest Caribbean, a major stop on the cruise ship circuit and a Spring Break hangout for partying North American youngsters.

Twenty years ago, Aruba was a different island. The economy was dominated by petroleum and many of the beaches were empty and there was barely anything that one might actually call a boutique. The transformation started in the mid 1980s when Exxon decided to close its huge oil refinery after operating for nearly a century. In 1986, Aruba split from the Netherlands Antilles and became a self-ruling territory within the Kingdom of the Netherlands. It was a tumultuous time for the island; the future of the Arubans was anything but assured. However, in less than two decades, Aruba was transformed into one of the rising stars of Caribbean tourism.

Aruba's rowdy tourist strip is a 10-km (6-mile) stretch of sand on the southwest shore. The strip is actually made up of separate strands—Palm, Eagle and Manchebo beaches—all of them flanked by beach bars and chic resort hotels. Name your water sport and chances are you will find something that satisfies your requirements. Offshore, the diving is great. Sites include the Malmok Reef and several World War II shipwrecks (like the German freighter *Antilla* and the oil tanker *Pedernalis*). Even older than these underwater relics is De Olden Molen (The Old Mill), a Dutch windmill built in 1804. Located near Eagle Beach, it has been converted into a restaurant.

aruba: casinos + shopping malls

Most of the casinos are found along the beach, but Aruba's oldest and most elegant gambling establishment is Crystal Casino in Oranjestad. Caribbean stud poker is the game of choice, but punters may also try their luck at baccarat, blackjack, roulette or one-arm bandits. The casino is open 24-hours a day and is modelled after Casino Royale in Monte Carlo. Do not forget your djucu. The djucu, good-luck charms that many Arubans use whenever they gamble, is basically a little sack of shiny black stones from the sea that becomes warm when rubbed.

Fort Zoutman, constructed in the late 18th century, is Aruba's oldest building. The museum behind its stout red-and-white tower displays artefacts of early Dutch colonial days. Oranjestad, with its countless boutiques and air-conditioned malls, is the best place on the island to shop. The bustling Caya Betico Croes in the middle of town and Seaport Village near the cruise terminal are the most popular shopping areas. In these areas you can buy Colombian emeralds, locally crafted gold jewellery, upscale sports clothes, ready-to-wear from around the globe, Swiss watches, Baccarat crystals; and a little bit of Holland thrown in for good measure: gouda cheese, wooden clogs and exquisite Delft porcelain.

THIS PAGE (FROM TOP): Oranjestad, the Aruban capital, glitters with the lights from casinos, boutiques and nightclubs; one-armed bandits await punters at the casinos in Aruba.

OPPOSITE (FROM TOP): Gruesome relics of the Afro-Caribbean slave trade in Curaçao's Kura Hulanda Museum; the windmill, De Olden Molen, was built in 1804 and stands at Aruba's Eagle Beach.

aruba: wide open spaces

The Aruban desert is studded with wildly contorted divi-divi trees, aloe vera plants, candelabra cactus and rocky outcrops. At Ayo and Casibari, there are even rock formations and ancient Arawak petroglyphs on cave walls and boulders. The best way to explore the interior is on horseback. Arikok National Park has more than 30 km (19 miles) of well-marked hiking and biking trails, as well as bat-filled caverns and the remains of a gold mine. The north coast is another nature lover's heaven, especially the dunes of Boca Prins, where sea turtles crawl ashore to lay eggs.

Strong offshore winds make Aruba great for windsurfing and kitesurfing, especially at the west coast enclave of Malmok and Boca Grandi in the northeast. Every summer, there is the Windsurfing Festival that includes music, food and an international competition. Another summer tradition—found nowhere else in the Caribbean—is drag racing at the Palo Marga Raceway near San Nicolas. The participants race anything they can get their hands on—motorcycles, muscle cars, pickup trucks or ordinary sedans.

curaçao: the fine art of tropical living

Curaçao was a bustling seaport and regional market for hundreds of years while the other two islands were slumbering in tropical reverie. It was also a haven for refugees such as British Pilgrims, Spanish Jews and Simón Bolívar, the South American liberator.

THIS PAGE (FROM TOP): Aruba's Natural Bridge Beach is framed by a mighty stone arch; ancient Arawak petroglyphs in a cave in the island's interior.

OPPOSITE (FROM TOP): The colourful Alto Vista Chapel is one of the few landmarks on Aruba's quiet north shore; Curaçao's landmark, the Queen Emma Bridge, is fondly called the 'Swinging Old Lady' because it moves sideways to allow ships to pass.

In recent years, there has been a flowering of art and architecture that has transformed Curaçao into one of the most vibrant destinations in the region.

Willemstad, the capital, is Amsterdam with a tropical twist. There are pastel buildings with gabled roofs along canals that reflect both the anchored schooners and the starry nights. Stone forts protect the entrance to St. Anne's Bay (Sinta Anna-baai), which you can cross either by ferry or by the famous Queen Emma Bridge—the 'Swinging Old Lady' that slowly floats open at least once per hour. Local painters and sculptors exhibit their works in their ateliers or the galleries of the Otrobanda district. Some of the island's homegrown artists, like painter Nena Sanchez and flamboyant metal sculptor Hubert Kirindongo, are renowned throughout the region.

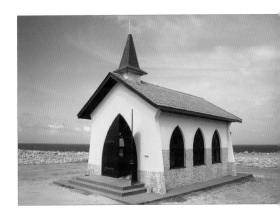

The local music scene is just as eclectic. On any given night, half a dozen clubs—many of them in Willemstad's trendy Salinja area—feature live bands. But instead of calypso and reggae, bands play local genres such as seu, tumba, zumbi, and tambu. Tambu was once banned by the Dutch as it was deemed to be too sexually suggestive and culturally subversive. African-American musical forms have also made a major impact. Much like baseball, jazz and blues were introduced by expatriate refinery workers after World War I. Cab Calloway and Louis Armstrong even performed in Willemstad in the 1930s. Soon Curaçao was producing its own jazz and blues maestros. This tradition continues today with nascent international stars like Randal Corsen who won an Edison Jazz World Music Award in 2004. Curaçao's most romantic jazz venue is the Blues Café at the end of the Avila Beach pier in Willemstad.

curaçao: architectural rebirth + renaissance

Curaçao is a regional leader in architectural renovation. Colonial buildings have not been replaced by modern structures, and the architectural heritage has been systematically conserved. The photogenic Punda district—nucleus of the city's duty-free shopping—never fell into disrepair. But the ramshackle Otrobanda area on the western flank of St. Anne's Bay had a different story. Many locals wrote it off as a lost cause as the

majority of its buildings were too dilapidated to save. After UNESCO declared Otrobanda a World Heritage Site in 1997, the government began searching for investors to refurbish the historic neighbourhood.

Dutch philanthropist Jacob Gelt Dekker took up the call, and poured millions of dollars into renovation. The end result was Kurá Hulanda, a cluster of 86 structures in the heart of Otrobanda resurrected as restaurants, galleries, shops and boutique hotels. Kurá Hulanda also has a remarkable museum that showcases art and artefacts from around the globe.

bonaire's beauty

Bonaire has the distinction of being one of the most ecologically sound islands in the Caribbean. The waters surrounding Bonaire have been declared a marine sanctuary. To appreciate the teeming sea life, simply wade into the surf at places like Thousand Steps and Nukove. Divers can feast their eyes in the more than 80 sites around the island.

Bonaire also offers some of the region's best bird watching. Around 200 species, including the yellow-shouldered Amazon, Bonaire green parrot and pink flamingo, can be seen here. Top feather stalking spots are Washington-Slagbaai National Park and a marshy lake called Goto Meer. Sprawling across more than 5,000 hectares (13,000 acres) of tropical desert terrain, Washington-Slagbaai was the first national park in the Dutch Antilles (1974) and is also a brilliant place to hike, bike or merely laze on the beach. For those who like to feel 'one with nature', Bonaire is also home to the only clothing-optional resort in the ABCs.

Kralendijk, the island's quaint little capital, is easily explored in a couple of hours. The waterfront Fish Market no longer deals in seafood, but there are plenty of other items on sale including fresh tropical fruit from Venezuela. But do not expect the urban delights of Aruba or Curaçao. Beyond a few duty-free shops, the town does not have an awful lot of distractions. Shopping is not why people come to Bonaire. Nature is what this island is all about..

THIS PAGE (FROM TOP): Outdoor cafés and duty-free shops grace the Punda waterfront in Willemstad; Curaçao liqueur continues to be produced in a 19th-century copper still.

OPPOSITE: A school of grunts under a pier in Bonaire, one of the Caribbean's most popular scuba destinations.

The waters surrounding Bonaire have been declared a marine sanctuary.

Bucuti Beach

THIS PAGE (FROM TOP): *The distinct contemporary style of Bucuti's recently refurbished guestrooms perfectly complements its original feel of European sophistication; one of the lounges in the wing housing the Tara Beach Suites.*

OPPOSITE: *Fortuitously positioned amid the tranquil, breathtaking beauty of Eagle Beach, Bucuti's renown as Aruba's most dreamy hideaway and the island's most elegant resort is well-deserved. Bucuti has also earned badges of honour for its impeccable service and genuine warmth.*

Lying lazily in the sun-drenched beauty of Southern Caribbean and tucked away on the soft, pure, palm-studded sands of Eagle Beach—celebrated as one of the 'Dream Beaches of the World'—is Aruba's most romantic escape, Bucuti Beach resort.

This blindingly white gem stands out against the azure allure of the Caribbean's waters and is surrounded by lush indigenous flora and the rich topography of its island home, which has magnetized the world for its spectacular coral bridges and plunging limestone grottoes. Here, the beaches curve like a wide, welcoming smile along Aruba's western shores, sloping into the glimmering turquoise translucence of the sea.

Gentle breezes bring the tang of the sea and the aroma of tropical blossoms into each of Bucuti Beach's stylish accommodations, which range from spacious rooms and suites to private studios for two and four exclusive

penthouse suites for couples. This first-class boutique resort is elegantly clad in simple European-style design and fronted by a palm-framed façade with wide verandahs running all through the length of its sides.

Inside, the clean, contemporary décor and dark wood furnishings are subtly lit. The fully-appointed guestrooms and suites all boast regally-sized beds, and a balcony or terrace from which to appreciate views of the setting sun. Granite counters and deep Kohler soaking tubs add an enduring quality to spotlessly white, cream and cherry wood tinted rooms. This pleasingly neutral colour scheme is the perfect counterbalance to the riotous blaze of colours outside.

For that special occasion, the resort's penthouses truly are the last word in ultimate luxury and indulgence. Bird's-eye views of the ever-shifting Caribbean; a smooth, white pedestal bath; a four-poster bed draped in white gossamer...honeymoons were created with dreamy spaces like this in mind.

Bucuti's acclaimed fame for its hallmark sensitivity and doting staff is testament to the genuine warmth and meticulous attention of its owners, who are hands-on in managing the resort. Their impeccable—and understated—thoughtfulness and service continue in the resort's latest addition, Intermezzo Spa. With top-notch services and treatment cabins, the spa features an oceanfront cabin on the beach to encourage a closer affinity with nature. Let the expert touch of Intermezzo's therapists dissipate the stresses of the real world under the watchful eye of the ever-smiling Aruban sun. Those who prefer to lull in the privacy of a quiet, intimate space will take to the spa's cosy indoor cabins.

As dusk melts into night, contemplate the moonlit beauty of this extraordinary beach while dining at the Pirates' Nest. A replica of a 16th-century Dutch galleon, this imaginative venue revels in its eye-popping buffets, scintillating champagne breakfasts and superb seafood and steaks. Seven Seas

Smoked Salmon, Filet Mignon and Pan-Fried Mahi-Mahi are the absolute specialities here. The ambience, surroundings and the cuisine itself perfectly capture the colourful style, spirit and distinct flair of Aruba.

FACTS		
ROOMS	48 superior rooms • 11 deluxe rooms • 2 one-bedroom junior suites • 38 Tara Beach Suites • 3 studios • 4 one-bedroom penthouse suites	
FOOD	Pirates' Nest: à la carte	
DRINK	Sand Bar	
FEATURES	Intermezzo Spa • fitness centre • freshwater pool • library • boutique • weddings • concierge arranges for off-site water sports, sailing and scuba diving courses	
BUSINESS	business centre	
NEARBY	Antilla shipwreck • Arikok National Wildlife Park • Bushiribana gold mill ruins	
CONTACT	LG Smith Boulevard 55B, PO Box 1347, Eagle Beach, Aruba • telephone: +297.583 1100 • facsimile: +297.582 5272 • email: info@bucuti.com • website: www.bucuti.com	

PHOTOGRAPHS COURTESY OF BUCUTI BEACH.

Tierra del Sol Resort, Spa + Country Club

Luxuriating in the Caribbean's shimmering blues off Venezuela's northern tip, Aruba is perhaps the most revisited of all the islands in the region. An island of unique contrasts, here windmills are nudged by cooling trade-winds, and trendy beachwear shares shelf space with wooden shoes.

Occupying a privileged location near Aruba's rugged northwestern tip, looking out across dramatic dunes and desert-like land-scapes to the famed California Lighthouse, is the all-encompassing paradise of Tierra del Sol. Here is, wrapped in an intimate and serene country club ambience, a sprawling 243-hectare (600-acre) property of luxuriously appointed condominiums, villas and estate homes, all perfectly tailored for the indulgent traveller or permanent visitor. The villas sport terracotta-tile roofs and creamy stucco walls reminiscent of a Mediterranean village setting and also feature spacious rooms and suites, private plunge pools and maid service.

Not merely a holiday option, Tierra del Sol is an exclusive and constantly evolving community—and one with a master plan. The estate's selection of posh accommodations is clustered into cosy neighbourhoods replete with a thoroughly spoiling menu of services

THIS PAGE (FROM TOP): The country club's championship golf course—inspired by Robert Trent Jones Junior—offers some of the most celebrated links in the region; gourmet cuisine is served at the golf course where, with its almost arid, desert-like landscaping, it is not difficult to imagine being transported somewhere along the coast of Spain.

OPPOSITE: Tierra del Sol offers an appealing alternative to the typical resort and country club. Arranged in a master plan, this is a community of luxury villas, condominiums and estate homes with premier amenities—just around the corner are spa, tennis and fitness facilities and, even a casino.

and amenities—an 18-hole championship golf course designed by Robert Trent Jones Junior, a state-of-the-art fitness centre, award-winning gourmet restaurants, world-class spa and beauty treatments, as well as exclusive boutiques and entertainment.

Surrounded by stunning white beaches and pristine shores, Tierra del Sol provides a superb outlet for the sportive to pursue their favourite pastimes in vast, beautiful settings. Complete your free weights routine with the heat-hazed horizon as your point of focus, or tee-off on the meandering links of Robert Trent Jones Junior's golf course, studded with giant cacti and intriguing rock formations.

For those seeking to be pampered, this is heaven on earth. The 372-sq-m (4,000-sq-ft) Body & Soul Spa, Salon and Fitness Centre offers delights ranging from hydrotherapy and Vichy showers to a Moroccan Cocoon and exquisite signature treatments such as the exotically named Desert Heat Body Wrap. Afterwards, relax with a cooling smoothie in the lounge or beneath the beaming rays by the pool. Nearby, Le Dôme restaurant serves Belgian-French cuisine amid the breathtaking scenery of the famous golf course.

Besides such winning elements, a large part of Tierra del Sol's enduring and magnetic appeal lies in its distinct blend of European sophistication, North American ingenuity and unparalleled service standards and, of course, the down-to-earth friendliness of Caribbean culture. The best thing about Tierra del Sol has yet, however, to be mentioned. Fabulous destinations often stir in travellers a desire to make it home once the vacation is over. In this particular paradise, the luxury villas can be purchased and made your own.

FACTS		
	ROOMS	clusters of luxury villas, condominiums and estate homes
	FOOD	Le Dôme • Lookout Bar and Grill
	DRINK	lounge
	FEATURES	Robert Trent Jones Junior-designed championship golf course • tennis centre • Body & Soul Spa, Salon and Fitness Centre • casino • boutiques • real estate sales and rental
	NEARBY	California Lighthouse • Malmok beach and reef • scuba diving • water sports • Antilla shipwreck • Oranjestad
	CONTACT	Malmokweg z/n, Oranjestad, Caya di Solo, Aruba • telephone: +297.586 7800 • facsimile: +297.586 4970 • email: tierra.rent@setarnet.aw • website: www.tierradelsol.com

PHOTOGRAPHS COURTESY OF TIERRA DEL SOL RESORT, SPA + COUNTRY CLUB.

continentalcaribbean

Gulf of Mexico

CUBA

Arrecife ○ Alacrán °○

Isla Contoy

San Felipe •
Chiquilá •
Isla Mujeres •
Puerto Juárez •
Cancún
Puerto Morelos •

Yucatán Channel

Mérida

Playa del Carmen •

> Maroma Resort + Spa
> Hotel Básico
> Deseo [Hotel + Lounge]

• Cozumel

Paamul •
Isla de Cozumel

Bahía de Campeché

Campeché •

Yucatán

▲ 250

• Tulum

• Punta Allen
Bahía de la Ascención

Bahía del Espírito Santo

Caribbean Sea

MEXICO

▲ 212

Chetumal

Banco Chinchorro

▲ 309

• Xcalak

Ambergris Cay

Orange Walk

BELIZE

Belize

Turneffe Is.

BELMOPAN

San Ignacio •

N

Dangriga •

▲ 858

1020
▲ 970
Maya Mountains
▲ 1122
▲ 1000

> Turtle Inn

Placentia •

Gulf of Honduras

San Antonio •

Punta Gorda

GUATEMALA

▲ 3141

HONDURAS

Legend	
=	Highways
▬	Main roads
—	Other roads
✈	Airport
●	Urban area
○	Lake
⊙	Dry Salt Lake
	3000 - 5000 m
	2000 - 3000 m
	1000 - 2000 m
	500 - 1000 m
	200 - 500 m

0 km   60   120   180 km

caribbean continent

The islands of the Caribbean are flanked by large continental landmasses to the south and to the west. However, despite the proximity, the offshore and continental Caribbean regions have long been treated as separate entities that have little in common with one another. This could not be further from the truth. The islands share much more than one might think with their continental counterparts including languages, landscapes and traditions. And on the holiday front, there are parts of the mainland that even offer a richer Caribbean experience than some islands.

It is not hard to see how this perception came about. During colonial times, the West Indies became increasingly cosmopolitan (and less Spanish), while most of the mainland continued to be domains of Spain. By the early 19th century, nearly all of South and Central America had gained independence. Yet all of the island territories (save Haiti) would remain colonies for another hundred years or more.

In recent years, diplomats and politicians from continental nations have forged much closer ties with the islands. Continental nations comprise about half the membership of the Organization of Caribbean States (OCS). As in many other parts of the globe, sports and games help foster strong international relations. Every four years, the Central American and Caribbean Games bring together more than 7,000 athletes from 31 island and mainland nations.

exotic yucatán

The vast Yucatán Peninsula—with its rainforests and ancient Mayan ruins—separates the Caribbean Sea from the Gulf of Mexico. The peninsula has a land area nearly as large as Spain but has only a fraction of the population. Apart from the shore, large parts of the peninsula are sparsely populated and remain mostly undeveloped. The Yucatán coast, on the other hand, is one of the Caribbean's fastest developing areas. Dubbed the 'Riviera Maya' in deference to the traditional people of the Yucatán, the coast is the region's hot new travel destination.

PAGE 222: *Young girls marching in a patriotic parade on Mexico's Day of the Revolution in the city of Izamal on the Yucatán Peninsula.*

THIS PAGE: *The chic hotels in Playa del Carmen provide the perfect getaway for those who love to snooze in the sun.*

OPPOSITE: *Giant stone sculptures among the Maya ruins at Tulum, south of the Riviera Maya.*

Geographically speaking, both Belize and northern Guatemala are part of the Yucatán, but the name generally refers to just the Mexican portion, which comprises the states of Campeche, Yucatán and Quintana Roo, plus the offshore resort islands of Cancún, Cozumel and Isla Mujeres. In the past, it was difficult (and sometimes impossible) to travel from one part of the Yucatán to another due to the lack of roads and airports. The development of tourism in the late 20th century, however, has led to improvements in local infrastructure. Visitors can now travel to many parts of the peninsula and cross international borders with relative ease.

The peninsula has become widely known in recent decades as the impact site of a massive asteroid that hit the earth around 65 million years ago. Scientists theorize that huge amounts of dust and particles thrown up by the impact dramatically altered the global climate. This climate change is believed to have led to the extinction of the dinosaurs on the planet. Most of Yucatán state, including the city of Merida, lies within the ancient crater, known as the Chicxulub crater.

the glorious mayan civilization

The Maya had settled in the Yucatán and developed an agriculture based on the cultivation of maize as early as 1500 BCE. By 200 CE, Mayan civilization had evolved into the most advanced in the entire western hemisphere with sophisticated mathematics, architecture, art, a hieroglyphic writing system, an incredibly accurate calendar based on precise astronomical observations, and a complicated social and religious structure.

As urban dwellers, the ancient Maya built great cities like Tikal, Uxmal and Chichén Itzá that may have supported as many as a million inhabitants. All of these cities were dominated by great stone pyramids and palaces that are now the most compelling of the region's attractions. The Mayan empire spread

into the highlands of central Mexico and deep into Central America, stretching as far south as modern-day Nicaragua. The Maya traded widely throughout the Americas and they may have even exchanged goods with mariners from across the great oceans. Around 800 CE, Mayan civilization went into a quick and catastrophic decline. Many of the great cities were abandoned and the empire fragmented. The Mayan collapse is still one of history's great mysteries. Archaeologists believe the collapse may have been due to drought, famine, civil war or a combination of all three.

THIS PAGE: El Castillo, also known as the Pyramid of Kukulcán, rises above the main plaza at the ancient Mayan city of Chichén Itzá, Yucatán Peninsula.

OPPOSITE (FROM TOP): Sombreros can be made of straw or of felt and protect locals from the sun; children dancing at the Sunday Festival in Merida, the capital of the Yucatán state.

enduring maya

By the arrival of the Spanish in the early 1500s, the great Mayan cities had faded into the jungle and the Maya were little more than fishermen and farmers. With no apparent treasures to plunder, the Spanish took their time conquering the Yucatán, a process that took nearly 200 years—and to some extent, never completed. Divided into three political spheres in the early 19th century, the peninsula continued to be ignored well into modern times. The glories of the ancient Mayan civilization remained secret until 1839 when American explorer John Lloyd Stephens struck out across the Yucatán in search of the legendary lost cities, many of which he actually found. This was perhaps the birth of the region's tourism industry.

Although immigrants from other parts of Mexico have drifted into the Yucatán in search of land and jobs, the Maya remain the region's dominant ethnic group. The Mayan language, with its nearly two dozen dialects, is still widely spoken. Although nominally Catholic, the Maya continue to hold on to their ancient religious beliefs. Rituals such as the burning of copal incense are still practised and the shaman continues to be important to village life. Many of the traditional Yucatec arts and crafts also continue to thrive, including hammock-making and the embroidery of huipiul skirts.

quintana roo, eastern yucatán

Perched on the peninsula's eastern shore, just north of Belize, the Mexican state of Quintana Roo reflects the modern face of the Yucatán. It is a place of gorgeous white-sand strands and hip little beach resorts, untouched coral reefs and wilderness areas that seem little changed from ancient Mayan times.

In 1967, the Mexican government initiated a three-year study to determine the ideal place on the Caribbean coast to create a purpose-built resort. Cancún, then virtually uninhabited, was identified. Today, the island has become one of the world's most popular beach resorts. Cancún's glitz eventually spread to the mainland, down the Quintana Roo coast. The region has since been called the 'Riviera Maya'.

Although it continues to expand, the heart of the Riviera Maya is the palm-shaded coast between Puerto Morelos and Tulum. Situated just 15 minutes south of Cancún's international airport, Puerto Morelos retains much of its bygone ambience, a town where fishing boats continue to outnumber Hobbie Cat sailboats and where the seafood is literally straight off the dock. On the outskirts of town, Yaax Che Botanic Gardens is a great place to wander amongst indigenous plants, while the nearby crocodile farm is the place to see the Yucatán's largest reptile. The crocodile may also be sighted in the Sian Ka'an Biosphere Refuge beyond Tulum.

playa del carmen

Playa del Carmen is the epitome of Riviera Maya chic. It is an oasis filled with championship golf courses, world-class spas, swank hotels and the Yucatán's finest dining. The streets of Playa are laid out in a grid, and one of the most famous streets is Quinta Avenida (literally, 'Fifth Avenue'), where the shopping experience is simply delightful. The perfect foil to Cancún's brash spring break vibe, Playa del Carmen charms with European savoir-faire and understated elegance that comes across in low-rise resorts scattered amongst the beachfront palms.

The spas of Playa offer indulgences from around the globe: everything from shiatsu and kundalini yoga to Swedish deep tissue massage and Egyptian milk baths. Many spas use local ingredients and Mayan treatments like the cenote clay sobada (massage), aromatherapy baths filled with Yucatán jungle flowers, and the legendary temazcal—a ritual that involves spiritual and physical cleansing in a traditional Mayan steam house.

The Mayan cuisine is just as inviting. Gourmands can savour old-time favourites like lime soup, seasoned chicken baked in banana leaves (pollo pibil) and pork marinated in sour orange juice (poc chuc). Many of the best eateries blend local and international cuisine, like the excellent Casa del Agua, which was voted one of the 50 best new restaurants in the world when it opened in 2001.

rolling down to tulum

The Riviera Maya continues south of Playa del Carmen. Here, the broad sweep of coast includes the posh Puerto Aventuras marina and residential development, and the intriguing Xcaret Eco Theme Park. The only one of its kind in the Caribbean, visitors to the Xcaret can snorkel in underground rivers, swim with dolphins and stop by the archaeological sites and re-creations of ancient Mayan life.

Continuing south, Highway 307 runs all the way down the coast to Tulum, where the most important ruins in all of the Yucatán are located. Protected within the city's thick limestone walls are 60 structures ranging from a grand palace and a stone well where human sacrifices were once carried out, to a stunningly well-preserved Mayan pyramid called 'El Castillo' which sits on the edge of a high sea cliff.

belize: jaguars + ruins

Wedged between Guatemala and Mexico, Belize is part of Central America. But its history, culture, atmosphere—and English dialect—are strongly reminiscent of other formerly British parts of the West Indies. With thick jungle, ancient Mayan ruins and

facilities for 'extreme sports', Belize offers a combination of culture and adventure that few places in the Caribbean can match. And that is not all. The longest barrier reef in the western hemisphere lies just offshore.

Scuba diving, snorkelling, hiking, mountain biking, sports fishing and beach horse riding are just a few of the outdoor activities available in Belize. Golden sand, and seawater that averages 27°C (80°F), are just footsteps away. Visitors can paddle down a river in a jaguar preserve, hike through virgin rainforest to reach cooling pools at the bottom of a 30-m (100-ft) waterfall, rappel into the mouth of a 90-m (300-ft) deep limestone sinkhole, or explore Mayan palaces and pyramids hidden in the jungle.

buccaneers + british protection

Trivia time: 'What was the former name of Belize?'. Anyone with more than a passing interest in history knows the answer to be 'British Honduras'. 'Belize' is a variant of the ancient Maya word for 'muddy water'—referring to the prevailing colour of most Belizean rivers, especially after heavy rain. Some historians claim the name is a Spanish corruption of 'Wallace', the surname of the English buccaneer who founded the first permanent settlement in 1638.

Like much of the continental Caribbean coast, Belize was ignored by the Spanish conquistadors, who made a beeline for the highlands and much more obvious riches. With so much of the shore lined by treacherous shoals and reefs, Belize could not even serve as a port. The Spanish considered it a coast best avoided, a fact that did not go unnoticed by the pirates of the Caribbean, who began to call on Belize as both a safe haven and booty cache. Many of the buccaneers who decided to settle down along this coast—and become respectable citizens—were British. The British government felt obliged to protect them from the Spanish and in 1862, London formalized the arrangement, creating a crown colony called the British Honduras. It eventually became the independent nation of Belize in 1981.

THIS PAGE (FROM TOP): Although better known for its beaches, Playa del Carmen has lush tropical greenery, perfect for exploring; a jaguar lies on its back and playfully gnaws on a branch in a preserve in Belize.

OPPOSITE (FROM TOP): The food at the Riviera Maya is just as chic as its hotels and spas; the Xcaret Eco Theme Park, complete with Mayan ruins and underground rivers.

Roughly two-thirds of the population are either creole (mixed European and African ancestry) or mestizo (mixed European and Amerindian). There are also pure-blooded Maya and the mysterious Garifuna (the descendants of escaped slaves), as well as Arab, Indian, Chinese migrants, and German-speaking Mennonite Christians who came in the late 1950s because they quite rightly thought that Belize had the wilderness solitude they could no longer find in the West.

preserving national treasures

Belize is all about adventure—with a cushy landing. The country boasts some of the most luxurious accommodations in the Caribbean. Visitors can stay in eco-lodges and wilderness retreats, where the pampering is as much a part of the experience as the jungle-covered Mayan temples.

Belizeans are determined to preserve their natural heritage and about a quarter of the country is given over to national parks and reserves. These reserves are among the best in Central America in terms of both wildlife protection and visitor enjoyment.

Six of the parks are managed by the Audubon Society, including the spectacular Cockscomb Basin Wildlife Preserve, which is the world's first jaguar reserve. Jaguars roam the 40,000-hectare (98,800-acre) park, which is also home to four other species of wild cats. Crooked Tree Wildlife Sanctuary is a haven for bird watchers. It is a maze of inland lagoons and waterways where hundreds of bird species can be spotted. Blue Hole National Park protects a sapphire sinkhole of the same name, as well as the fascinating underground world of St. Herman's Cave. While the Blue Hole is strictly protected, the limestone landscapes outside the park provide venues for adventure sports like potholing and tubing down subterranean rivers in the Maya Mountains.

Most of the nation's Mayan treasures are also protected within the confines of national parks. The Cayo District of Western Belize boasts the greatest concentration of ancient ruins. It includes the Mayan city of Caracol (where more than 36,000 structures have been discovered) and the Maya ceremonial centre of Xunantunich with its towering stone temples. There are more impressive ruins at Lamanai (with its giant stone heads) in the north and near Punta Gorda in the south. Located in an area that remains largely occupied by the Maya even today, Punta Gorda is also a staging point for visits to indigenous villages, where visitors can enjoy unique home stays and get a chance to snooze in hammocks beneath thatched roofs.

belize barrier reef

Stretching nearly 300 km (186 miles) from north to south, the Belize Barrier Reef is the largest coral formation in the western hemisphere. The reef marks the outer edge of a giant limestone plateau that underpins the Yucatán.

East of the reef, the seafloor plunges into the deep blue Caribbean where submerged walls, sunken caves and other underwater formations offer spectacular sights for divers. The visibility here can reach an astounding 60 m (197 ft). These offshore waters are also teeming with big game fish. West of the reef, the shallow

THIS PAGE: Jaguars and other wild cats roam freely in the dense tropical forest of the Cockscomb Basin Wildlife Preserve.

OPPOSITE (FROM TOP): A handprint adorns the wall of a Mayan cave in Roaring Creek Valley; Tiger Cave, in southern Belize, opens into a massive limestone labyrinth where ancient Mayan artefacts can be seen.

coastal waters, about 5 m (16 ft) deep, are dotted with 175 sandy islands that locals call 'cayes' (pronounced 'keys'). The waters here are ideal for swimming, snorkelling, sailing, water skiing and kayaking.

Accommodation in the islands ranges from secluded, thatched-roof palapas to über-hip resorts with lavish suites and gourmet eateries. Ambergris Caye and Caulker Caye are the major isles, and can be reached by ferry (daily) and puddle-jumper airline service from Belize City. Beach resorts have also started to sprout on the mainland in recent years. Perched on miles of empty sand and turquoise water, they can be reached by roads that have whimsical names like 'Hummingbird Highway'.

a true city

With more than 60,000 people, Belize City is the country's largest urban area and the only place in Belize that can be truly called a city. In recent years, it has become a major cruise port. However, the harbour is not deep enough for large ships, which have to anchor offshore, like great floating castles.

Founded in the 17th century, this seaport on the banks of Haulover Creek has been the focus of Belizean politics and culture for more than 350 years. Built of bricks formerly used as ship ballast, St. John's Cathedral (built in 1847) has survived many storms and is now the oldest Anglican church in Central America. The courthouse overlooking Battlefield Park is said to be even older (built in 1820) and for years housed the colonial administration. Travelling back even further in time, the oldest grave in Yarborough Cemetery dates from the old pirate days in the mid-18th century.

Belize City is also the starting and ending point for the country's oldest and biggest international event—the annual Cross Country Classic, a 225-km (140-mile) bicycle race into the Belizian countryside that takes place on the Saturday before Easter Sunday. The first race was staged in 1928 and now attracts avid cyclists from all over. The Classic is concluded inside Marion Jones Stadium, named after the Olympic gold-medal winning sprinter, who holds dual American-Belizean citizenship.

THIS PAGE (FROM LEFT): The waters off Belize is home to the second longest barrier reef on earth; a sign advertising a bar greets visitors to Caulker Caye.
OPPOSITE: The Lighthouse Reef Atoll surrounds the Blue Hole, a sunken cave system that is a haven for scuba divers.

Blue Hole National Park protects a sapphire sinkhole...

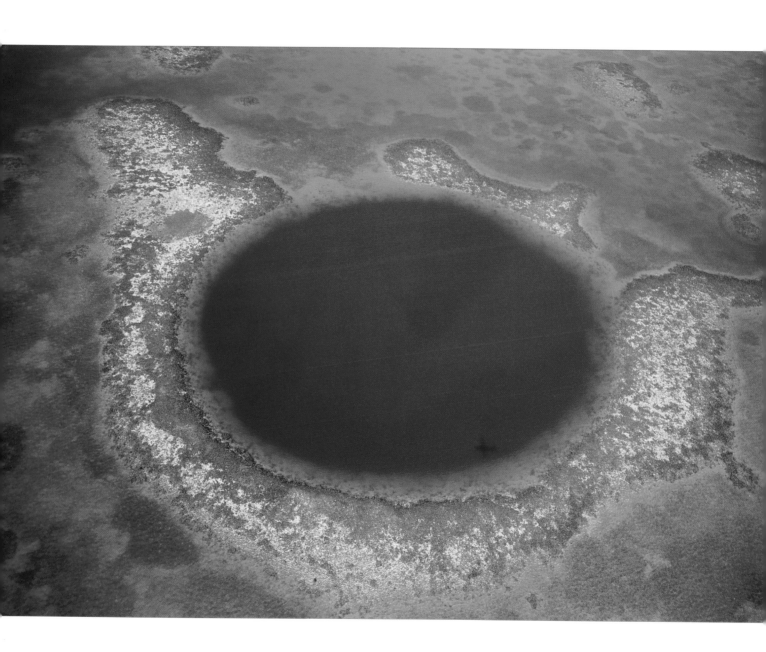

Turtle Inn

Film director Francis Ford Coppola is perhaps not the likeliest of candidates to be running a luxury 'eco-tourism' resort nestled in verdant Belize. Yet, at Turtle Inn, this is exactly what he does.

What started out as a private retreat for close friends soon grew into a business—Coppola now runs several environmentally-friendly resorts in Belize, of which one is powered by clean, hydroelectric energy.

Turtle Inn is based in the seaside community of Placencia. The scope for diving and snorkelling is tremendous, being adjacent to the Belize Barrier Reef, the longest in the Western Hemisphere. You may also add an ecological dimension to your vacation by joining a reef tour, or simply kayak, scuba dive or do some leisure sailing. For other simple pleasures, you can opt to chill out by the freshwater pool or recline on the beautiful beaches with the book you've always wanted to read.

This is also the ideal base for wildlife lovers, where they can visit the Cockscomb Basin Wildlife Sanctuary and Jaguar Preserve, or steal glimpses of howler monkeys and crocodiles in Belize's rainforests. Fishing enthusiasts can indulge in saltwater flyfishing as they will get a chance to jump aboard 'Something Fishy' to stealthily stalk bone fish.

If it is tranquillity that you crave for, settle into the Sunset Spa, a striking building in the style of a Balinese Rice House. A sea salt body glow or Thai massage will soon restore your spiritual equilibrium.

In terms of accommodation, the Family Pavilion would be worth checking out for its hand-carved wood finishing and stone sculptures. It also comes with a terrace for oceanfront dining and a private pool surrounded by burgeoning tropical flowers. Roofed with traditional thatch, pleasant temperatures are maintained throughout the day inside the room.

Another highlight would be the Seafront Villas with Balinese-themed rooms and private walled gardens featuring outdoor showers.

All accommodations are within walking distance from the pristine sands of the Caribbean Sea.

It also comes as no surprise that Coppola's personal ethos have been subsumed into the preparation of dishes at The Mare Italian Restaurant. With organic produce supplied from Blancaneaux Lodge, guests can enjoy super-fresh cuisines.

As TV and the Internet are available only in the main lodge, Turtle Inn not only provides an absolute respite from life's daily bustle but also offers a glimpse into another reality where a luxurious yet sustainable lifestyle is evidently possible.

You've marvelled at Coppola's films like Apocalypse Now and The Godfather. It's time to do likewise with Turtle Inn.

FACTS

ROOMS	4 seafront villas • 1 seaview villa • 8 pool-side seaview cottages • 1 family pavilion • 2 garden view villas • 1 honeymoon cottage • 1 Chinese matrimonial suite • 1 seafront cottage • 4 seaview cottages • 2 garden view cottages
FOOD	The Mare Italian Restaurant: Italian
DRINK	Skip White Bar • beach bar
FEATURES	spa • 2 freshwater pools • beach • dive shop
NEARBY	jaguar preserve • Monkey River • Maya ruins
CONTACT	Central Reservations Office • telephone: +501.824 4912 • facsimile: +501.824 4913 • email: info@blancaneaux.com • website: www.blancaneaux.com

PHOTOGRAPHS COURTESY OF BLANCANEAUX RESORTS.

Hotel Básico

THIS PAGE: *Rooftop swimming pools assume the form of oversized oil drums.*

OPPOSITE (FROM LEFT): *The cocktail bar at the terrace; the unique design of the hotel speaks volume of its ingenuity—with its stripped-down, quasi-industrial look.*

U p until a few years ago, visitors to the Riviera Maya were restricted in their choice of accommodation to palapa-style beach huts at one end of the spectrum, and thousand-room mega-resorts at the other, with not much in between. Overlooked and ignored was the possibility that among the million or more people who travelled to the area each year, some would be looking for something a little bit more bespoke, something a little bit more eclectic, something a little bit more special.

All that changed with the recent arrival in the area of a dynamic quartet of Mexico City hoteliers, Carlos Couturier and brothers Moises, Rafael and Jaime Micha—founders and owners of the landmark HABITA and CONDESAdf hotels in Mexico City. They instinctively understood that a destination with as high a worldwide profile as the Mexican Caribbean deserved better. They recognized that a new generation of younger travellers was emerging onto the tourist scene whose tastes and requirements were more sophisticated than those of the average backpacker or family of four. They realized that there was a gaping hole in the market and proceeded to look for a way to fill it. The result is the Hotel Básico.

Do not be fooled by the name, Básico is anything but basic. Along with its sister hotel, Deseo [Hotel + Lounge], this 15-room lifestyle hotel, strategically located between the Caribbean Sea and downtown Playa del Carmen, is at the cutting-edge of cool—an ultra-savvy, ultra-cosmopolitan, ultra-hip hangout that breaks all the rules of hotel design and startles as much as it satisfies. In fact, it's no exaggeration to say that Básico is nothing less than a bold and brilliant attempt to single-handedly thrust Playa del Carmen into the forefront of the world's most stylish tourist destinations. And it works!

How did they do it? Well, for a start, there's the architectural style. They've

eschewed the usual clichés that characterize so many other five star hotels. You won't find the superficial fixtures and features, intended to hide the rough edges of the building's structure. Here, the emphasis is on a stripped-down, quasi-industrial appearance, with exposed support beams, walls of polished cement and floors covered with recycled tyres. Nor are there the usual objets d'art or pretentious artworks to clutter the view—the décor here is more likely to come in the form of inner tubes and functional pipe work. The end result is as utilitarian as it is beautiful, and like a work of modern art it has

traditional Mexican recipes and served with a selection of local side dishes such as beans, deep-fried bananas, and rice.

As an alternative, guests can take the freight elevator to the rooftop terrace where the Azotea bar serves seafood ceviche and some of the best mixed drinks in the region, including a wide variety of 'Latin cocktails', such as margaritas, mojitos, caipirinhas. At night this area transforms itself into an open-air lounge bar, with local DJ's and an electric 'marimba' sound to chill out to. Here, you will also find the twin rooftop swimming pools which resemble oversized oil drums—incongruous at first sight, but perfect for sipping one's drink while enjoying spectacular views of the sea or stars.

The bedrooms, too, are startlingly original in design and execution. Sure, they have all the usual amenities that come with a five star experience, such as flat screen TV's, DVDs, air conditioning and 100 per cent cotton sheets. But they also come complete with a host of unique features, including unique multi-use high beds with integrated desks, fins for skin diving and complimentary Polaroid cameras.

But it's not just the bold design and clever details that mark Hotel Básico out from the herd of other hotels in the area. The staff, for example, are an international bunch, stylishly attired and looking like

THIS PAGE: Guests will be tempted to suntan in the open-air terrace and lounge.

OPPOSITE (FROM LEFT): The cleverly conceived bathroom design is not only functional but warm and inviting in its own way; the bedroom renders a spartan yet cosy feel, providing a sanctuary for the somnolent.

a tendency to leave the beholder challenged yet pleasantly surprised.

This revolutionary attitude to the everyday aspects of life extends even to the food and drink on offer. The restaurant on the first floor, has a kitchen set up to look like a regional Mexican market, open to all and allowing guests to select which ingredients they'd like and the manner in which they'd like to have them. Specialities of the house include fresh local fish and seafood, prepared by local chefs according to

This 15-room lifestyle hotel is at the cutting-edge of cool...

they'd just stepped off a nearby catwalk. They can relate to their clientele and won't cramp anyone's style.

The owners also put a great deal of thought into its superb location. Step out of the door on one side and you'll find yourself in the hustle and bustle of downtown Playa del Carmen. Bars, restaurants, nightlife, shopping—they're all there just yards from the hotel entrance, making this the perfect choice for those who want to get the most out of their holiday—24/7.

On the other side, just one block away, is one of the finest beaches on the Costa Maya. And, as if that wasn't enough, Playa del Carmen allows easy access to many of the nearby attractions, including the magnificent Mayan ruins at Tulum, Coba and Chichén Itzá, and the various cenotes—or sinkholes—which dot the surrounding landscape and make for such excellent swimming.

FACTS		
	ROOMS	12 rooms • 3 suites
	FOOD	Mexican
	DRINK	rooftop bar • lounge bar • juice bar
	FEATURES	2 pools
	NEARBY	Playa del Carmen • Tulum • Coba • Chichén Itzá
	CONTACT	5th avenue and 10th street, Playa del Carmen, Quintana Roo 77710, Mexico • telephone: +52.984 879 4448 • facsimile: +52.984 879 4449 • email: info@hotelbasico.com • website: www.hotelbasico.com

PHOTOGRAPHS BY UNDINE PRÖHL COURTESY OF HOTEL BÁSICO.

Deseo [Hotel + Lounge]

The Caribbean coast of Mexico, or the Riviera Maya as it is now known, only sprung onto the tourist map in the last few decades. Why it took so long for its merits to be recognized is something of a mystery. Physically, it has everything a tourist could desire, from spectacular white sand beaches and the most magnificent turquoise waters, to a lush tropical landscape and climate that

is the envy of the world. Further inland, there are cenotes—limestone sinkholes once used for religious worship, but perfect as exotic swimming pools—colonial haciendas which are steeped in history, and some of the most impressive ancient ruins in existence. Then there is the unique Mayan culture, with its cuisine and handicrafts, as well the gentle Mayans themselves. Few destinations can boast such a wonderful array of attractions, and the area can rightly be described as offering one of the most perfect and varied tourist experiences there is.

Until recently, however, visitors to the region often found themselves let down by the selection of accommodations on offer. There was plenty of it, but much of that consisted of enormous mega-resorts with little appeal to the more discerning, independently minded traveller, with the only alternative being the down-to-earth and often

down-at-heel palapa-style beach hut. What was needed was something that bridged the gap between the two—something which combined some of the glamour, facilities and luxury of the larger hotels, with the charm, individuality and personalized service of their smaller counterparts.

This predicament did not go unnoticed, at least not by a group of four hoteliers from Mexico City—Carlos Couturier and brothers Moises, Rafael and Jaime Micha. This intrepid quartet, founders of the capital's groundbreaking HABITA and CONDESAdf hotels, quickly realised that there was plenty of room for improvement and set about applying their consummate skills to the

challenge. The result was the Deseo [Hotel + Lounge] and its sister hotel, the Hotel Básico, which together are helping to transform the former fishing village of Playa del Carmen into the style capital of the Riviera Maya.

Located on 5th Avenue, in the heart of the downtown area and just a short walk from the beach, Deseo—Spanish for

'desire'—lives up to its name in every respect. It's a hip, youthful, hedonistic paradise, exuding a heady mix of cutting-edge modernity and laid-back lounging the likes of which are more usually found in cities like Los Angeles or Miami's South Beach. Indeed, the inclusion of the word 'lounge' in its name is no coincidence. The

whole place has been created and designed to have the intimate feel of a private club, where guests are encouraged—indeed expected—to mingle and interact with each other, in pleasant contrast to the sometimes stuffy formality of other more run-of-the-mill hotels.

Activities are concentrated around the central courtyard—which includes a bar, swimming pool, oversized sun beds and piped house music—now a well-established magnet for the beautiful people of Playa del Carmen and often used as the backdrop for model shoots and music videos. The entertainment doesn't stop at dusk either. As the sun begins to set, the whole place transforms itself effortlessly into a hip lounge-style nightclub, complete with starlight and resident DJ, making it a 24-hour party hangout to remember.

Rooms here share the stark minimalist design of the common areas, but they're not without their own unique fixtures and fittings, and a stunning degree of attention to detail is evident throughout. Thoughtful touches include hammocks, king-sized beds, slide-away bedside tables, party packs of incense and condoms, and a wire clothesline hung with unexpected amenities: sun hat, boxer shorts, beach bag, flip-flops, bananas, and the room-service menu. Apart from room service, there's a self-service kitchen that provides American breakfasts, all-day tapas and complimentary health snacks, and there are plenty more eating and drinking options on the nearby streets. In fact, step outside and it's sometimes hard to believe that 30 years ago, Playa del Carmen was just a sleepy fishing village. Now the town is a fun, sexy, savvy place with everything from chic dining experiences and funky bars, to designer shops and stalls selling locally made handicrafts.

Nor is there any shortage of nearby attractions. For a start, there's the beach—one of the hippest and prettiest in the whole of the area—and the offshore snorkelling, scuba diving and deep-sea fishing that are world class.

To the south, the world-famous Mayan ruins of Tulum and Coba are within easy driving distance, and the island of Cozumel is but a 40-minute ferry ride away. Further

THIS PAGE (FROM TOP): The library offers comfortable surroundings in which to relax; innovative artwork with a practical twist decorates the stylish bedrooms.

OPPOSITE (FROM LEFT): Bedrooms come with king-size beds; giant sunbeds for 24-hour lounging and socializing.

afield, there's Chichén Itzá, another Mayan archeological zone and a UNESCO World Heritage Site.

So it's little wonder that the Deseo [Hotel + Lounge] has been such a roaring success since its doors were opened to the public several years ago, and it's no surprise that the clientele is mostly young, hip, international, sophisticated and urbane, drawn by the lure of the minimalist design, funky character, louche trappings and 24-hour party atmosphere.

FACTS

ROOMS	12 rooms • 3 suites
FOOD	room service • complimentary American breakfast and tapas
DRINK	poolside bar
FEATURES	pool • lounge • jacuzzi • music
BUSINESS	Internet access
NEARBY	Playa del Carmen • Tulum • Coba • Chichén Itzá
CONTACT	5th avenue and 12th street, Playa del Carmen, Quintana Roo 77710, Mexico • telephone: +52.984 879 3620 • facsimile: +52.984 879 3621 • email: info@hoteldeseo.com • website: www.hoteldeseo.com

PHOTOGRAPHS BY UNDINE PRÖHL COURTESY OF DESEO [HOTEL + LOUNGE].

Maroma Resort + Spa

The Maroma experience starts the moment you walk into the arrivals hall at Cancun's international airport. There, a smiling employee will greet you by name and transport you some 32 km (20 miles) to an unmarked turning on the highway south. After that, it's a 15-minute drive along a bumpy road through the jungle before the hotel's white stucco walls and thatched turrets emerge from the 25 acres (10 hectares) of lush tropical gardens in which they are set.

There are 65 rooms and suites, all of which offer ocean or garden views, original artwork, and king-size beds draped with mosquito nets. Outside, private terraces, some with outdoor showers and plunge pools, are bedecked with sofas and hammocks. These secluded terraces provide the perfect place for long, lazy breakfasts or a romantic evening meal for two.

Alternatively, Maroma boasts three excellent and highly rated restaurants. El Sol, with its superb wine cellar, offers innovative Yucatecan-inspired fusion cuisine and dramatic ocean views. El Restaurante, also overlooking the sea, has a more casual atmosphere, and features traditional dishes and all-day dining. Cilantro serves up lighter, healthier alternatives—such as antojitos, Mexico's version of tapas—in a poolside setting. There are also three superb bars, including one by the beach.

More than anything, it's the sense of relaxed wellbeing that permeates the atmosphere that makes Maroma special. It has a way of seeping into your system, no matter how stressed out and exhausted you are on arrival - a phenomenon facilitated by the presence of two world-class facilities: the Mayan-inspired Kinan Spa and the newer Wellness Centre.

The Yucatán Peninsula is surely one of the world's greatest tourist playgrounds...

overlook the other attractions the resort has to offer. The private beach is regularly rated as one of the world's best, and for good reason. They just don't come any prettier or more idyllic. Offshore is the world's second longest barrier reef, which helps to create a perfect swimming environment whilst providing world-class scuba diving and snorkelling. Replete with ancient Mayan ruins, colonial haciendas, and limestone sinkholes which are perfect for swimming in, the Yucatán Peninsula is surely one of the world's greatest tourist playgrounds and more than worthy of the odd excursion.

The first has a wide array of spa features, including a saltwater flotation tank and treatment rooms. The second offers an air-conditioned gym, massages and yoga, as well as a traditional temazcal, the Mayan equivalent of a sauna. Together, these combine to provide the most complete health, fitness and rejuvenation package in the region, and have a reputation that reaches much further afield.

Tempting as these facilities are, guests at Maroma would be well-advised not to

FACTS		
	ROOMS	65 rooms
	FOOD	El Sol: European-inspired Mayan Yucatecan • Cilantro: health bar • El Restaurante: traditional dishes
	DRINK	Maroma Bar • beach bar
	FEATURES	3 pools • 2 tennis courts • spa • jacuzzi • wellness centre • temazcal
	NEARBY	Chichén Itzá, Coba, Tulum and Uxmal ruins • Sian Ka'an Biosphere Reserve • Great Mayan Reef • Cozumel • Isla Contoy • Cancún • Playa del Carmen
	CONTACT	Highway 307, Rivera Maya km 51, Quintana Roo 77710 • telephone: +52.998 872 8200 • facsimile: +52.998 872 8220 • email: reservations@maromahotel.com • website: www.maromahotel.com

PHOTOGRAPHS COURTESY OF MAROMA RESORT + SPA.

Jamaica Itinerary

The mere mention of an impending Caribbean vacation will probably elicit a standard response from most people: turquoise waters and white sandy beaches. That's fine if a simple beach holiday is all you're looking for, but Jamaica has so much more to offer. For a start, there's the lush tropical interior with its rivers, waterfalls, mountains and views, taking the viewer's breath away with its sheer beauty. In addition, you will get to sample its musical tradition and cuisine as well as its rich and varied history which encompasses pirates, fortresses and colonial-era plantations. But most of all, Jamaica has some of the friendliest people you're ever likely to meet. Not only will they make your stay completely magical but they'll change the way you look at life in the process. It's no wonder that so many artists, writers and musicians have gone to the island over the years in search of inspiration—it truly is the quintessential Caribbean destination.

Highlights:

Dunn's River Falls • Plantation Great Houses • golf courses • rafting on the Rio Grande • Blue Mountains

Suggested Itinerary:

- Fly into Montego Bay international airport direct with Virgin Atlantic or Air Jamaica.
- Transfer from the airport and check in for a two-night stay at Round Hill. You can enjoy a few days lazing by your own private pool or relaxing on the beach. Alternatively, there are several world-class golf courses nearby.
- Drive east along the coast towards Ocho Rios. En route, stop for a tour of the historic (and haunted!) Rose Hall Great House just east of Montego Bay. Lunch can be had at any one of the many jerk chicken stands along the way, but leave some time for a visit to Dunn's River Falls where you can enjoy a cooling dip in one of the most beautiful settings imaginable.
- Check in at the Jamaica Inn and Spa or the Royal Plantation Resort for a few days of pampered luxury.
- Continue east along the coast to Goldeneye for a couple of nights and experience the lifestyle of James Bond's creator Ian Fleming. While you're there, be sure to visit Firefly, the former home of Noel Coward, just a short distance away. Also highly recommended is a day trip to Port Antonio to soak up the unspoiled atmosphere of this old banana port. Afterwards, spend a few hours rafting down the Rio Grande.
- Drive on to Strawberry Hill in the foothills of the Blue Mountains. From there, you can explore mountain trails on foot and visit the nearby coffee plantation. Kingston, Jamaica's capital, is just an hour's drive away, giving you a perfect chance to experience this vibrant and historic city.
- Fly back from Kingston international airport with British Airways or Air Jamaica.

SEASONS
IN STYLE

Winner of Condé Nast Traveller magazine's award for the best UK Tour Operator in 2005, Seasons in Style specializes in creating tailor-made, fully flexible luxury holidays for the discerning, independent-minded traveller. With a wealth of experience, an unbiased perspective and huge portfolio of carefully selected destinations, they pride themselves on being able to offer holidays which best suit the requirements of their clients. In order to arrange a holiday with Seasons in Style, call +44.1244.202 000 or visit their website at www.seasonsinstyle.co.uk.

THIS PAGE: *Round Hill—always known for low key luxury and timeless glamour.*

OPPOSITE (CLOCKWISE FROM TOP LEFT): *At Round Hill, a sumptuous meal paired with candlelight makes for a memorable experience; get close to the edge at Strawberry Hill's unique infinity-edge pool; crystal-clear waters at the beach off Goldeneye.*

Turks + Caicos Itinerary

Despite having more than 322 km (200 miles) of pristine white sand beaches, some of the finest waters in the Caribbean and the third largest coral reef in the world, the Turks and Caicos Islands may be unheard of for most people. That's part of the attraction of this tiny archipelago of 45 islands and cays southeast of the Bahamas—it's a long way off the beaten track. Such anonymity brings other advantages too, foremost amongst which is the complete sense of peace and tranquillity which pervades the whole place. The pace of life here is measured not by clocks or by timetables, but by the rise and fall of the tide and the passage-migrating whales. Throw in some of the most exclusive and luxurious hotels in the Caribbean and you've got something that's pretty close to paradise, as those who have been there will testify. Let's just hope they don't tell everyone about it. Some things are best kept secret!

Highlights:

White sand beaches • snorkelling • scuba diving • deep-sea fishing

Suggested Itinerary:

- Fly into Providenciales from London with British Airways.
- Transfer directly to The Palms and spend a few days relaxing in the timeless elegance and sumptuous surroundings of this brand-new resort. Inspired by the works of the legendary theatrical designer, Oliver Messel, The Palms is set in 5 hectares (12 acres) of tropical landscaped gardens and lies alongside the 19-km- (12-mile-) long Grace Bay Beach, regularly rated as one of the world's most beautiful. Scuba diving and snorkelling are easily arranged, and with more than 2,590 sq km (1,000 sq miles) of coral reef lying just offshore in near-perfect visibility, there's plenty of exploring to do.
- For a change of scene, transfer to Parrot Cay, a short speedboat ride away. Parrot Cay is a 20-hectare (50-acre) resort on a 405-

hectare (1,000-acre) private island with its own stretch of white sand beach. With butler service and a 511 sq m (5,500 sq foot) infinity pool, the only distractions to the peace and quiet here are the temptations posed by the excellent restaurants and the spa—the latter offering a wide range of Eastern-style body treatments, massages and therapies. Using the hotel as a base, you might like to arrange an excursion to one of the many deserted islands that lie offshore or try your hand at deep-sea fishing in the surrounding waters.

• Transfer back to Providenciales by boat for the flight home.

SEASONS
IN STYLE

Winner of Condé Nast Traveller magazine's award for the best UK Tour Operator in 2005, Seasons in Style specializes in creating tailor-made, fully flexible luxury holidays for the discerning, independent-minded traveller. With a wealth of experience, an unbiased perspective and huge portfolio of carefully selected destinations, they pride themselves on being able to offer holidays which best suit the requirements of their clients. In order to arrange a holiday with Seasons in Style, call +44.1244.202 000 or visit their website at www.seasonsinstyle.co.uk.

THIS PAGE (FROM LEFT): Leave your cares behind in the breathtaking private island resort of Parrot Cay; regain spiritual equilibrium in peace and quiet.

OPPOSITE (FROM TOP): Recline by the pool and watch the clouds drift by at The Palms; get that top-of-the-world feeling with exquisite penthouse living.

Leeward + Windward Islands Itinerary

The Caribbean is deservedly one of the world's foremost tourist destinations. It offers everything a relaxing beach holiday should, whether it's sheer natural beauty and exotic cuisines you're looking for, or crystal clear waters and welcoming hosts. The only challenge is that you will be bombarded by so many choices of excellent destinations that it gets difficult to decide where to head to. For this reason, a growing number of travellers to the area are choosing to stay in several different destinations on the same trip, of which the Leeward and Windward Islands would be ideal as they are located in close proximity to the rest. Together, this string of beautiful islands, stretching over some 805 km (500 miles) along the eastern rim of the Caribbean, offers a combination of destinations, including some of the finest hotels and resorts in the region. A few possible itineraries are suggested here.

Highlights:

Snorkelling • scuba diving • sailing • deep-sea fishing, bonefishing • golf

Suggested Itinerary:

- Fly direct to Antigua international airport from London with British Airways or Virgin Atlantic. Alternatively, fly direct from Manchester with BMI.
- Transfer for a stay at either Carlisle Bay, Blue Waters, The Inn at English Harbour, or Curtain Bluff. All four hotels are notable for the highest levels of service and customer satisfaction, enabling guests to seamlessly adjust to their new surroundings. Then there's the beautiful island of Antigua itself, with its rolling, rustic landscape and deliciously slow pace of life. The sailing here is also well-known and other water sports can easily be arranged.
- Fly to Virgin Gorda in the British Virgin Islands via Antigua and transfer by boat to Biras Creek, or Caneel Bay on the island of St. John. These two hotels offer a wonderful sense of seclusion and relaxed elegance. During your stay, you may also want to try your hand at scuba diving or deep-sea fishing. The bonefishing is also excellent.
- Fly to Barbados and transfer to either Sandy Lane or Treasure Beach. Sandy Lane's near-legendary reputation as the jet set elite's favourite Caribbean resort speaks for itself. Treasure Beach offers a more intimate and low key experience and is perfect for those in search of a little romance. Barbados has plenty of other diversions, from golf courses to some of the most sophisticated dining experiences in the region.
- Fly to Canouan, a tiny island in The Grenadines, and transfer to the Raffles Resort for a few days. Here, apart from the dining and sporting facilities, guests have the opportunity to play golf on the newly completed Jim Fazio designed course.
- Fly home to London or Manchester via Barbados.

SEASONS
IN STYLE

Winner of Condé Nast Traveller magazine's award for the best UK Tour Operator in 2005, Seasons in Style specializes in creating tailor-made, fully flexible luxury holidays for the discerning, independent-minded traveller. With a wealth of experience, an unbiased perspective and huge portfolio of carefully selected destinations, they pride themselves on being able to offer holidays which best suit the requirements of their clients. In order to arrange a holiday with Seasons in Style, call +44.1244.202 000 or visit their website at www.seasonsinstyle.co.uk.

index

Numbers in *italics* denote pages where pictures appear. Numbers in **bold** denote map pages.

A
African 15, 16, *75*, 135, 170, 211, 232
Aloe vera 214
Altos de Chavón 64, 69
Amber Coast 63
Amerindian 15, 129, 161, 232
Anegada 99, 101, 125
Anse du Gouverneur 137
Appleton 18, 43
Arab 15, 25
Arawak 15, 25, 211, 214
Aruba **209**, *211*, 212–214, 216, 218–221
Ash Wednesday 20, 140, 171

B
Bacardi 18
Baie de St-Jean **133**, 137
Bajan 162, 163, 179, 183, 185, 189
Baker, Dow 25
Banana 25, 26, 40, 161, 165, 240, 244
Baseball 58, 215
Beguine 135
Belize 14, 231–234
Bequia *159*, 166, 167, 201
Black River Morass **23**, 25, 34, 36, 47
Blackbeard 99
Blue Mountain 25, 31, 52, 53, 249
Blue mahoe 33
Bonaire **209**, 211, 216, *217*

C
Calabash 36, 43
Calypso 13, 17, 20, 25, 28, 75, 101, 166, 170, 171, 215
Campeche **223**, 226
Cancún 226, *228*, 229, 246, 247
Cannibalism 161
Caribs 15, 16, 161, 172
Carnival 17, 19, 20, *21*, 75, 101, 170, 171
Carriacou 172
Cassava 16
Christian 15, 123, 232
Cibony 15
Cockscomb Basin Wildlife Preserve *233*
Coffee *33*, 52, 53, 249
Coleridge, Samuel Taylor 13
Columbus, Christopher 13, 16, *57*, 63, 70, 75, 99, 100, 146, 161
Conch *76*, 78–80, 85, 87, 93, 141
Cordillera Central 64
Coward, Nöel 27, 249
Cozumel **223**, 226, 244, 247
Creole 17, 61, 62, 149–153, 157, 165, 168, 195, 197, 211
Cricket 15, 98, 100, 105, 106
Cuba libre 18
Curaçao **209**, 211, 212, 214–216

D
Daiquiri 18
Dessalines, Jean 15
Divi-divi 214
Dreadlocks 28, 136
Dunn's River Falls 30, 249
Dutch 19, 100, 138, 211–213, 215, 216

E
El Castillo *227*, 230
European 15, 16, 19, 45, 47, 61, 62, 63, 68, 98, 136, 161, 229, 232

F
Fern Gully 30
Fleming, Ian 27, 40, 249
Fort-de-France *135*, 140
Fort King George 170, 207

G
Gambling 138
Ganja *28*
Garrison Savannah 164
Garvey, Marcus 15
Grace Bay 10–11, **73**, *75, 78*, 90–93, 250
Grand Cul de Sac **133**, 137
Guadeloupe 16, 97, **133**, 135, 142, 148
Gustavia **133**, 137, 144, 145, 147

H
Hindu 15

I
Independence 15, 19
Iles des Saintes **133**, 142
Isla Mujeres **223**, 226

J
James Bond 27, 30, 40, 249
Jazz 28, 60, 115, 135, 168, 215
Jerk 25, 31, 36, 47, 249
Jewish 15, 63
Jones, Marion *15*, 234

K
Kingston **23**, 28, 33, 53, 249
Kingstown *159*, 165
Kipling, Rudyard 26

L
La Soufriere Volcano 165
L'Ouverture, Toussaint 15

M
Mambo 20
Marley, Bob 15, *25*, 28, 33, 34
Martinique 19, 135, 136, 139–142, 156, 157, **159**, 172
Maya 16, 225–233, 237, 238, 241–247
Mento 28

Merengue 20, *57*, 60
Michelin 85, 141
Mofongo 60
Molasses 17, 18
Mondongo 60
Montego Bay **23**, *29*, 30, 49, 249
Montserrat **95**, 97, 135
Motto 15
Mojito 18
Musgrave market 30
Muslim 15
Mt. Pelée **133**, 140, 142

N
Naipaul, V.S. 161
Negril **23**, 34–36, 38, 39, 46, 47
Nobel 15, 161

O
Ocho Rios *29*, 30, 44, 50, 249
Otrobanda 215, 216

P
Papiamento 211, 212
Parang 171
Pétanque *138*
Petroglyphs 214
Pico Duarte 64
Piña colada 18, 45
Pirates 15, 19, 75, 79, 98, 99, 146, *166*, 202, 203, 219, 234
Piton peaks 168, 194–197
Playa del Carmen **223**, *225*, 229–231, 239, 241–245, 247
Ponce de León 13, 75
Port Antonio **23**, *29*, 30, 31, 33, 249
Providenciales 10–11, **73**, 76, 77, 82–87, 89, 250, 251
Puerto Rico 14, 18, 20, *57*, 60, 62, 97
Puerto Morelos 229
Puerto Plata *57*, 60, 62, 63, 70
Punda 215
Punta Cana **55**, *57*, 62, 68, 69
Punta Gorda **223**

Q
Quintana Roo 226, 228, 241, 245, 247

R
Rap 25, 33
Rastafarian 15, 20, *28*, 34, 43
Red Stripe 25, 36, 47
Reggae 20, 25, 28. 30, 33, 34, 166, 168, 215
Ripsaw 75
Rocksteady 28, 33
Route de la Traversée
Rubirosa, Porfirio 59
Rum 17–19, 27, 43, 53, 80, 99, 141, *142*, 168, 172

Rumba 135

S
Salsa 20, 60
Salt Cay 80
Sancocho 60
Santa Maria *57*, 63
Santo Domingo **55**, *57*, 60, 61, 62, 64
Seven Years' War 135, 142
Ska 20, 28
Slave 15–17, 19, 31, 75, 79, 171, 211
Sobers, Garfield 15
Soca 171
Sosa, Sammy 15
Spice 48, 124, 161, 172, 173, 190–192, 201
St-Pierre *133*, 140
St. Barts **95**, 108, 109, **133**, 136–138, 144–149, 155
St. Croix 102, 125, 135
St. John's Cathedral 234
St. Kitts **95**, 97, 98
St. Maarten **95**, *138*, 150
St. Martin **95**, 108, 109, *135*, *138*, 139, 144, 150, 151, 153–155
Sugarcane 15, 17, 18, *57*, 97

T
Taino 15, 63, 103
Tassa 171
Temazcal 229, 247
The Careenage 164, *165*
Tortola 99–101
Tulum **223**, 229, 230, 241, 244, 245

U
UNESCO World Heritage Site 61, 216, 245

V
Virgin Gorda *100*, 124–127, 253

W
Walcott, Derek 15
Waterfalls 51, 93, 126, 127, 166, 231, 248
Weston, Garfield 26
Whale 62, 63, 68, 80, 166
Whitby **73**, 80
Willemstad **209**, 215, *216*

X
Xaymaca 25
Xcaret Eco Theme Park *230*
Xunantunich 233

Y
Yaax Che Botanic Gardens 229
Yucatán 35, **223**, *225*, 226, 228–230, 247
Y.S. Falls 36

Z
Zona Colonial 61, 62

The publisher would like to thank the following for permission to reproduce their photographs:

Al Rod/Corbis 106 (below)
Amanyara front flap (top)
Amos Nachoum/Corbis 5, 94
Angelo Cavalli 79 (top)
Bettmann/Corbis 59 (below)
Blaine Harrington III/Corbis 72, 158
Blue Waters front cover (boat)
Bob Krist/Corbis 18 (centre), 138 (below), 213 (below), 229
Bradley Smith/Corbis 27 (centre)
Bucuti Beach 212 (below), 215 (top)
Buddy Mays/Corbis 103 (below), 107, 214 (below), 228 (below)
Bureau L.A. Collection/Corbis 166
Caneel Bay 253 (below)
Catherine Karnow/Corbis 19
Corbis 75 (top), 103 (top), 214 (top), 215 (below)
Creasource/Corbis 14 (top)
Curtain Bluff 99 (right)
Dallas and John Heaton/Free Agents Limited/Corbis 139 (below)
Daniel Lainé/Corbis 28 (below)
Danny Lehman/Corbis 17 (below)
Dave G. Houser/Corbis 105 (top)
David Samuel Robbins/Corbis 234 (top)
Deseo [Hotel + Lounge]/Jean Luc Laloux 225, 228 (top)

Durand Patrick/Corbis 21
Envision/Corbis 60 (centre)
Fridmar Damm/zefa/Corbis 31, 213 (top)
Galen Rowell/Corbis 104 (left)
Gary Braasch/Corbis 224
Glowimages/Getty Images front cover (raft), 26
Goldeneye back flap (top), 248 (centre)
Grace Bay Club front flap (centre)
Jake's back cover (balcony)
James Marshall/Corbis 60 (below)
James Strachan/Riser/Getty Images 233
Janet Jarman/Corbis 222
Jay Dickman/Corbis 33 (top)
Jean Pierre Amet/Corbis Sygma 138 (top)
Jeff Albertson/Corbis 20 (below)
Jeff Hunter/Getty Images front cover (fish), 13 (below), 234 (below)
Jonathan Blair/Corbis 18 (below), 164 (left), 165
Jonathan Smith/Cordaly Photo Library Ltd./Corbis 2
Karl Weatherly/Corbis 211
Kennan Ward/Corbis 231 (below)
Kevin Philips front flap (below), 63 (top), 136 (below), 168 (right and below), 169 (top)
Kit Kittle/Corbis 98
La Samanna 13 (top)
Lawson Wood/Corbis 81
Layne Kennedy/Corbis 63 (below)
Lee Snider/Photo Images/Corbis 138 (centre)
Louie Psihoyos/Corbis 62 (right)

Ludovic Maisant/Corbis front cover (mural), 16 (top), 56, 134, 162 (below)
Macduff Everton/Corbis 8–9, 232 (below)
Marcos Larrain/epa/Corbis 54
Mark Downey/Getty Images 29 (below)
Maroma Resort and Spa front cover (dish), 230 (top)
Mexican Tourism Board 226 (top), 230 (below), 231 (top)
Michael S. Yamashita/Corbis 34 (top)
Michele Westmorland/Corbis 226 (below)
Mustique Villas 167 (below)
Necker Island front cover (hammock), back cover (sunset), 14 (below), 17 (top)
Neil Rabinowitz/Corbis 100 (below), 101
Nic Bothma/epa/Corbis 99 (left)
Nik Wheeler back cover (steel drums, waterfall, festival, harbour, cactus), 20 (top), 27 (top and below), 30 (top and below), 32, 36 (top, right and below), 57 (top and below), 60 (top), 61 (top and below), 62 (left), 64 (top), 65, 74, 75 (below), 76 (top, centre and below), 77 (top and below), 78 (top), 79 (below), 80 (below), 96, 97, 100 (top), 102, 104 (right), 105 (below), 106 (top), 135 (top and below), 137, 139 (top), 140 (left), 141 (top), 142 (centre), 160, 161 (top), 162 (top), 167 (top), 172 (top and below), 173
Nik Wheeler/Corbis 212 (top), 216 (top and below)
Owen Franken/Corbis 142 (top and below)
Pablo Corral V/Corbis 170, 171 (top)
Parrot Cay 251 (left and right)

Patrick Molnar/Riser/Getty Images 35
Paul Seheult/Eye Ubiquitous/Corbis 171 (below)
Peter Power/Zuma/Corbis 58–59
Phil Schermeister/Corbis 80 (top)
Philip Gould/Corbis 136 (top), 140 (right)
Philippe Giraud/Goodlook/Corbis 15 (below), 132, 141 (below), 143
Raffles Resort Canouan Island 168 (top), 253 (top)
Reinhard Eisele/Corbis 33 (below)
Richard Klune/Corbis 163 (top), 210
Ron Watts/Corbis front cover (lifeguard), 22, 24, 235
Round Hill Hotel and Villas 248 (top and right), 249
Royal Plantation 4
Sakis Papadopoulos/Riser/Getty Images 208
Sandy Lane Hotel and Resort 252
Stefan Matzke/NewSport/Corbis 16 (below)
Stephen Alvarez/National Geographic/Getty Images 232 (top)
Stephen Frink/Corbis 29 (top), 78 (below), 217
The Caves back cover (grottoes), 37
The Palms 250 (top and below)
Thom Lang/Corbis 227
Tony Arruza/Corbis 18 (top), 34 (below), 64 (below), 163 (below), 164 (right)
Turtle Inn back flap (centre), 14 (top)
Wolfgang Kaehler/Corbis 161 (below)
Yann Arthus-Bertrand/Corbis front cover (cays), 12, 169 (below)

Amanyara (page 82)
Northwest Point, Providenciales
Turks and Caicos Islands
telephone: +65.6887 3337 (central reservations)
facsimile: +1649.941 8132
amanyara@amanresorts.com
www.amanresorts.com

Anse Chastanet Resort (page 194)
PO Box 7000, Soufrière
1 Anse Chastanet Road, St. Lucia
telephone: +1758.459 7000
facsimile: +1758.459 7700
ansechastanet@candw.lc
www.ansechastanet.com

Biras Creek (page 124)
Virgin Gorda, British Virgin Islands
telephone: +1284.494 3555
facsimile: +1284.494 3557
gm@biras.com
www.biras.com

Blue Waters (page 110)
Boon Point, Soldiers Bay, Antigua
telephone: +44.870.360 1245
facsimile: +44.870.360 1246
bluewaters@threesixtyhotels.com
www.bluewaters.net

Bucuti Beach (page 218)
LG Smith Boulevard 55B, PO Box 1347
Eagle Beach, Aruba
telephone: +297.583 1100
facsimile: +297.582 5272
info@bucuti.com
www.bucuti.com

Caneel Bay (page 128)
PO Box 720, Cruz Bay, St. John
US Virgin Islands 00831-0720
telephone: +1340.776 6111
facsimile: +1340.693 8280
caneel@rosewoodhotels.com
www.rosewoodhotels.com

Carlisle Bay (page 114)
Old Road, St. Mary's, Antigua
telephone: +1268.484 0000
facsimile: +1268.484 0001
info@carlisle-bay.com
www.carlisle-bay.com

Casa Colonial Beach + Spa (page 66)
PO Box 22, Playa Dorada, Puerto Plata
Dominican Republic
telephone: +1809.320 3232
facsimile: +1809.320 3131
reservascc@vhhr.com
www.casacolonialhotel.com

Curtain Bluff (page 118)
PO Box 288, Old Road, Antigua
telephone: +1268.462 8400
facsimile: +1268.462 8409
curtainbluff@curtainbluff.com
www.curtainbluff.com

Deseo [Hotel + Lounge] (page 242)
5th Avenue and 12th Street, Playa del Carmen
Quintana Roo 77710, Mexico
telephone: +52.984 879 3620
facsimile: +52.984 879 3621
info@hoteldeseo.com
www.hoteldeseo.com

François Plantation Hotel + Restaurant (page 146)
Colombier, 97133 St. Barthélemy
French West Indies
telephone: +590.590 298 022
facsimile: +590.590 276 126
info@francois-plantation.com
www.francois-plantation.com

Fustic House (page 182)
Bajan Services Ltd, Newton House, Battaleys
St. Peter BB26094, Barbados
telephone: +1246.422 2618
facsimile: +1246.422 5366
villas@bajanservices.com
www.bajanservices.com

Gallows Point Resort (page 130)
PO Box 58, Bay Street, St. John
US Virgin Islands
telephone: +1340.776 6434
facsimile: +1340.776 6520
information@gallowspointresort.com
www.gallowspointresort.com

Goldeneye (page 40)
Oracabessa, St. Mary, Jamaica
telephone: +1876.975 3354
facsimile: +1876.975 3620
goldeneye@cwjamaica.com
www.islandoutpost.com

Grace Bay Club (page 84)
PO Box 128, 1 Grace Bay Circle Road
Providenciales, Turks and Caicos Islands
telephone: +1649.946 5757
facsimile: +1649.946 5758
info@gracebayclub.com
www.gracebayclub.com

Hotel Básico (page 238)
5th Avenue and 10th Street, Playa del Carmen
Quintana Roo 77710, Mexico
telephone: +52.984 879 4448
facsimile: +52.984 879 4449
info@hotelbasico.com
www.hotelbasico.com

Jake's (page 42)
Calabash Bay, Treasure Beach
St. Elizabeth, Jamaica
telephone: +1876.965 3000
facsimile: +1876.965 0552
jakes@cwjamaica.com
www.islandoutpost.com

Jamaica Inn + Spa (page 44)
PO Box 1, Main Street, Ocho Rios
St. Ann, Jamaica
telephone: +1876.974 2514
facsimile: +1876.974 2449
reservations@jamaicainn.com
www.jamaicainn.com

Ladera (page 196)
PO Box 225, Soufrière, St. Lucia
telephone: +1758.459 7323
facsimile: +1758.459 5156
reservations@ladera.com
www.ladera.com

Laluna (page 190)
PO Box 1500, Morne Rouge, Grenada
telephone: +1473.439 0001
facsimile: +1473.439 0600
info@laluna.com
www.laluna.com

La Samanna (page 154)
PO Box 4077, 97064 St. Martin
French West Indies
telephone: +590.590 876 400
facsimile: +590.590 878 786
reservations@lasamanna.com
www.lasamanna.com

Leamington Pavilion (page 184)
Bajan Services Ltd, Newton House, Battaleys
St. Peter BB26094, Barbados
telephone: +1246.422 2618
facsimile: +1246.422 5366
villas@bajanservices.com
www.bajanservices.com

Le Cap Est Lagoon Resort + Spa (page 156)
97240 Le François, Martinique
telephone: +596.596 548 080
facsimile: +596.596 549 600
info@capest.com
www.capest.com

Le Christopher (page 144)
Pointe Milou, 97133 St. Barthélemy
French West Indies
telephone: +590.590 276 363

facsimile: +590.590 279 292
lechristopher@wanadoo.fr
www.hotelchristopherstbarth.com

Le Domaine de Lonvilliers (page 150)
Anse Marcel, 97150 St. Martin
French West Indies
telephone: +590.590 523 535
facsimile: +590.590 291 081
resa@hotel-le-domaine.com
www.hotel-le-domaine.com

mangobay (page 176)
Second Street, Holetown, St. James, Barbados
telephone: +1246.432 1384
facsimile: +1246.432 5297
reservations@mangobaybarbados.com
www.mangobaybarbados.com

Maroma Resort + Spa (page 246)
Highway 307, Riviera Maya km 51
Quintana Roo 77710, Mexico
telephone: +52.998 872 8200
facsimile: +52.998 872 8220
reservations@maromahotel.com
www.maromahotel.com

Marquis Hotel Resort + Spa (page 152)
Pigeon Pea Hill, Anse Marcel
97150 St. Martin, French West Indies
telephone: +590.590 294 230
facsimile: +590.590 874 633
info@hotel-marquis.com
www.hotel-marquis.com

Mustique Villas (page 204)
PO Box 349, St. Vincent & the Grenadines
telephone: +1784.488 8000
facsimile: +1784.488 9000
villarentals@mustique-island.com
www.mustique-island.com

Necker Island (page 126)
PO Box 1091, The Valley, Virgin Gorda
British Virgin Islands
telephone: +44.208.600 0430
facsimile: +44.208.600 0431
enquiries@limitededition.virgin.co.uk
www.virgin.com/necker

Parrot Cay (page 88)
PO Box 164, Providenciales
Turks and Caicos Islands
telephone: +1649.946 7788
facsimile: +1649.946 7393
res@parrotcay.como.bz
www.parrotcay.como.bz

Port St. Charles (page 186)
Port St. Charles Development
St. Peter, Barbados
telephone: +1246.419 1000
facsimile: +1246.422 7447
reservations@caribsurf.com
www.portstcharles.com

Raffles Resort Canouan Island (page 198)
Carenage Bay, Canouan Island
St. Vincent & the Grenadines
telephone: +1784.458 8000
facsimile: +1784.458 8885
info@raffles-canouanisland.com
www.raffles-canouanisland.com

Rockhouse (page 46)
West End Road, Negril, Jamaica
telephone: +1876.957 4373
facsimile: +1876.957 0557
info@rockhousehotel.com
www.rockhousehotel.com

Round Hill Hotel + Villas (page 48)
PO Box 64, Montego Bay, Jamaica
telephone: +1876.956 7050
facsimile: +1876.956 7505
reservations@roundhilljamaica.com
www.roundhilljamaica.com

Royal Plantation (page 50)
Main Street, PO Box 2, Ocho Rios, Jamaica
telephone: +1876.974 5601
facsimile: +1876.974 5912
rpres@jm.royalplantation.com
www.royalplantation.com

Sandalo (page 188)
Bajan Services Ltd, Newton House, Battaleys
St. Peter BB26094, Barbados
telephone: +1246.422 2618
facsimile: +1246.422 5366
villas@bajanservices.com
www.bajanservices.com

Sandy Lane Hotel + Resort (page 178)
St. James, Barbados
telephone: +1246.444 2000
facsimile: +1246.444 2222
mail@sandylane.com
www.sandylane.com

Sibarth Villa Rentals + Real Estate (page 148)
La Maison Suédoise, Rue Samuel Fahlberg
97133 St. Barthélemy, French West Indies
Sibarth Villa Rentals
telephone: +590.590 298 890
facsimile: +590.590 276 052
villas@sibarth.com
Sibarth Real Estate
telephone: +590.590 298 891
facsimile: +590.590 278 522
estates@sibarth.com
www.sibarth.com

Siboney Beach Club (page 122)
PO Box 222, St. John's, Antigua
telephone: +1268.462 0806
facsimile: +1268.462 3356
siboney@candw.ag
www.siboneybeachclub.com

Sivory Punta Cana (page 68)
Sivory Beach, Uvero Alto, Punta Cana
Dominican Republic
telephone: +1809.552 0500
facsimile: +1809.552 8686
reservations@sivorypuntacana.com
www.sivorypuntacana.com

Strawberry Hill (page 52)
Newcastle Road, Irish Town, St. Andrew
Jamaica
telephone: +1876.944 8400
facsimile: +1876.944 8408
strawberry@cwjamaica.com
www.islandoutpost.com

Tamarind Beach + Yacht Club (page 202)
Canouan Island, St. Vincent & the Grenadines
telephone: +1784.458 8044
facsimile: +1784.458 8851
info@tamarind.us
www.tamarindbeachhotel.com

The Caves (page 38)
PO Box 3113, Light House Road, Negril
Westmoreland, Jamaica
telephone: +1876.957 0270
facsimile: +1876.957 4930
thecaves@cwjamaica.com
www.islandoutpost.com

The Copper + Lumber Store Hotel (page 116)
Nelson's Dockyard, English Harbour, Antigua
telephone: +1268.460 1058
facsimile: +1268.460 1529
clhotel@candw.ag
www.copperandlumberhotel.com

The Crane Resort + Residences (page 174)
Crane, St. Philip, Barbados
telephone: +1246.423 6220
facsimile: +1246.423 5343
reservations@thecrane.com
www.thecrane.com

The Inn at English Harbour (page 120)
Freeman's Bay, English Harbour, Antigua
telephone: +1268.460 1014
facsimile: +1268.460 1603
theinn@candw.ag
www.theinn.ag

The Palms (page 86)
Providenciales, Turks and Caicos Islands
telephone: +1649.946 8666
facsimile: +1649.946 5188
info@thepalmstc.com
www.thepalmstc.com

The Palms Villa Resort (page 206)
Signal Hill, Old Road
PO Box 1070, Tobago
telephone: +1868.635 1010
facsimile: +1868.635 1011

info@thepalmstobago.com
www.thepalmstobago.com

The Somerset on Grace Bay (page 92)
Princess Drive, Grace Bay Road
Providenciales, Turks & Caicos Islands
telephone: +1649.946 5900
facsimile: +1649.946 5944
kwhitt@thesomerset.com
www.thesomerset.com

The Villa Book (page 108)
12 Venetian House, 47 Warrington Crescent
London W9 1EJ
telephone: +44.845.500 2000
facsimile: +44.845.500 2001
info@thevillabook.com
www.thevillabook.com

Tierra del Sol Resort, Spa + Country Club (page 220)
Malmokweg z/n, Oranjestad
Caya di Solo, Aruba
telephone: +297.586 7800
facsimile: +297.586 4970
tierra.rent@setarnet.aw
www.tierradelsol.com

Treasure Beach (page 180)
Paynes Bay, St. James, Barbados
telephone: +1246.432 1346
facsimile: +1246.432 1094
reservations@treasurebeachhotel.com
www.treasurebeachhotel.com

True Blue Bay Resort + Villas (page 192)
PO Box 1414, Grand Anse
St. George's, Grenada
telephone: +1473.443 8783 or
888.883 2482 (US toll-free line)
mail@truebluebay.com
www.truebluebay.com

Turks + Caicos Club (page 90)
West Grace Bay Beach, West Grace Bay
Providenciales, Turks and Caicos Islands
telephone: +1649.946 5800
facsimile: +1649.946 5858
info@turksandcaicosclub.com
www.turksandcaicosclub.com

Turtle Inn (page 236)
Central Reservations Office
telephone: +501.824 4912
facsimile: +501.824 4913
info@blancaneaux.com
www.blancaneaux.com

Victorian House (page 70)
Calle Dr Alejo Martinez 1, El Batey, Sosúa
Puerto Plata, Dominican Republic
telephone: +1809.571 4000
facsimile: +1809.571 4545
info@starzresorts.com
www.starzresorts.com